73 NORTH

73 NORTH

THE BATTLE OF
THE BARENTS SEA

DUDLEY POPE

with a Foreword by Admiral of the Fleet Lord Tovey,
G.C.B., K.B.E., D.S.O.

NAVAL INSTITUTE PRESS

Published and distributed in the United States
of America by the Naval Institute Press,
Annapolis, Maryland 21402

Library of Congress Catalog Card No. 88–61812

ISBN 087021–660–0

Reprinted 1989

Printed in Great Britain

TO A. AND T.S.W.

Contents

CONTENTS

Illustrations

Illustrations 6, 10, 11, 12, 13, 14, 15, 17, 18, 19, 20, 23 and frontispiece are reproduced by courtesy of The Imperial War Museum; 1, 2 and 3 of Capt. J. M. A. Wilson, D.S.C., RN; 4, 8 and 9 of Kevin Walton, D.S.C.; 5 of Cdr D. C. Kinloch, D.S.O., O.B.E.; 7 and 22 of Rear-admiral Sherbrooke, V.C., C.B., D.S.O.; 16 of Planet News Ltd; 21 of Lt H. Aisthorpe, D.S.O., RCN

Foreword

by Admiral of the Fleet Lord Tovey, G.C.B., K.B.E., D.S.O.
Commander-in-Chief, Home Fleet 1940–1943

THE Battle of the Barents Sea was one of the finest examples in either of the two World Wars of how to handle destroyers and cruisers in action with heavier forces. Captain Sherbrooke saved his convoy by going straight in to attack his far heavier enemy, using his guns to do what damage they could but relying on his torpedoes, the real menace to the heavy ships, to deter them from closing the convoy.

Sherbrooke knew the threat was lost once his torpedoes were fired. When in position for firing he turned his ships to simulate an attack—the mere threat was sufficient to persuade the enemy to break off their attack.

In spite of the smallness of his force Captain Sherbrooke had not hesitated to detach two destroyers to cover the convoy from possible attack from the other side.

As Sherbrooke went in to attack the Commodore turned his convoy away and it was quickly covered by smoke from the *Achates*. Throughout the action the Commodore handled his convoy with great skill.

Smoke-laying may not appear a very exciting way of fighting but I know few things more unpleasant than being fired at when you cannot shoot back. Apart from preventing the enemy getting a sight of the convoy, there is always the chance of a torpedo attack developing out of the smoke. The sinking of the smoke-layer is essential if the enemy is to get a chance of damaging the convoy and the *Achates* was constantly coming under heavy fire, but she stuck to her job right up to the time she sank—truly a noble little ship and company.

11

When Captain Sherbrooke was himself put out of action his second in command, and when his wireless failed the next in command, continued the same tactics.

It was no sudden inspiration that Captain Sherbrooke acted under; he had thought it all out before sailing and had discussed every move with his subordinate commanders and the Commodore of the convoy, and I am sure he would be the first to pay tribute to the previous training given to his flotilla by Captain Armstrong, whom he had very recently relieved.

I doubt if many who did not actually serve in the cruiser escorts of the Russian convoys appreciated the extremely difficult conditions under which they operated. Normally when a convoy had completed only a quarter of its trip it had three or four enemy submarines in its vicinity. Later there might be twelve or more.

To close and sight the convoy was, therefore, asking to be torpedoed—two cruisers were lost in this way. Wireless silence was necessary for escorts and the convoy to avoid the enemy detecting their position or, if they had been lucky enough not to have been sighted, of giving away the fact they were at sea. Wireless signals could be made only when it was obvious the enemy knew their position or a ship had been detached and was some distance from the convoy.

So cruisers seldom knew at all accurately the position of the convoy they were escorting. Is it to be wondered at that Admiral Burnett closed that very suspicious radar contact on his way to support the destroyers?

Admiral Burnett had more experience than any other officer in escorting Russian convoys and was in more actions in their support, finally shepherding the *Scharnhorst* to her destruction by the *Duke of York*, flying the flag of Admiral Fraser, and her destroyers. I never knew Admiral Burnett to take anything but the right action promptly and with the greatest gallantry.

Dudley Pope tells his fine tale magnificently with no embellishments, and the way he has woven in the German information and the personal experiences of those concerned makes thrilling and fascinating reading.

The Battle of the Barents Sea was an action of which we can

all be enormously proud, but it was only one of the many convoys that were run and not all were so successful. Altogether they carried to Russia a total of £428,000,000 worth of material, including 5,000 tanks and over 7,000 aircraft and also large quantities of high explosives and high octane spirit—unpleasant cargoes when hit by a torpedo.

Sixty-two outward-bound merchant ships were lost while twenty-eight of those homeward-bound failed to arrive. Two cruisers, six destroyers, three sloops, two frigates, three corvettes and three minesweepers were sunk with the loss of 1,840 officers and men.

For at least twelve days the convoys were liable to submarine attack; in the summer for six days they were within range of ever-increasing air attack. In winter they experienced bitter cold and some of the worst weather ever met with, as well as dense fog, which no sailor likes. As with other convoys, there was the ever-present risk of being torpedoed, but with the water never far off freezing the hope of ever being picked up alive was very slim.

The officers and men of the ships in convoy and of their escorts were heroic. Masters of ships, some over seventy, men and boys only sixteen years old, after having their ships sunk under them sometimes two or three times, came back for more and insisted on ships going to Russia. I hope that perhaps one day Dudley Pope will tell the story of the Russian convoys as a whole as some tribute to the gallant men who, while never catching the spotlight, gave such service.

Introduction

'This brilliant action fought by the Royal Navy to protect an Allied convoy to Russia at the end of the year [1942] led directly to a crisis in the enemy's naval policy and ended the dream of another German High Seas Fleet.'
—WINSTON CHURCHILL, *The Second World War*, Vol. IV

A T the end of the First World War the German High Seas Fleet surrendered and scuttled itself in Scapa Flow. In the Second World War, however, the Fleet was paid off and partly scrapped in the middle of the war on the express orders of its infuriated Supreme Commander, Adolf Hitler. This was one of the more startling discoveries made by Allied Intelligence officers whose task was to unravel the facts contained in the German naval archives captured at the end of the war. The full story of Hitler's fantastic decision has not been told before.

It is possible that the idea to scrap his Fleet came to Hitler gradually over a long period of time; but we now know for certain that the final and (for the Germans) disastrous decision was made because he was angered by two events of quite minor importance which happened in quick succession.

The first was a clash at Christmas, 1942, between the Navy and Hermann Göring, the head of the German Air Force, over the control of transport ships in the Mediterranean; the other was the failure, on New Year's Eve, of an attack by the pocket battleship *Lützow*, the heavy cruiser *Hipper* and six destroyers on a small convoy of four British and ten American merchantmen bound for Russia through the Arctic with munitions for an ungrateful ally.

This massive attack was initially beaten off in the half-light

15

of the Arctic by only four destroyers commanded by Captain R. StV. Sherbrooke, D.S.O., in a gallant and classic action which won him the Victoria Cross, the highest British award for gallantry in war.

With his ship HMS *Onslow* thrice hit by 8-inch shells, set on fire and sinking, and himself almost completely blinded by a severe face wound, Sherbrooke drove off the *Hipper* and three destroyers and held the ring for nearly two hours until two small British cruisers came to his rescue. The *Lützow*'s attempts to sink the convoy were beaten off by the three remaining destroyers, and not one merchantman was sunk.

This colossal failure by the German Navy in the Battle of the Barents Sea—caused partly by his own orders that no risks were to be taken with the big ships—sent Hitler into a screaming fury.

'The entire action,' said Hitler, 'shows that the ships are utterly useless and nothing but a breeding ground for revolution, idly lying about and lacking any desire to get into action. This means the passing of the High Seas Fleet; it is now my irrevocable decision to do away with these useless ships. . . .'

As a result Grand Admiral Raeder, the Commander-in-Chief, resigned in protest and Admiral Dönitz took over, putting all the German naval effort into the U-boat war. But this was in the spring of 1943, when the Battle of the Atlantic was reaching its bloody crisis. Within a few months the Allies had beaten the U-boats' final and most desperate challenge.

The full story of the Battle of the Barents Sea is told for the first time in the following pages; and because of its tremendous effect I have also dealt fully with Hitler and his relationship with his Navy. It is not enough to say that Hitler became angry and scrapped his Fleet: we need to know more about his psychological make-up.

I have been more than fortunate with my sources. The Lords Commissioners of the Admiralty allowed me to see hitherto-secret British and German records concerning both the battle and Hitler; and many officers who fought in the battle itself have given me a great deal of help and also filled in the 'human' details.

In the following narrative I have tried to present the story three-dimensionally, so that the reader sees it from the point of view of the historian, impartially concerned only with the true facts; from that of the Germans, Hitler, Raeder, the Naval Staff and the men who fought in the battle (particularly the Flag Officer, Admiral Kummetz); and from that of the Allies, ranging from Mr Churchill and Mr Roosevelt to the admirals, captains, junior officers and ratings who fought the convoy through to Russia.

The battle was a confused one—it was only after the British destroyer captains met in Russia later that it dawned on them (the phrase is theirs) that they had fought off not one but two German capital ships. Until the German naval archives were read after the war it was impossible to fit the details of the battle together correctly.

However, it is inadequate just to describe the battle—itself one of the classic destroyer actions of the war. Much that happens in battle is conditioned by what goes on in men's minds and is the result of national and individual character, training and tradition.

Sherbrooke fought with great gallantry in order to save the convoy; he could not know that by a quirk of fate the whole future of the German Fleet depended on his actions. In the battle he beat a German cruiser—and in doing so defeated a Fleet comprising three battleships, two battle-cruisers, two pocket battleships, two heavy and four light cruisers.

It was by no means only a British action: ten of the merchant-men were American; and although British warships escorted them, they freed American warships to fight in other theatres. Indeed the convoy only sailed because of Anglo-American co-operation in the matter of sending arms to Russia.

It should also be remembered that no battle in the last war solely concerned the nation to which the combatant ships, aircraft or troops belonged: the Battle of the Barents Sea affected the fortunes of every enemy-occupied country, as well as Britain, the United States and Russia. In the same way, for instance, the great victories in the Coral Sea and at Midway, won by United States warships, were victories for the Allies as a whole.

17

It is my personal opinion that in the bickering following any war, when each country is striving to claim its share of credit for final victory, we frequently forget that final victory is simply the sum total of all the small victories, whether at sea, on the land or in the air.

Many people have helped to provide the facts contained in this narrative, but I would particularly like to thank the following: The Lords Commissioners of the Admiralty for access to documents; the Records Section, and in particular Mr J. Davy, for his patience in finding those documents; the Historical Section, especially Cdr L. J. Pitcairn Jones, D.S.C. and Cdr W. B. Rowbotham (who also read through the MS and made several valuable suggestions). I am grateful to Cdr M. G. Saunders, head of the Foreign Documents Section, and Mr J. Lawson for much help and advice concerning German documents.

The former Chief of Naval Information, Captain A. W. Clarke, C.B.E., D.S.O., RN(Retd), who also commanded HMS *Sheffield* in the action, Mr M. Ellis and Mr E. G. A. Thompson of the Department of the Chief of Naval Information have all given me a lot of assistance.

The men who fought in the action have given me many hours of their time, and I must express my gratitude to: Rear-admiral R. StV. Sherbrooke, V.C., C.B., D.S.O., who commanded the *Onslow*; Cdr T. J. G. Marchant, D.S.C., his second-in-command; and Captain P. J. Wyatt, D.S.C., his Navigator, all of whom also read the MS; Captain J. M. A. Wilson, D.S.C.; Dr C. B. Holland, D.S.C.; Cdr R. Bird, V.R.D., R.N.V.R.; Cdr G. A. Henderson; E. W. K. Walton, Esq., D.S.C.; and D. Williams, Esq., all of the *Onslow*.

Cdr D. C. Kinloch, D.S.O., O.B.E., commanding the *Obedient*, and Cdr P. G. Satow, D.S.C., Navigator of the *Orwell*, helped me enormously and also read the MS; Captain N. H. G. Austen, D.S.O. and Bar, commanding the *Orwell*, Captain H. J. Lee, D.S.C. and three Bars, his second-in-command, and Captain R. H. Tribe, M.B.E., his Engineer, have patiently answered my questions.

Cdr L. Peyton Jones, D.S.O., O.B.E., D.S.C., senior surviving officer of the *Achates* and Lt H. C. Aisthorpe, D.S.C. of the *Northern Gem*, gave me a good deal of information about their ships; and I am grateful to D. Mackness, Esq., one of the *Orwell*'s radar operators, for his vivid account of life on the lower deck.

Concerning Force R, I have had much help from Admiral Sir Robert L. Burnett, G.C.B., K.C.B., D.S.O., its Flag Officer; Captain A. W. Clarke, mentioned earlier, commanding the *Sheffield*; Cdr E. F. S. Back, D.S.C., her Navigator; Captain H. H. R. Moore, D.S.C., Navigator of the *Jamaica*; and Captain J. E. Scotland, D.S.C., her Gunnery officer.

Cdr J. E. Poulden, of HMS *Anson*, and L. Matthews, Esq., who was the Convoy Commodore's Yeoman, have also been a great help. It remains to thank certain people unconnected with the Royal Navy—Count Henry Bentinck and David Wainwright, two friends whose advice has helped considerably.

Finally I must express my gratitude to my wife, without whose encouragement, criticism and sheer hard work in typing letters, drafts and the final MS, this book would never have been written or even attempted; and to Admiral of the Fleet Lord Tovey, G.C.B., K.B.E., D.S.O., for the Foreword.

D. P.

Chancery Lane, London, W.C.2.

All times are Greenwich Mean Time: all ranks are RN unless otherwise stated. Material enclosed within square brackets which appear in signals and quotations has been interpolated by the author.

19

1

Route Green

AT a quarter past two on the afternoon of Tuesday, 22nd December 1942, the windlasses on the fo'c'sles of fourteen merchant ships gathered in Loch Ewe, on the north-west coast of Scotland, wheezed and clattered mournfully as they hove in anchor chains. The ships were travel-stained; patches of dull red rust mottled their grey hulls, and they seemed slab-sided because they were loaded down to their marks with the heavy munitions of war. Straight stems, bluff bows and flat sheerlines made them chunky, the ugly sisters of the lean destroyers anchored nearby; but designers had drawn out the lines of their hulls to cram in the maximum amount of cargo. Speed was, in wartime, a vital consideration; in the competitive days of peacetime charter rates, however, it meant higher fuel bills, and so the fastest of the fourteen ships could do but eleven knots, and the majority only nine. At least, they were the speeds their masters gave; but being wary men, they knew their chief engineers would have a knot or so in hand for emergencies.

Four of the ships flew the Red Ensign, nine the Stars and Stripes and one the pale blue and red flag of Panama. From each ship's halyards flew a two-figure hoist representing its number in the convoy formation. The once-gay colours of the flags were darkened by soot and by the heavy rain, but they seemed to be trying to stream out bravely in the chill wind which squalled its way across the loch.

Soon the windlasses stopped their asthmatic grumbling: anchors were aweigh and engine-room telegraphs on the bridges were swung over to bring the propellers to life. One by one, in a pre-arranged order, the ships steamed out through the boom gate in a long single line stretching for more than two miles.

Soon the convoy was in the North Minch, the long channel of water shielded from the full winter fury of the North Atlantic by the rocky outcrop of islands known as the Outer Hebrides.

This was indeed the convoy's Hebrides Overture, for the merchant ships were bound for North Russia, by sea more than 2,000 miles away, taking succour to an ungrateful and suspicious ally. Much of the voyage would be beyond the Arctic Circle. The convoy's track was listed as Route Green and consisted of geographical positions labelled alphabetically from A to H in the convoy orders. It was through the track of the great winter gales that swept in from the broad wastes of the Atlantic, raged across the seas round Scotland and Iceland for days on end and then howled their way across the Greenland Sea to die away, their phrenetic energy expended, in the high latitudes between Spitzbergen and Norway.

The tracks of these centripetal depressions were often the same as the routes of the convoys bound for Russia. After passing Iceland many of these storms advanced only slowly to the north-east, so slowly that the convoys often steamed along with them, and heavy seas and foul weather stayed with them for much of the voyage.

Day after day the wind screamed in the rigging, overwhelming their senses with its noise. Freezing spray driving across the decks in blinding sheets clung to the guns and steel plates of the ships' superstructure. The fearful cold numbed men's bodies until limbs felt like bent bars of wrought iron, and their spirits were attacked by the almost continual darkness of the Arctic winter.

With these great winter storms came heavy, mountainous seas which could force a thirty-two-knot cruiser, with 75,000 h.p. engines, to a struggling, pounding eight-knot crawl, and fling about its 600-ft length and 10,000-ton bulk as if it were a waterlogged tree trunk; seas which overpowered merchantmen and forced them to heave-to or steer contrary courses; seas which could in a few hours scatter a convoy across hundreds of square miles, like chaff before a March wind.

At the moment, as the ships steamed up through the North Minch, the gales were not yet blowing, but the 'glass' was falling. Each hourly tap on the barometer dropped the hand another millibar; white crests rose up on the waves in automatic response to the increasing but unseen pressure of the wind.

Leading the line of ships was the *Empire Archer*, built two years earlier in Dundee and, with her engine-room and funnel right aft, looking more like a tanker than the dry-cargo ship that she was. For this convoy she was the Commodore's ship and carried—in addition to her normal master, officers and crew—Captain R. A. Melhuish, now retired from the Royal Indian Navy, and his staff.

He would be responsible for JW 51B (the convoy's official designation) though not for its escorts. Locked in the *Empire Archer*'s safe, and now known almost by heart, were the convoy orders; the route it was to take; action if attacked by U-boats, bombers or surface raiders; the position of ships in the convoy formation; the meaning of various cryptic code signals; what stragglers were to do, and a host of other instructions necessary for the safe passage of the convoy.

Down below in the *Empire Archer*'s holds was ton upon ton of war equipment. Apart from 4,376 tons of mixed cargo, she carried 141 lorries, 18 tanks, and 21 fighters. If she arrived safely in Russia those weapons should be in action on the Eastern Front within three months.

The Commodore and his staff were veterans, although this was their first Russian convoy. Most of them had been on survivors' leave and were naturally rather disappointed to receive telegrams of recall just before Christmas. There was, for instance, L. F. Matthews. Slim, young and quick-thinking, he was the Yeoman of Signals and as such the senior rating. His previous voyage had been the first with Captain Melhuish (the two of them were destined to sail together for the rest of the war, for voyages to such diverse places as India, New York, the Sicily landings and eight trips to the Normandy beaches).

The pair of them had been unlucky in North Africa because, after landing their troops at Bougie, their ship, the three-funnelled P & O liner *Narkunda*, had been bombed and sunk. Matthews had been enjoying his survivors' leave when his telegram arrived, and the 17th December saw him on the night train for Liverpool. Arriving dirty and tired at 0500[1] he reported for duty. He spent the next two days correcting and bringing up to date the Confidential Books needed for the next voyage and on the 20th, with Captain Melhuish and the rest of the staff, boarded the night train for Loch Ewe.

'We were carrying warm coats and thick gloves in our gear, so we deduced we were in for a nice Russian trip in the depths of winter,' Matthews wrote later. 'I had been in Liverpool when the survivors of the ill-fated PQ 17 had arrived, so I had a fair idea of the pleasures that might await us.'

At 1300 on 22nd December, an hour and three-quarters before the convoy was due to weigh anchor, Captain Melhuish and his staff had boarded the *Empire Archer*, met her master, Captain Maughan, and stowed their gear.

Astern of the *Empire Archer* steamed the *Daldorch*, registered in Glasgow, her holds loaded with 264 lorries as well as 1,744 tons of mixed cargo. Third in line was a modern-looking tanker, the *Empire Emerald*, built on the Tees a year earlier and registered at Middlesbrough. Her crew received extra danger pay, and they deserved it since for the whole voyage they would be living on top of 7,400 tons of highly inflammable aviation spirit and 2,580 tons of fuel oil. One mine, one torpedo, one bomb or shell could, in a second, reduce her trim lines to a flaming and exploding hulk. If she sank without blowing up, then that innocent-looking fuel oil, if swallowed by men gasping as they swam for their lives in the water, could kill them with the slow certainty of poison.

The fourth ship was also a British tanker, the *Pontfield*, built in Sweden in 1940, the year after Hitler's march on Poland. Her hull was electrically welded, and her owners, Hunting & Son, had registered her in Newcastle. Now her master, Captain L. B. Carr, had the task of getting his ship and her vital cargo of aviation spirit and fuel oil safely through to Kola Inlet.

Those four ships were the only ones flying the Red Ensign. There should have been a fifth, the *Dover Hill*, but she had

---

[1] The 24-hour clock will be used throughout. To obtain p.m. times 1200 must be subtracted from all times over 1200 (noon). 1300 is thus 1 p.m.

developed an engine defect at the last moment and could not sail. Together they were manned by a total of 43 officers, 128 seamen, and 74 DEMS[1] gunners served the ancient 4-inch guns mounted on the poop, the Oerlikon 20-mm. cannon and the machine-guns with which they had been fitted.

Fifth in the line of ships was the *Executive*, flying the Stars and Stripes. Owned by the American Export Lines, registered in New York and built twenty-two years earlier at Hog Island, Pennsylvania, she now carried 130 lorries and 4,210 tons of mixed cargo in her holds with four bombers, in huge crates, lashed to her deck. Her eight officers and thirty seamen were backed up by the twenty-four DEMS gunners.

Astern of her came the *Puerto Rican*, with tanks, fighters, bombers and lorries, as well as 5,300 tons of mixed cargo loaded in her holds or secured on her decks; and she was followed by the Texas Company's *Vermont*, built a year after the end of the Great War at Alameda, California, and registered in Wilmington, Delaware. She had a similar cargo.

So the ships slowly—for this was an eight-knot convoy—left the safety of Loch Ewe behind them . . . the *Jefferson Myers*, whose master was the Rear Commodore of the convoy, carried 376 lorries and thousands of tons of mixed cargo in her holds. Four bombers now in crates on her decks forward and aft were well snugged down; but were to cause a lot of trouble later when a powerful gale hit the convoy. Owned by the Pacific-Atlantic Steamship Company, she was registered in Portland, Oregon.

Following close in her wake was the *Calobre*, whose American master was the Vice-Commodore and thus second-in-command to Captain Melhuish, the Commodore. He would have to take over should the *Empire Archer* be sunk or become detached from the convoy. Tenth in the line came the *John H. B. Latrobe*, which was going to be forced to heave-to in the fury of a gale in seven days' time; then came the *Ballot*, registered in Panama and now under charter to the United States Maritime Commission.

---

[1] From the designation: Defensively-Equipped Merchant Ships. These men in the British ships were volunteers from the Royal Navy and the Army, the latter forming the Maritime Regiment of Royal Artillery.

The last three ships in the line were also American. There was the *Chester Valley*, which in company with a trawler was to lose touch with the convoy in a big gale. At the same time she was to miss a great battle as well as mislead the radar of two British cruisers seeking the enemy. Finally came the *Yorkmar* and the *Ralph Waldo Emerson*.

These fourteen ships formed the smallest convoy yet to leave for Russia; but few as they were, they carried a valuable help for Stalin's hard-pressed armies now fighting for their very existence—2,040 lorries, 202 tanks, 87 fighters, 33 bombers, 20,120 tons of oil fuel (many of the merchant ships carried some in their deep tanks), 12,650 tons of aviation spirit, and 54,321 tons of mixed cargo, ranging from copper to explosives, and zinc to shells. (The individual cargoes are given in Appendix 2.)

Once in the open water and steering north, the Commodore ordered Matthews to run up the pre-arranged flag signal RZ 2. When these signal flags were hauled down it was the executive order for the formation of a second column. Slowly each alternate ship, starting with the *Daldorch* immediately astern of the Commodore, hauled out to port and increased speed until it had moved up a place.

By now the escorting warships were getting into position: the minesweeper *Bramble*—her fate nine days later was to become a mystery until after the war—whose captain, Cdr H. T. Rust, D.S.O., was the Senior Officer of this escort force, three of the small Hunt class destroyers, *Blankney*, *Chiddingfold* and *Ledbury*, three corvettes, *Hyderabad*, *Rhododendron* and *Circe*, and two trawlers, *Northern Gem* and *Vizalma*.

The three Hunts and the *Circe* would be leaving the convoy at Position C, the third geographical position detailed in their orders merely as a spot on the chart one hundred and fifty miles east of Iceland. Seven of the larger fleet destroyers, their fuel tanks freshly topped up at Seidisfiord (on the east coast of Iceland), would take over as escorts for the convoy's passage through the Greenland and Barents Seas, where the main threat of attack by the enemy was to be expected.

As soon as they were well clear of Cape Wrath and the Butt

26

of Lewis, Captain Melhuish ordered the signal RV to be hoisted in the *Empire Archer*. When all ships had understood the signal it was hauled down. Slowly, almost hesitantly— since some of the American masters were new to convoy work— the last of the three ships in the port (left-hand) column hauled out to port and moved up, while the last four in the starboard column hauled out to starboard and moved up. Thus the fourteen ships of JW 51B were now steaming northwards in four columns, *Calobre* (Vice-Commodore) leading the first, *Daldorch* the second, *Empire Archer* (Commodore) the third, and *Jefferson Myers* (Rear-Commodore) the fourth.

These were standard convoy positions for the Commodores. It had proved a wise arrangement, since the more experienced captains were given these tasks and were naturally better at leading the columns. However, it presupposed the Germans never guessed this, but they did, and U-boats made a practice, if they had the chance, of sinking the leading ships and thus disposing of the Commodore and his deputies.

The merchantmen were now in the formation which it was intended they should keep all the way to North Russia, and Captain Melhuish set a course for Position A, sixty-five miles north from Loch Ewe. Night came down and with it the wind increased, the audible herald of the barometer's pointing finger. By midnight Captain Melhuish reckoned the convoy had passed through Position A, and the ships steamed on the same course for Position B, eighty miles ahead and midway between Shetland and the Færöes.

To some merchant seamen, no less brave than other mortals, the Russian run was a death sentence with little or no chance of a reprieve. Even in a security-conscious Britain and America, some of the horrors and perils of war at sea beyond the Arctic Circle were common knowledge; and there was also plenty of rumour, gossip and fact surrounding the official secrets of many epics in these waters.

There were rumours that convoys were being decimated by heavy and bitter attacks by the Luftwaffe and U-boats; there was gossip that something terrible had happened to convoy PQ 17 the previous summer—that the Navy had left the merchantmen to their fate and only eleven out of thirty-three got through to Russia.[1]

How long did you survive in the freezing sea if your ship sank —was it two minutes or five? And how many hours in a life-boat (even if you could launch it in time, and row it away)? One? Or was it three? The law was not very strict about life-boats: only one was supposed to have an engine—the rest relied on oars which were nearly always broken or lost, often through exhausted men collapsing over them. There was, the men said cynically, always the Pool (the organization which supplied seamen for the merchantmen) and it was a deep one, so the Ministry of Transport did not have to worry itself unduly.[2] Lest anyone should think the warships were more fortunate, it should be remembered that their life-saving equipment was no better.

It did not need a very vivid imagination to realize that if your ship was sunk your chances of survival were extremely slender. Nor was it hard to guess that a good half of the convoy was likely to be sunk—perhaps more, with a small convoy like this. One out of two; five out of ten . . . every alternate finger on both hands.

A fifty-fifty chance of death, in fact; either the sudden all-obliterating death from the explosion of mine, bomb, shell or torpedo (and that, if one had to choose, was the way one would prefer); or the somewhat slower death from exposure in bitterly cold waters of the Arctic—just above freezing point; or the struggling, choking strangulation that is drowning.

In each of the merchantmen the cold wind whined in the rigging, searching for gaps in protective clothing, making half-

---

[1] A prevalent but unfair report circulated at the time. PQ 17 was heavily attacked from the air. The First Sea Lord, Admiral Sir Dudley Pound, guessed that German surface ships would join in. Knowing they would overwhelm the escort and then be able to sink the convoy, he ordered the escort to withdraw and the merchantmen to scatter—thus making it harder for the German warships to find them. The surface attack never materialized. Admiral Pound has since been severely criticized for his decision and for some loosely-phrased signals. The full story could not be told at the time for security reasons.

[2] Contrary to general belief, legislation covering merchant ships and seamen even in 1942 was crude and ineffective. Apart from life-boats, there was the question of pay. The author's pay, for instance, stopped the day his ship was torpedoed. Any sojourn in a life-boat or on a raft was an unpaid holiday.

closed eyes water and blur. Slowly the seas began to build up in size on the beam as the protective lee of the Hebrides was left astern, making the ships roll, pitch and yaw convulsively, a nightmare to officers of the watch trying to keep station in their columns and to helmsmen trying to steer a reasonable course; and a misery to the men off watch trying to snatch some sleep.

The ship in the next column was theoretically one thousand yards off—less than five ships' lengths; the ship next ahead was, theoretically, four hundred yards away. There were no lights to help them—or you—keep position. A minute or two off course, engines a few revolutions (perhaps half a knot) too fast, and the result could be a collision—or the convoy lost to sight. As the seas increased in size, slamming into each ship as it clawed its way north, and the wind got extra leverage on those great crates of bombers lashed to decks, the bows would yaw through twenty degrees and no one would blame the quarter-master at the wheel.

And all the while, at predetermined intervals, the convoy zigzagged. A special clock with electrical contacts which sounded a buzzer was used. These contacts were adjusted for the zigzag diagram ordered by the Commodore so that at the sound of the buzzer the officer of the watch would alter course the prescribed number of degrees.

For the escorts it was even worse, particularly the corvettes and trawlers. For days on end, in heavy weather, these small ships would be more like half-tide rocks than ships of war, heavy seas sluicing over them and making the upper deck impassable.

This was the picture at the beginning of the voyage: soon, as will be seen later, came the danger of ice forming inches thick on decks, guns, deckhouses, wires—on anything exposed to which spray, sleet or snow could cling and freeze. The most dreaded conditions came when rain or sleet fell with the thermometer down around 28° Fahrenheit. This happened in the waters east of Iceland when rain falling from warmer clouds was driven on to the ships by colder winds at sea-level and froze instantly it arrived aboard.

29

With the ice came one of the mariners' greatest fears, excessive topweight—tons upon tons not allowed for in the stability calculations made by ship designers. Weight forming high up in the ship meant the danger of capsizing . . . warning being given by the ship pausing at the end of each roll, heavy in the water, and reluctant to come upright again.

Yet this was almost entirely the war waged by Nature; the physical problem of sailing ships to North Russia to a calendar schedule in wartime. There was also the problem of fighting: of keeping the guns and their allied apparatus free of ice and manned, of conserving precious fuel oil, of even seeing the enemy—these winter convoys sailed in almost perpetual darkness. Daytime as known in lower latitudes was simply a lightening of the southern sky for three or four hours either side of noon. At this stage in World War II radar was fitted to few ships and was, at best, a temperamental and comparatively crude device.

In those dreary hours just after a convoy sailed, with the various jobs on deck completed, one's thoughts wandered—providing they were not dragged into the narrow, miserable, and retching confines of seasickness—beyond the bulkheads of one's cabin, mess-deck, or defence station: to wives, sweethearts, mothers and children left behind. Now one was at sea the link with them was tenuous: simply memories, tattered letters, creased and much-handled photographs kept carefully in wallets, all to be looked at or remembered when the chance came.

It was those thoughts which, when one was at sea, but without the guns firing, made one frightened of death: it was then the fear for one's loved ones, a fear that the bureaucratic machine inevitably enmeshing a government would deal harshly with one's next of kin. A sudden picture would thrust itself into the edge of one's reluctant imagination, a picture of trembling hands opening an impersonal buff telegram envelope, and unbelieving eyes reading the stereotyped words, 'The Minister of War Transport regrets . . .'

That, when there were no guns firing, no enemy in sight, and time to think, was what death meant to the average sailor:

30

the shattering of his home, without him being there to provide the buffer, the cushioning against harsh realities.

Quite an impersonal feeling in one way; yet one which brought the rebellious thought that one was caught up in an awful, slow-moving machine. After the first couple of days at sea—less if one was ever seasick—it wore off a bit, to attack only when one was on watch, hunched down in heavy, thick and soggy clothes, and trying to speed on reluctant, heavy-footed hours and minutes before the watch changed.

When the shooting started, if it was on the other side of the convoy, death took on a different aspect: then it became personal, and each explosion, each burning ship, capsized lifeboat, surging, spray-topped sea had but one meaning.

As it became closer, it changed once again, to become an all-pervading fear and, if one was not completely craven, a fear of fear itself: the fear that cowardice would make one unconsciously crouch, sprawl or run when it was one's duty to stand to a gun, signal lamp, searchlight—or just stand and wait for an order.

If one was honest, it was often only the fear of cowardice which kept one free of it; ingrained tradition, personal pride, the inability to face afterwards the scorn of the men whose opinions one valued, proved greater than the fear of being killed. Or maybe physiologists, to whom tradition is perhaps a conditioned reflex, can explain it in terms of glands secreting, or failing to secrete, too little or too much of the right or wrong kind of chemical into the bloodstream. Either way, it was a lousy feeling.

However, the men of JW 51B, thrashing their way north from the lee of the Butt of Lewis into grim wintry wastes of the North Atlantic, were, although they did not know it, sailing into a series of events and circumstances which, they could claim, had almost nothing to do with them.

This was a small convoy, but the battle to rage round it in a few days' time was to alter the course of the war at sea decisively. We must, therefore, examine why the convoy was at sea, what were the factors which caused it to be attacked

31

and why the outcome of the naval action had such far-reaching consequences.

War is not all shooting, heroism and violence; much that is of interest to historians and the general reader alike took place in men's brains, was affected by remote happenings in childhood, environment, the love of a wife, the lack of a wife, or strange quirks hard to explain without delving into the phraseology of the psychiatrist.

Looming ominously and unpredictably in that background is Adolf Hitler. One cannot ignore him, on the basis that most people know about him already, because although much has been written about his actions as the German war lord, very little is known about him as a 'sea lord'. It is Hitler as his own admiral that we must now briefly study.

2

The Sea Lord

WHO and what was Hitler? Before and during the war we had many and varied reports on the man; nearly all were from his enemies or from diplomats in contact with him. The former were unfortunately disregarded, since they had an axe to grind; the latter were listened to. But, it is now clear, they were nearly all wrong.

With their orderly, trained brains, cultured minds and polished manners, the diplomats were puzzled by this dull-eyed, harsh-voiced man, physically insignificant, so obviously a vulgar bluffer with a crude mind.

Hitler was a supreme opportunist: the ruthless gambler with a superb sense of the psychological moment to strike. At this time during the war the rest of the world saw him as a shrewd war lord, a man with a master plan on which the road to the Thousand Year Reich was carefully drawn. Years later, after the war, a surprised world was to find this was not the case. Hitler was a successful batsman if he could rely on bad bowling and inept fielding.

Born in 1889, at Braunau on the frontier between Bavaria and Austria, third son of a Customs official's third marriage, Hitler as a boy wanted to be an artist, refusing his father's demand that he become a civil servant. He worked at what he liked and left the rest; at school he was no great success, failing the usual leaving certificate examination. When his father died the boy, spoiled by his mother, grew up lazy and rebellious, a day-dreamer who refused to settle down. One of his few pleasures was to listen to Wagner's operas.

Going to Vienna Hitler tried and failed to get into the Academy of Fine Arts of the School of Architecture. In order to live he took labouring jobs. In *Mein Kampf* he refers to that

33

time as 'five years in which I had to earn my daily bread, first as a casual labourer, then as a painter of little trifles'. He frequently slept on park benches and in doss-houses when he could not pay his rent.

'During these years,' he wrote, 'a view of life and a definite outlook on the world took shape in my mind. These became the granite basis of my conduct at that time. Since then I have extended that foundation very little; I have changed nothing in it. . . .'

The scruffy little Austrian stayed out of active politics in those days, but nevertheless politics fascinated him. By the time the First World War began Hitler had become the man who was to stay unchanged until he was the master of Europe, almost of the world. Although an Austrian, he was a violent German nationalist; he was violently anti-Jewish and anti-Socialist.

When war broke out he joined a Bavarian regiment, fought in the First Battle of Ypres as a runner, won an Iron Cross Second Class in 1914 and, as a corporal, an Iron Cross First Class in 1918. And those brooding years of danger, blood and sacrifice in the trenches—which were to form his staple topics of conversation for the rest of his life—rounded off the man. From then on he had a contempt for democracy, an overwhelming feeling of the superiority of Germany as the master race (although he was of the opposite type: short, dark and Austrian) and a certainty that, with the Allied victory, the German nation had been 'stabbed in the back' by the German General Staff.

Merely one of millions of unemployed ex-Servicemen, Hitler went to Munich. There, at the age of thirty, he read voraciously, storing vast numbers of unrelated facts in his incredible memory, entered beer-cellar politics, and dreamed of restoring Germany to her previous greatness—and more. He dreamed of Germany as the Great Power of Europe.

Neurotic, shabbily dressed, pale, the famous forelock then plastered back on his scalp, a black moustache the width of his nostrils looking as if it was stuck on with spirit gum for a knock-about burlesque act, Hitler plunged into the whirling, swirling, cut-and-thrust politics that characterized the Germany of the 1920s.

Swiftly, from the unemployed ex-corporal of 1920, a rebel against society—though perhaps not a rebel without a cause —he became the leader of the National Socialist Party, a German citizen, and on 30th January 1933, Chancellor of the German Reich. The fantasy had become reality.

For thirteen years Hitler had studied history (selecting facts he wanted for his case, rejecting the rest). He had schemed, plotted, waited for the psychological moment, and then acted. He alone of the men active in German politics during those years knew what he wanted and pursued it with a single-mindedness usually given only to young lovers and crackpots.

Too many people were misled by the ranting, screaming, hectoring voice they heard, punctuated with the exhilarated 'Sieg Heil' of the enraptured thousands in his audience, coming over their wireless sets; too many diplomats cabled home assessments of this strange man based on his bad accent, ill-kempt appearance and lack of the salon manners expected of the leader of a government.

They did not penetrate behind those dull eyes, gesticulatory hands and excitable manner, to see the powerful, narrow, brutal and ruthless mind which watched and waited, planned and prepared for the time to act, and which had the hypnotic ability to bend men to his ways.

Apparently they assumed he was a coarse adventurer; they did not know the incredible amount of reading and study he got through, so that he could blind even the German General Staff with his knowledge. As Field Marshal Keitel, Chief of the High Command of the German Armed Forces (OKW) told the International Military Tribunal at Nuremberg: 'Every professional soldier will confirm that Hitler's grasp of strategy and tactics commanded admiration.'

'Nights of the war,' he said, 'were passed at his headquarters in study of all the General Staff books by Moltke, Schlieffen, and Clausewitz, and his remarkable knowledge not only of all the armies, but of the navies of the globe, amounted to genius. Far from the Chief of the OKW advising Hitler, it was Hitler who advised him.'

Hitler had become, in the minds of many people, simply a machine or a mad dog. A machine which overran Europe and then wore itself out; a mad dog who bit at nations viciously and without selection.

But he was neither of these. His mind and actions can be likened to those of Stalin—calculating and ruthless; they bear a tolerable resemblance to the modern style of business executive.

Even as a demobilized corporal he planned Germany's fight to greatness. Without education, contacts in the 'old boy' style, or even physical presence, he pulled himself up by his own bootstraps into a position where he could and did put his visions and plans into practice. That required incredible willpower. It is a 'success story'—if that is the right phrase—unparalleled in history.

An adventurer? Not in the accepted sense: that is the role of a Franco, a Kruschev, a career politician or a Napoleon. He was given no golden opportunity which he could seize to launch himself on the road to power. He created his own opportunities, knowing he had the courage to make the most of them. He thought and planned and schemed on a grand scale when the men about him—in the rest of Europe as well as Germany—were provincial in the extreme.

A megalomaniac? Yes—that is perhaps the key to his power. From his own highly-selective study of history, plus the ideas culled from the welter of crazy pseudo-philosophy spawned in the early twentieth-century Germany, he realized there was a golden opportunity for Germany to create her own Golden Age, her own Thousand Year Reich with its built-in culture, autobahns teeming with People's Cars, Strength-through-Joy cruises, auto-change Wagner, and slave labour provided by the rest of Europe.

Germany could achieve this, he believed, only under his own divine leadership. 'At long intervals in human history,' he had written in *Mein Kampf*, 'it may occasionally happen that the practical politician and political philosopher are one. . . .

Such a man does not labour to satisfy demands that are obvious to every Philistine; he reaches forward towards ends that are comprehensible only to the few. . . .'

(The few, regrettably, did not include among their members the foreign offices of Western Europe. The first volume of *Mein Kampf* came out in 1925. Even when Hitler came to power in 1933, and *Mein Kampf* became the Bible of the National Socialist Party and was published in most European languages, the diplomats failed to take heed of Hitler's written warning of his plans.)

How did he achieve all this?

We must remember that during his early life Hitler was deprived—of sufficient food, parental discipline and a secure family life. And these we know are necessary to produce a mentally well-balanced youth. The lack of these factors in childhood can—and in Hitler's case did—lead to a child creating his own world of fantasy; and he can live in this world for the rest of his life. As a compensation for his misery and deprivation Hitler, in fantasy, dreamed of himself not as an unhappy, unemployed weakling but a great leader. He saw Germany broken, corrupt and inefficient. He dreamed of re-creating its greatness. In this fantasy world he evaded harsh realities; to him there was no real obstacle to a Thousand Year Reich, with himself marching at the head of it.

Coupled with this (and it was of extreme value in overcoming his physical insignificance and lack of presence) was his hypnotic ability to persuade people and imbue them with loyalty to him.

Thus he was able, over the span of a very few years, so to persuade people that his fantasies became realities. In addition he used his fantastic memory to such purpose that he could often beat a man with a more logical mind but a lesser memory in a particular argument. Memory is a manifestation of intelligence, although naturally memory is not itself intelligence.

Reading over his speeches, statements, orders and remarks at various conferences and meetings, two things are now strikingly clear: Hitler considered that no one 'understood' him—he was alone; and he also considered that whereas mortals had ordinary appetites, he was above them. Both point to the fact he was the sole inhabitant of his own world of fantasy, the king—or prisoner—of the product of his own neurotic disorder.

He always identified himself with the country: Germany was part of himself. At the same time, once he had come to power, he wanted the men about him to give him frequent reassurances of their sycophantic obedience. Any criticism or argument from them could be—and nearly always was—interpreted as an action against Germany, and something to be smashed. It was the reaction of a spoilt child against the chiding of a doting parent.

(Jumping ahead in time for a moment, it is easier to understand why Hitler fought on, when every front had collapsed. Having in his fantasy world created Germany as part of himself, he wanted Germany to share in his own destruction. It was the spiteful action of a narcissistic child: if he could not have Germany then no one else should: he would break the toy rather than have another child play with it.)

Hitler's mental condition was no rarity; but fortunately the combination of a fantasy-builder with an hypnotic ability to persuade and enjoin loyalty is. The fantasy-builder is met frequently—the man, for instance, with delusions of grandeur, the man who thinks how heroic he would have been given the chance. Danny Kaye, in his film, symbolized it in the character of Walter Mitty.

Small wonder Hitler dismissed Europe's diplomats as little men, able to see only as far as next week's cocktail-party. He was seeing far into the future, to this Golden Age. Yet even so, he worked without a long-term plan showing how it was to be reached.

When Britain and France did come into the war Hitler found himself involved in a struggle in which he had too few U-boats and a comparatively small fleet. As Raeder had noted ruefully on 3rd September 1939, the Navy (having planned to build a balanced fleet with which Britain could be challenged in 1945) was 'in no way very adequately equipped for the great struggle with Great Britain', and the surface forces were 'so inferior in number and strength to those of the British Fleet that, even at full strength, they can do no more than show they know how to die gallantly'.

The speed with which Poland crumbled under the German tanks and Stuka dive-bombers gave the world a new and awful word, *blitzkrieg*, and partly convinced a doubting and suspicious General Staff that Hitler had something which might pass for genius, and they waited patiently for Hitler to produce his next master move.

But for ten months Hitler had nothing more in mind than the defeat of France, and hoped he would later come to agreement with Britain. The next move came about because of Germany's dependence on Swedish and Norwegian iron ore, a third of which was sent in ships down the Norwegian coast.

British attempts to stop this traffic, and the rescue of the British prisoners of war in the German ship *Altmark*,[1] led Hitler and Grand Admiral Raeder to fear a British invasion of Norway; the result was the German invasion of Norway and Denmark on 9th April 1940. The invasion of Holland, Belgium and France followed in May.

The German Navy learned a bitter lesson in the invasion of Norway—that the Royal Navy was ready to strike, and strike hard, wherever it could find the *Kriegsmarine* at sea. Even though much of the invasion of Norway was through the sheltered, near-landlocked waters of the Skagerrak and Kattegat, the Germans lost three cruisers sunk and two severely damaged, nine destroyers sunk and one severely damaged, and twelve merchant ships sunk or damaged.

These losses were high; they gave Hitler and Raeder an indication of what they might expect if and when they attempted to invade England. From dawn on 4th June, with the end of the Dunkirk evacuation, Hitler was in control of nearly three thousand miles of coastline, stretching from Norway's North Cape, inside the Arctic Circle, to the coast of Spain. The Royal

---

[1] These prisoners were from ships sunk by the pocket battleship *Admiral Graf Spee*: the British Government ordered the destroyer *Cossack* to go into Norwegian territorial waters and release them.

Navy had lost many valuable warships to the Luftwaffe; and from now on Britain was fighting alone.

When he saw a Britain that refused to make peace and was determined to fight on, Hitler realized he would have to invade, and made his plans. It was then his mistake became apparent.

Germany had not given any thought to war with Britain. Neither the Supreme Command nor the Naval Staff had worked out any strategical study or operational plan, and since the German Navy was so comparatively weak, this was vitally necessary so that the *Luftwaffe* could make up for deficiencies. In the event, Grand Admiral Raeder and Göring, head of the *Luftwaffe*, had bitter personal quarrels. As men they abhorred each other; as Service heads they distrusted each other.

Perhaps Hitler then finally realized the difficulties which faced Phillip II of Spain, Louis XIV, Napoleon and Kaiser Wilhelm II—and turned his thoughts to the East, to the vastness of Russia.

Why, as he paused on the banks of the English Channel, looking across that narrow sleeve of water which was all that separated him from final victory, did Hitler turn aside, to make an even greater enemy in the East? Was it fear that he would meet defeat on those rolling green English fields, flat fens, crowded industrial areas and windswept downlands?

Not exactly. There were several reasons, the basic one being that his victory in Europe had been so fast that no plans had been made for following it up with a swift cross-Channel invasion. No military landing-craft were available. Barges from Europe's waterways had to be hurriedly assembled.

Yet he wanted to keep up the pretence to his allies.

He told Mussolini later, on 19th January 1941, before his attack on Russia, 'The general situation in the East can be judged correctly from the situation in the West. The attack against the British Isles is our ultimate aim. . . . In this respect we are in the position of a man with only one round remaining in his rifle. If he misses, the situation is worse than before. . . .' If the invasion failed, Germany would have lost too much equipment—from tanks to landing-craft and warships—to try again.

Hitler was always conscious of the great power of Russia. The German-Soviet friendship pact, for instance, was signed in August 1939, and only when it was signed, thus settling with Stalin, did Hitler feel it was safe to start his attack on Poland.

When Stalin moved in on the Baltic states of Latvia, Lithuania and Estonia in July 1940, Hitler was very conscious of the nearness of Russian troops to the Homeland. Allied with that was his disappointment with Britain. He could not understand why Britain would not negotiate for peace after the collapse of France; he hoped—indeed believed—that Britain could be persuaded to leave him a free hand on the Continent in return for his agreement that he would not interfere with Britain and her vast overseas possessions and interests.

Perhaps because he was so sure of his own skill, but more possibly because of his own insular ignorance, and because of Ribbentrop's well-meant but ill-formulated advice, Hitler completely misjudged the British character. The lion was mangy, but mange is far from being a fatal disease.

When Britain refused to compromise his wrath fell on 'that drunkard Churchill', whose sturdy resilience, courage and determination seemed to be putting new life into the beleaguered island which, up to then, had apparently been a ripe plum waiting to be picked by an arm reaching from Berlin.

His newly-won friendship with Russia did not last long: neither Hitler nor Stalin trusted each other—with good reason; and Russia had begun to worry over Germany's increasing influence in the Balkans. So Hitler decided to eliminate Russia —'the last vassal on the Continent'—and with this completed he hoped then to force Britain to surrender.

Fantastic as such a decision may seem today, and inviting as the comparison with Napoleon's great blunder more than a century before may seem, let us see what was in Hitler's mind.

It is probably best described by Professor Trevor-Roper, the first man to unravel the last fantastic weeks of Hitler's life. Hitler, he says, reasoned thus. Just as the Roman Empire had sickened before the German barbarians fell on it and destroyed

it, so the civilization of the West, in Hitler's belief, was now
sickening and would slowly die.

Or would it be allowed to die? Would it not rather, like the
Roman Empire, be conquered and absorbed by the new barbarian
power which would ultimately replace it? But what would that new
barbarian power be? On this topic also Hitler had brooded long, and,
following 'the iron law of historical development', thought he had
found the answer.

First of all, it was clear that the new power, whatever it was, must
be a land power. This was determined by technical fact. The day of
maritime empires such as the empires of Portugal, Holland and
Britain was, in his opinion, over. In the old times, indeed, the sea had
provided the only smooth and cheap communications with the distant parts of the earth, and great land masses had been the barriers,
not the means of travel; but now, thanks to roads and railways,
motor power and air power, that was reversed: the new empire,
which would conquer and absorb and replace the society of Western
Europe, must be a great land empire, bound together not by ships
and trade but by giant roads and massive armies, the real nexus of
the new age.

Hitler was naturally a landsman: he came not from the Baltic or
the Mediterranean but from the heart of Europe, and he had probably
seldom seen the sea. Certainly he never understood sea power; and
distant colonies, which depended on sea power, he rejected altogether.

It was continents, not islands, that interested him. So he brooded
over maps and planned vast roads and studied the new science of
'geopolitics' which, inspired by Sir Halford Mackinder in 1919,
had found a more sympathetic reception in Central Europe than in
its native England. . . . But if the new age was to be the age of a great
land-empire dominating what Sir Halford Mackinder had called
'the Heartland', 'the Citadel of the World Empire'—the area, that
is, invulnerable to sea power in Central Europe and Asia—what
people, what government could claim this empire?

Clearly it could not be any of the old maritime peoples—and in
them therefore Hitler was fundamentally uninterested: it must be—
if it were to be a European people—either the Germans or the

Russians, for those people alone had the land-armies, the land-ambitions, the 'geopolitical' outlook on such an achievement.

The German geopoliticians, on the whole, had assumed that it would be the Russians, who were, after all, both more numerous and already there; and they advocated, for Germany, rather an alliance with Russia than an attempt to conquer it. And yet, Hitler asked himself, was that really inevitable? Were not the Germans the real *Kulturtrager*, the culture-bearers of Europe? Was it not the Germans, who, when the Roman Empire had been rotted inwardly by Jewish Christianity and a declining population, had conquered and inherited it?

The Germanic Middle Ages had indeed been frustrated by the 'Christian' Renaissance, the rise of the plutocratic capitalist civilization of Western Europe; but now that that plutocratic capitalist civilization was in its turn decaying, might not the Germans re-awake and, awakened, resume and redirect their splendid mission? The old German Emperors, for good technical reasons, had looked south to Italy; the new German Reich, for similar reasons, must look east.

Might it not, even now, by some heroic effort, wrest from the Russians their dominion and impose upon the Heartland a German instead of a Russian Empire?'[1]

So it was, then, that misunderstanding sea power and the strength it gave to Britain, failing to appreciate that there was one place where Britain could bring him to battle on land—the Middle East—and underestimating Russia's strength and powers of recovery after the first shattering *panzer* blows, he turned from the unquiet waters of the Channel and told Grand Admiral Raeder of his plans.

Raeder was a very worried man. He was head and shoulders above Hitler, the Party and the General Staff—who by now had completely knuckled under to Hitler and were in the position of mesmerized lackeys, anxious and willing to do his bidding —as a strategist. It was Raeder's fears for Norway which led to its invasion; it was his fear—as he warned Hitler—that an

[1] H. R. Trevor-Roper, Introduction to *Hitler's Table-Talk* (Weidenfeld & Nicolson, 1953).

43

attempt to invade Britain involved the risk of losing the entire force engaged.

So he was greatly relieved when Hitler announced on 26th December 1940 that 'the German Armed Forces must be prepared, even before the end of the war against England, to overthrow Soviet Russia in a rapid campaign (Operation Barbarossa)'.

3

Zone of Destiny

THE opening months of the war had not gone too well for the German Navy, and from the beginning there had been a worrying material and mental unpreparedness: neither Raeder nor the Naval Staff shared the view of Hitler and others on the General Staff that successes on the Continent of Europe would prove decisive and bring final victory. How was war against world powers to be fought without sea power?

During 1940 the U-boats had a fair success, but the British blockade began to make itself felt. The loss of the pocket battle-ship *Admiral Graf Spee* on 13th December 1939, giving Britain a splendid propaganda—as well as sea—victory, had a great psychological effect on Hitler.[1]

In the spring of 1941 Coastal Command slowly began to score successes against U-boats in the Atlantic. It was in May of that year that the *Bismarck*, with the *Prinz Eugen* in company, sailed on a foray into the Atlantic to attack Allied shipping. At first she scored a big success by sinking the *Hood* and then escaping into the Atlantic; but, thanks to Coastal Command and Fleet Air Arm planes, she was finally caught by the Royal Navy and sunk, amid a flurried exchange of loyal greetings. The *Bismarck*, a few hours before the end, signalled: 'To the Führer of the German Reich Adolf Hitler: we fight to the last in our belief in you my Führer and in the firm faith in Germany's Victory,' to which Hitler replied: 'I thank you in the name of the German people.'

With the loss of one of his latest and greatest battleships, Hitler began to have serious doubts about his surface fleet; but he had plenty of other things to worry about around this time.

German troops marched into Jugoslavia and Greece and

[1] See the author's *The Battle of the River Plate* (Kimber, 1956).

advanced rapidly, and before dawn on 22nd June almost the whole of Germany's armed might was flung against Russia in an attack Hitler was sure would take him to Moscow before the winter set in. He was so confident that he dismissed any idea of preparing suitable clothing, and gear for planes, tanks and guns which would allow his forces to continue fighting when the sub-zero Russian winter set in. Victory would have been achieved by then, he declared.

By this time, Hitler was taking an increasing hand in Army operations; he was now about to begin his interference in naval operations. In September, the Naval Staff under Raeder drew up a plan for commerce-raiding in the Atlantic. They proposed that the battle-cruisers *Scharnhorst* and *Gneisenau* and heavy cruiser *Prinz Eugen*, then bottled up in Brest and being regularly bombed by the RAF, should be joined by the battleship *Tirpitz* and heavy cruiser *Hipper* from home waters. There was violent opposition from the Naval Group Commanders who maintained that the ships would be running an unnecessary risk.

The plan was put up to Hitler and he vetoed it. With the invasion of Russia slowing up, he was finding another bogy to frighten himself with—Norway. As it has a considerable bearing on the fate of convoy JW 51B and her escort we must examine this fear in more detail.

The first hint came on 17th September when there was a big conference at *Wolfschanze* (Fort Wolf), Hitler's headquarters hidden among the pine trees at Rastenberg, in East Prussia. In a widespread survey of the war at sea, Raeder reported that 'the British realize the vital importance of the sea route off the Arctic coast for supplies of the German Armed Forces, and they are operating in the northern area with several cruisers, destroyers, one or two aircraft carriers and submarines. Our own naval and air resources are slight. . . . As the activities of the *Luftwaffe* are reduced by the approaching winter, the threat from surface forces increases.'

Hitler nodded at this but made no reply. Then Raeder went on to describe his big ships. They were undergoing repairs, overhauls or trials. 'Operations in the Atlantic will not be possible before the beginning of 1942,' he said.

Then Hitler said: 'Would it not be better to station them along the Norwegian coast, in order to defend the northern area? They cannot be protected from air attacks at Brest.'

Basically, replied Raeder, the idea of using these ships to wage war against merchant shipping in the Atlantic is the correct one. Originally the battleships were not supposed to remain in Brest very long, since at that time it was definitely hoped they would be able to use the Spanish bases, 'from which the battle of the Atlantic could have been fought very advantageously'.[1]

A month later Raeder reported once again to Hitler at Fort Wolf and complained about Norway: the most important task was that of bringing up supplies and strengthening coastal defences in the Arctic area. Turning to the surface fleet, he said the *Tirpitz* would go to Norway in December while the Brest squadron would be ready for operations in February. 'In view of the existing danger of air attacks it is not advisable to keep the ships in Brest after they are ready for operations,' he added. Then he outlined the Naval Staff's conclusions—arrived at after full consideration of the 'very difficult oil situation'.

No lengthy operations against merchant ships in the Atlantic were to be undertaken. When the ships were ready, it could be decided whether the ships should operate off the French Atlantic coast against convoys, or 'whether steps could be taken to transfer the ships to home waters or to the Norwegian area. The decision will depend on the enemy situation and the oil situation'.

In the event, it was neither which caused the decision to be made; but Hitler asked, 'What are the chances for a surprise withdrawal of the ships through the Channel?'

Raeder explained that it was thought it might be possible for the *Prinz Eugen* 'but not so far for the battle-cruisers: the matter is to be further studied'.

He said the Naval Staff wanted to send the *Admiral Scheer*, a pocket battleship, on another commerce-raiding operation into the Atlantic and Indian Oceans; but Hitler said that the

---

[1] Operation Felix, the conquest of Gibraltar and the establishment of German bases in the Canary Islands and along the Spanish coast, had fallen through—thanks mainly to Franco's wariness.

possible loss of the ship at present 'would be a heavy blow to prestige', and, he added: 'The vital point at present is in the Norwegian sea.' He would rather see the *Scheer* transferred to the Norwegian coast—to Narvik or Trondheim.

By the time the next naval conference was held, the world situation had changed drastically: Japan—without warning the other two partners of the Rome–Berlin–Tokyo Axis— attacked Pearl Harbour on 7th December and brought America actively into the war.

Raeder told Hitler that the effect should be a withdrawal of American ships from the Atlantic and 'the strain on British merchant shipping will increase'.

But it was at the conference at Fort Wolf on 29th December 1941, that Hitler really came out in the open: Raeder reported that 'an enemy surprise undertaking of considerable pro- portions' was being carried out against focal points in the trade route of Narvik and near Bergen 'to destroy coast de- fences, disrupt shipping, and to reconnoitre the terrain and the defences with a view to the later establishment of bridgeheads for the purpose of disrupting and blocking supply routes'. (A somewhat alarmist view of Allied Commando activities.)

The *Scharnhorst*, *Gneisenau* and *Prinz Eugen*, all at Brest, would be ready in a few days, although because of the lack of training 'it is out of the question to send the ships on opera- tions before March'. The possibilities were attacks on British north- and south-bound convoys, he said, or transfer to the northern area. . . .

But he had said too much. Hitler immediately said: 'If the British go about things properly they will attack Northern Norway[1] at several points. By means of an all-out attack with their fleet and landing troops, they will try to displace us there, take Narvik, if possible, and thus exert pressure on Sweden and Finland. This might be decisive for the outcome of the war.

'The German Fleet must therefore,' he declared, 'use all its forces for the defence of Norway. It will be expedient to transfer all battleships and pocket battleships there for this purpose: the

[1] In fact Mr Churchill had wanted to do this during 1942 but was overruled by the Chiefs of Staff Committee.

pocket battleships can be used, for instance, for attacking convoys in the north, although the Naval Staff do not consider them suitable for the task in this area.'

A marginal note, probably made by the Naval Staff, in the Navy's minutes of the conference says: '*How come? In winter perhaps?*'

Hitler had got into his stride: once again the sea lord was functioning at full power. That he knew nothing of naval strategy mattered little; he had, he was certain, figured out the Allies' next move. He did not need to ask a question of the Naval Staff, whose head, Raeder, was sitting round the table; he knew, and that was enough.

'The return of the Brest ships,' he declared, 'is therefore most desirable. This can be accomplished best if the vessels break through the Channel, taking the enemy completely by surprise—that is without previous training movements and during bad weather which would make air operations impossible.'

The Naval Staff pencilled on the minutes: '*Navigational difficulties would be greatest then.*'

Having given his views, the Führer gave a warning—a warning not then taken very seriously by Raeder, but one which was to have a vast effect on the Navy and which provides the subject of this narrative.

'If the surprise break-out through the Channel is impossible, therefore, it would be best to pay off the ships and use the guns and crews for reinforcements in Norway.'

He went on to talk of torpedo-carrying aircraft, which he rated very highly. In the discussion that followed the value of battleships in future was brought up. Raeder found himself in a minority, since their value was denied; but he made a sharp and detailed reply.

The presence of battleships in Brest, even if under repairs, he said, forces the British to protect their convoys with heavy forces which are then not available for other purposes[1]: it

---

[1] A simple statement of the classic concept of 'a fleet in being'. It gives some idea of Hitler's lack of knowledge of the use of sea power that Raeder felt it necessary to give this 'child's guide'.

would be impossible, he declared, to justify the paying off to the Italians and especially to the Japanese. He asked for permission to go into the whole question once more before a decision was made. The Führer agreed.

The Navy worked quickly before the next conference with Hitler on 12th January. In the opening weeks of 1942 Germany was thoroughly enmeshed in the war against Russia: the bitter winter was proving to be Russia's most effective ally. By now, supplies from the Empire and America were pouring into Britain by sea despite the U-boats waiting in ambush; and the British were fighting desperately in Libya and Abyssinia. Many Commando raids were being made against the German-held European coast. They were simply pinpricks, designed more to irk the Germans and to keep them constantly on the alert; but in fact the small raids on Norway alarmed Hitler.

With his imagination fed by rumour—and also by Raeder's own views on Norway—Hitler became more and more convinced that an Allied invasion of Norway was imminent. With neither Keitel nor Jodl able or willing to argue with him, he saw in his imagination, bolstered up by a close inspection of relevant maps and sweeping gestures indicating armoured movements, Sweden on the point of joining the Allies.

Then, he declared, the attack on Norway would become a pincer movement: Britain would attack by sea while the Swedes and the Russians would attack by land. The immediate outcome would be that Russia and the Western Allies would be able to join forces and thereby slow down and damage the German advance on the Eastern Front.

How, then, was he to meet such a threat?

It was, he considered, comparatively simple. The main thing was not to take any troops, tanks or guns away from the Russian front. There were three methods by which Germany could defend Norway against a possible invasion: by attacking the sea routes to Britain; by attacking Britain's towns and factories; and by attacking the invaders in or off Norway itself.

As the first two methods were already being used, there remained only the strengthening of Norway's sea and air defences. The Navy and the *Luftwaffe* would be responsible for the country's defence.

A reluctant Raeder turned up at the conference on 19th January 1942 with his staff and said that although he did not believe that he should take the initiative in advocating a breakthrough operation in the Channel, plans had been worked out that ought to be followed, should it be decided upon. The officers with him would report on how it could be carried out 'to enable you, my Führer, to make the final decision afterwards'.

But Hitler, without waiting to hear the expert and considered view of his admirals, had already made up his mind. After saying he might have left the ships at Brest if he could be sure they would not be damaged by bombing, he added: 'On the basis of incoming reports and in view of the increasingly unfriendly attitude of Sweden, I fear there will be a large-scale Norwegian-Russian offensive in Norway.

'If a strong force of battleships and cruisers, practically the entire German Fleet, were stationed along the Norwegian coast, it could, in conjunction with the *Luftwaffe*, make a decisive contribution to the defence of the Norwegian area. I am therefore determined to have the main strength of the German naval forces shifted to that area.'

At the next naval conference, on 22nd January, Hitler was scaring himself even further about Norway. Vice-admiral Fricke reported that the latest news had 'thoroughly convinced the Führer that Britain and the United States intend to make every effort to influence the course of the war by an attack on Northern Norway. Several places along the coast from Trondheim to Kirkenes will probably be occupied shortly. Sweden's support in the spring offensive is expected, for which she would receive Narvik and ore deposits near Petsamo'.

Anglo-Saxon domination of the area, Hitler said, would gradually eliminate all freedom of action in the Baltic Sea. He was convinced that 'Norway is the zone of destiny' in this war. Therefore he demanded the 'unconditional obedience' to

51

all his commands and wishes concerning the defence of the area.

Thus on the evening of 11th February 1942 the battle-cruisers *Scharnhorst* and *Gneisenau* and the heavy cruiser *Prinz Eugen* slipped out of Brest and ran up through the Channel. Commanded by Admiral Ciliax, screened by smaller warships and a large number of fighters, the ships got through even though in Britain it was appreciated they might make the attempt and plans had been made accordingly.

'Vice-admiral Ciliax,' said *The Times*, 'has succeeded where the Duke of Medina Sidonia failed . . . nothing more mortifying to the pride of the sea power has happened in home waters since the 16th century.' Hitler was very pleased—particularly so since he felt he had forced the Navy to take ships through the Channel.

In the spring of 1942 he made far-reaching plans for the two major theatres of war—Russia and the Mediterranean. For the former, he planned a spring offensive by the Army, and he was also concerned to stop British and American aid reaching Russia.

Since 22nd June 1941—the day Hitler attacked in the East and Mr Churchill had promised all possible British help for Russia—the Allied assistance had, with America's entry into the war, increased considerably. It had grown from a modest beginning of a seven-ship convoy in August 1941 until in June 1942 quite large convoys were sailing at least twice a month. It did not take Hitler long to realize that help on this scale would soon start to affect the position on the Eastern Front. The Arctic convoys, therefore, were to become one of the German Navy's priority targets. Operations were worked out for a combined sea and air offensive in June, followed by surface raiders later, when almost perpetual darkness stopped effective flying.

Now Hitler's lack of understanding of the use of sea power, and his timidity over the use of his warships, began to make itself felt. The Navy and Luftwaffe planned a massive attack on the next Allied convoy to Russia (PQ 17 in July). At his conference on 15th July Hitler assumed that the Royal Navy

would sail an aircraft carrier with PQ 17 and warned Raeder
that he considered they were a great threat to heavy warships
of the German Fleet. 'The aircraft carriers must be located
before the attack,' he said, 'and they must be rendered harm-
less by our Ju 88 planes before the attack gets under way.'

Raeder asked that the naval forces 'be sent to their stations
in the north in good time'. Hitler agreed, but he insisted that
they must await the order to attack, and this order was to be
subject to his approval.

It was now that the earlier British successes at sea were
beginning to pay dividends. A victory at sea is not only a
question of sinking enemy warships. Hitler obviously had a
vivid picture in his mind of the *Graf Spee* blowing up off Monte-
video, and also of those last dramatic signals from the *Bismarck*.
He had earlier changed the name of the pocket battleship
Deutschland to *Lützow*, because if she was sunk while still
named *Deutschland* it would be a great propaganda victory for
the Allies.

By this time Hitler had pretty well assumed tactical, as well
as strategical, control of the Army: instead of merely setting
the over-all objective, he interfered so much that within a few
months he was juggling with individual battalions, let alone
brigades, divisions or armies. And as spring gave way to summer
in 1942 the German offensive in Russia was renewed. By
August they had pushed into the Caucasus. Rostov and Stalingrad were reached.

The U-boat war was going well, with heavy sinkings of
Allied ships. Rommel had attacked again in the Mediterranean,
aiming for Suez. Hitler knew the British and Americans must
be preparing some counter-attack, and he was satisfied he had
discovered the spot and made adequate plans and dispositions
to defend it. That place, he thought, was Norway. Hitler was
partly right, as at that moment the British and Americans *were*
planning their first counter-attack; only it was not against
Norway. It was to be against North Africa.

However, since Hitler was determined to stop the Allied
convoys to Russia, we must now see the problems facing the
Royal Navy in trying to fight these convoys through.

4

'In Defeat, Defiance'

WHEN Germany invaded Russia in June 1941 there were only two practicable ways in which Britain could send help to Russia—by sea through the Arctic to Murmansk and Archangel, or by sea round the Cape of Good Hope to the Persian Gulf and then 1,000 miles overland on a single-track railway.

The best and most obvious way was through the Arctic; and the first convoy to Archangel sailed in late summer of 1941. More convoys sailed through that winter, with little opposition from the Germans, and surprisingly few losses.[1]

But as the spring of 1942 came, the 'Russian Run' as it was often called, became one of the most bitterly contested naval and air operations of the whole war. This was due, of course, to Hitler's decision to move his fleet to Norway to prevent an invasion and to put an end to any Allied aid to Russia.

On paper, it was impracticable to sail convoys from Britain to North Russia without heavy and unbearable losses. But Mr Churchill's promise to Stalin—'We shall do everything to help you that time, geography and our growing resources allow'— had to be implemented.

The Germans held the whole of Norway: more than 1,320 miles of coastline liberally supplied with bases for U-boats and surface ships, as well as with airfields. The convoys had to sail between 1,500 and 2,000 miles, depending on the time of the year—roughly the distance from London to Moscow. For more than half that time they were well inside an area where the *Luftwaffe* could bomb and torpedo them with fast Ju 88s and the heavier He 111s.

---

[1] Raeder reported after the war that the first six PQ convoys were detected by wireless intelligence but could not be attacked.

For the last part of the voyage they had to pass within two hundred miles of Altenfiord, where the Germans kept big surface raiders; towards the end of the voyage they sailed to within one hundred and fifty miles of the German-held bases at Petsamo and Kirkenes. Even when they docked at Murmansk, the *Luftwaffe* had only ninety miles flying from Petsamo and were able to attack the merchantmen and their escorts at will.

Protection of the convoys was one of the tasks of the Commander-in-Chief, Home Fleet, Admiral Sir John Tovey and he thus had to provide for their safety along a route on which they could always be attacked by U-boats, limited as it was in the north and west by ice and to the east and south by the proximity of German naval and air bases in occupied Norway. Support for these convoys from Russian forces was negligible, despite their tremendous value to the Russian war effort.

In addition, the convoy bases at either end of the route— Scotland–Iceland and Murmansk–Archangel—could be and were inspected by German planes, and the route was crossed by at least two regular German meteorological and reconnaissance flights.

These were the purely geographical features. But always there was the constant battle against Nature.

Almost everywhere, in the spring of 1942, the Allies were on the edge of defeat. It had become almost too much even to hope. In the Far East the Japanese had carried all before them (Singapore fell in February) and the Americans were still reeling from the treacherous blow at Pearl Harbour. Java surrendered, Rangoon had been occupied, and the world waited for the Japanese to begin their march on India. There was precious little to stop them if they so chose. Their landings on New Guinea menaced Australia.

In the Mediterranean the Germans had advanced three hundred miles into Cyrenaica, threatening the Suez Canal itself; the problem of keeping Malta supplied was wearing down Admiral Cunningham's forces. Britain was on the verge of being beaten in the only place where she could bring the Germans to battle on land and thus ease some of the pressure on Russia. As if this were not enough, the Battle of the Atlantic was entering in March its worst phase: it looked as though Britain might fall simply because she could not be fed and armed from abroad—a minimum of a million tons of supplies had to be brought in by sea every week if the island was to survive.

The Royal Navy was suffering—as, indeed, were the Army and the RAF—the results of the muddled political and diplomatic thinking of the inter-war years. The fleet in peacetime had been tied in size by treaties which were now merely the epitaphs of well-meaning but naïve and stupid diplomacy; now it had to fight in every ocean of the world. Heavy losses in 1941 included the carrier *Ark Royal*, the *Barham*, *Prince of Wales* and *Repulse*.

The Admiralty was pitifully short of almost every type of warship. There were not nearly enough battleships—needed to contain the German Fleet in Europe—to defend the sea lanes of the Indian Ocean against the Japanese Fleet and to help the Americans still recovering from the blow of Pearl Harbour.

Cruisers, vital vessels for patrolling the shipping routes of the world and guarding against surface raiders—witness the three cruisers which forced the destruction of the pocket battleship *Admiral Graf Spee* in the Atlantic—were few and far between.

And as for aircraft carriers of all sizes, wanted to protect capital ships and convoys in the Atlantic, Mediterranean, Arctic, Indian and Pacific Oceans, there were hardly any at all.

But our most desperate shortage was of convoy escorts—destroyers, frigates and corvettes. We had traded naval bases for fifty over-age American destroyers, but they could be only a palliative. Convoys sailed with only token groups of escorts—for example a convoy on a less important route, Britain to West Africa, comprising thirty ships might, at this time, have an escort of three small corvettes. If U-boats or bombers attacked, they had a more or less free hand to deal with the convoy.[1]

It was a discouraging and dismal picture which faced the Combined Chiefs of Staff Committee in Washington; but they agreed that the Allies had three main tasks at that moment:

(1) to keep Russia effectively in the war;
(2) to prevent Germany and Japan from joining hands in the Indian Ocean area;
(3) to check the Japanese advance on India and Australia.

The first was rated the most important, and it could be achieved in two ways—by keeping on hammering at the Germans in the Mediterranean, thus preventing reinforcement of the *Wehrmacht* on the Eastern Front and by keeping up a continuous flow of supplies to Russia.

The bulk of these supplies, of course, were to come from America, which by the beginning of 1942 was sufficiently well geared up to be called the 'Arsenal of Democracy'. America was to supply most of the material, but Britain was to supply most of the escorts for the convoys: a fine example of Allied co-operation, since each partner was giving of his utmost in the only way possible.

To Admiral Tovey, commanding the Home Fleet, who naturally knew nothing of Hitler's modesty over Norway, the arrival of the *Tirpitz* and *Scheer* in northern waters meant one of two things—attacks on our Russian convoys or German raiding forays into the Atlantic. Thus, with a depleted fleet, he had to face two ways.

The long dark nights of the winter of 1941 had sheltered the convoys; but the lengthening days of the summer of 1942 brought unbroken daylight, which resulted in prolonged attacks on the merchantmen. But the long hours of daylight were not the only natural hazard: the icefields come much farther south in the spring and the convoys were forced to pass south of Bear Island, and thus much nearer German air and naval bases.

[1] One such convoy, SL 125 in which the author sailed, was attacked in 1942 by nine U-boats, and thirteen merchant ships were sunk in a seven-day battle. No U-boats were sunk. Those lessons, learned in three centuries of war at sea, and at such a dreadful and dangerous cost, seem now, in 1958, to have been forgotten again, as always happens in the inter-war years, those sporadic outbreaks of peace which enervate democracies.

It was clear to Admiral Tovey that big ships from the Home Fleet would have to cover the convoys; but they would, because of the increasing threat from U-boats, need plenty of destroyers to screen them. That meant fewer destroyers available as close escorts for the convoys, and in any case escorting destroyers became so short of fuel that they could not afford to hunt U-boats to the kill. They could only drive them from the convoy, which meant they lived to attack another day. Usually, since the convoys were so slow, the next day.

Admiral Tovey, in February 1942, said in an appreciation of the situation that probable air and U-boat attacks would be concentrated on the eastern end of the route (i.e. close to the Norwegian-Russian coast) and surface attacks by the big ships would be to the westwards, where there was more sea room.

'The protection of these convoys,' he wrote, 'is a major commitment for the Home Fleet; but in it lies a hope of bringing enemy surface ships to action. On the other hand the operation covering a northern passage and the time spent in northern waters must be the minimum.'

The attacks on the convoys increased in severity but President Roosevelt, in a cable to Mr Churchill, pointed out the possible political repercussions in Russia if they were stopped, and added, 'We have made such a tremendous effort to get our supplies going that to have them blocked except for most compelling reasons seems to me a serious mistake.'

Mr Churchill in reply explained the difficulties: not only anti-submarine vessels were needed, but heavy ships as well. 'Admiral King (the American Chief of Naval Operations) has expressed opinion that our transatlantic escorts are already too thin. Reduction proposed [of the number of escorts to each Atlantic convoy, with bigger convoys] would dislocate convoy system for eight weeks, during which, if enemy switched [his heavy U-boat attacks] from your east coast to mid-ocean, disastrous consequences might follow to our main life-line.'[1]

Three days later Marshal Stalin cabled to Mr Churchill: 'I have a request for you. Some ninety[2] steamers loaded with

[1] Churchill, *The Second World War*, Vol. IV, p. 231.
[2] Actually 107.

various important war materials for the USSR are bottled up at present in Iceland, or in the approaches from America to Iceland. I understand there is a danger that the sailing of these may be delayed for a long time because of the difficulty to organize convoy escorted by the British naval forces.

'I am fully aware of the difficulties involved and of the sacrifices made by Great Britain in this matter. I feel it however incumbent upon me to approach you with the request to take all possible measures in order to ensure the arrival of the above-mentioned materials in the USSR in the course of May, as this is extremely important for our front.'

The climax of those signals was convoy PQ 17 of which only eleven out of thirty-four merchantmen got through.

Admiral Tovey then suggested to the First Sea Lord, Admiral Sir Dudley Pound, that the Russian convoys should be temporarily suspended until the period of perpetual daylight was over, or smaller and handier convoys sailed.

However, neither suggestion could be accepted: too much was at stake, and the American munitions and supplies were piling up at the same time as the Russians were clamouring for them.[1]

Apart from that, Mr Churchill was inclined to increase the stakes, on the principle of 'in defeat, defiance', and suggested that practically all our aircraft carriers, supported by heavy ships, should be used. The Admiralty did not agree. In fact the urgent necessity to run a convoy to Malta, then almost starving, intervened, and at the same time American ships were being slowly withdrawn for Pacific operations. The shortage of escorts thus caused Mr Churchill, in co-operation with President Roosevelt, to decide the time had come to call a halt, at least during the summer months of perpetual daylight. He cabled a long signal to Marshal Stalin explaining the situation. 'My naval advisers tell me,' he said, 'that if they had the handling of the German naval surface, submarine and air forces, in

---

[1] An interesting sidelight on the Russian attitude is shown by the fact that a medical unit sent out from Britain to help tend the sick, wounded and frost-bitten British seamen, who had been bringing in arms and ammunition, and for whom there had been no adequate facilities, was refused permission to land. No reason was given, although insults were exchanged at high levels.

present circumstances, they would guarantee the complete destruction of any convoy to North Russia . . . it is therefore with the greatest regret that we have reached the conclusion that to attempt to run the next convoy, PQ 18, would bring no benefit to you and would only involve dead loss to the common cause.'

Marshal Stalin replied in a way which, in post-war years, one got to know and expect. At the time, however, it was brutal—especially considering the number of Allied seamen who had already perished in their attempts to help supply the Russians.

Two conclusions could be drawn from Mr Churchill's message, said Stalin. 'First, the British Government refuses to continue the sending of war materials to the Soviet Union via the northern route. Second, in spite of the agreed communique concerning the urgent tasks of creating a second front in 1942 the British Government postpones this matter until 1943.

'Our naval experts,' he added, 'consider the reasons put forward by the British naval experts to justify the cessation of convoys to the northern ports of the USSR wholly unconvincing. They are of the opinion that with goodwill and readiness to fulfil the contracted obligations these convoys could be regularly undertaken and heavy losses could be inflicted on the enemy. . . .'

Perhaps Mr Churchill's comment is all that need be said. He did 'not think it worth while to argue out all this with the Soviet Government, who had been willing until they were themselves attacked to see us totally destroyed and share the booty with Hitler, and who even in our common struggle could hardly spare a word of sympathy for the heavy British and American losses incurred in trying to send them aid'.[1]

Up to now—since the heavy losses sustained by PQ 17 were the result of a mistake rather than anything else—the Navy had been able to keep up with the attacks of U-boats and the *Luftwaffe*; but the greatest danger, the Admiralty could see, would come if and when the Germans threw in the surface ships.

And this is just what the Germans were proposing to do.

[1] Churchill, *Second World War*, Vol. IV.

By the beginning of June the German Naval Staff had decided that the fuel situation had improved sufficiently to let them sail the big ships. Admiral Klüber, the German Flag Officer, Northern Area, had repeatedly suggested this; and though Admiral Schniewind, the head of the Operations Division, was not particularly anxious to get involved with British or American heavy ships, he realized the bad effect staying at anchor in fiords had on the morale of the crews when their comrades of the U-boats were constantly in action.

But, as mentioned earlier, Hitler had said his approval would be necessary before the cruisers and battleships could sail. Fortunately for the Allies he refused it. By constantly harping on the fact that he could not bear to expose them to any sort of risk, he had got his admirals into the frame of mind that, once they were at sea, their overwhelming object in life was to get back to harbour safely, rather than to inflict damage on the enemy.

This factor is an important one in this narrative—indeed in one's whole assessment of the conduct of German surface ships at sea.[1] Frequently the captains appeared to turn and run from battle through cowardice. It was, in effect, cowardice—but often due to their fear of Hitler rather than of the British. The U-boat commanders, for instance, who were not hedged round with restrictions, fought extremely bravely, though not always honourably.

When the Home Fleet was strong enough to allow the Russian convoys to start again Admiral Tovey settled down to plan their sailings and decided to change his tactics. He was firmly convinced that from now on he would have to fight every convoy through to the Russian ports, and his problem was how best to defend it from the triple menace of air, surface and U-boat attacks. He realized that if the Germans used their surface forces—the big ships—intelligently, there was little to stop further disasters on the scale of PQ 17.

[1] I exclude the *Graf Spee*: as can be seen from my book *The Battle of the River Plate*, there was no such factor in Langsdorff's decision to run.

He finally decided that the defence against surface ship attack must come from the convoy escort itself and developed the idea of the 'fighting destroyer escort' of twelve to sixteen fleet destroyers.[1]

These would sail and remain with the convoy and its normal close escort of destroyers, frigates, corvettes and trawlers. If bombers or U-boats attacked, it would be a powerful reinforcement for the close escort. If surface ships—cruisers and battleships for instance—attacked the convoy, the 'fighting destroyer escort' would be powerful enough to keep them at bay.

The next convoys to sail were PQ 18 to Russia and QP 14 from Russia to Iceland. The former suffered badly because the Germans, having broken several of our ciphers and codes, 'had an ear in the Admiralty'.

The German radio intelligence worked in this way. All along the German-held coasts of Norway, Denmark, Holland, Belgium and France the German Navy had set up special wireless stations, called 'MPS' (literally 'Navy Bearing Stations'). They were manned day and night and they listened in on all the frequencies which the Royal Navy used.

When a British shore station or ship sent a wireless signal, German operators at the nearest group of MPS took it down and, with the help of radio direction-finders, took the bearings. The coded or ciphered signal and the bearings were then sent by teleprinter direct to the Operations Division in Berlin. The bearings were drawn in on special charts and the position of the sender of the signal plotted: a process which took only a few seconds.

At the same time, the signal was fed into several electronic brains which, in a matter of minutes, tried every permutation and combination possible—a job which would take skilled cryptographers very many hours. The brains gave the 'answer' in less than half an hour.

The intercepted message could be an Admiralty order to a distant base about some seaman's pay—or it could describe

[1] Which are larger, faster and better armed and equipped than escort destroyers.

some future operation. It could be a plea for help from some stricken and overwhelmed convoy escort in the Atlantic or an Admiralty order diverting it from U-boats discovered to be waiting in ambush along its path.

Whatever it was, the signal was sent to the Operations Division of the Naval Staff and, if necessary, Admiral Gerhard Wagner, head of the division or his deputies, would act, passing the information on to various commands or even to the *Luftwaffe*, if their help was needed and available.

The Germans had been breaking our codes and ciphers since the beginning of the war, but these were changed in 1940. However, it did not take long for the Germans to break many of the new ones. By 1942 they 'had achieved another substantial penetration of our ciphers; nor was it until the end of that year that our counter-measures began to take effect . . . it was not until May 1943 that the discomfiture of the highly skilled German cipher breaker was made complete and final'.[1]

PQ 17 had sailed to disaster in June and, because of their success against it, the Germans were naturally very anxious for a repeat performance when PQ 18 sailed. Their aircraft flew regular reconnaissance flights over the Icelandic anchorages on the watch for it, but the Naval Staff were not to know whether the Allies had any ruse or stratagem up their sleeves.

July and August passed, with still no sign that the Allies were sending another convoy. Then the MPS picked up signals, took the usual bearings, and sent them on to Berlin. When the answers came out of the electronic brains, they were just what Raeder and Wagner wanted to know: the date and position where the escort of PQ 18 would change over to QP 14, which would have sailed from Russia.

Wagner then made his plans. The *Luftwaffe* was warned, and U-boats, minelayers and destroyers were sent to put down mines along the convoy's proposed route into the White Sea. By the time PQ 18 sailed, more than two hundred of the *Luftwaffe*'s bombers and torpedo planes and twelve U-boats were waiting. Out of the forty merchantmen in PQ 18, thirteen were sunk. QP 14 lost three of her fifteen merchant ships, a

[1] Captain S. W. Roskill, D.S.C., *The War at Sea*, Vol 2 (HMSO, 1957).

destroyer, fleet oiler and minesweeper. It was indeed a victory for MPS.[1]

But there was another side to it. The *Admiral Scheer*, *Hipper*, *Köln* and some destroyers had been sent up from Narvik to Altenfiord, the northernmost anchorage, but when the time came to sail them against the convoy, Hitler warned Raeder that since these ships were vitally important for the defence of Norway, he 'must not accept any undue risks'. Raeder cancelled the plan and it was left to the *Luftwaffe* and the U-boats to deal with the convoys.

After the arrival of these two convoys, the Allies were concerned over the North Africa landings, planned to begin on 7th November. It was to be the greatest seaborne armada in history, and it required a lot of warships. Many of them had to come from the Home Fleet; but even before this the Allied naval strength in northern waters had been drastically reduced. The United States battleship *Washington* with four destroyers was withdrawn in July, and the heavy cruisers *Wichita* and *Tuscaloosa* left for other operations. They had formed Task Force 99 and, said Admiral Tovey, 'had been a welcome reinforcement'.

From PQ 18 until after the North Africa landings there were no convoys to Russia, although at the end of October, aided by the arrival of the period of almost complete darkness, several merchant ships sailed singly from Iceland and QP 15, which will be referred to later, sailed for home.

---

[1] It should be mentioned that the British were having a good deal of success in breaking German ciphers and codes, but because of the need for security, these cannot be discussed.

5

The Problem

THE regular convoys to Russia began again in the middle
of December, and by then the war situation had changed
drastically in the Allies' favour, more than anyone had
dared to hope—although many hard battles were still to be
lost and won.

The Allied blow so much feared by Hitler, and against which
he had moved his fleet north, had fallen. But it had not fallen on
Norway—instead North Africa had been the target.

As far as the Navy was concerned, Hitler decided that
because of the oil shortage—by now the ships were being fuelled
on a hand-to-mouth basis—only the *Lützow* was to be transferred to the north while the *Prinz Eugen* was to stay in Germany. The *Scharnhorst* was still under repair after her Channel
dash and he would decide about moving her north in January.
But he ordered that light naval forces should be sent to Norway
and desired 'Norway to be heavily stocked with supplies, since
all available reports lead me to fear the enemy will attempt an
invasion during the Arctic night'.

At the same time he ordered that the North Sea coast should
be reinforced with a 'West Wall' and Albert Speer was given
orders to get on with this immense undertaking.

Meanwhile Hitler was facing a major crisis: in North Africa
itself the Allies were pushing on towards Tunis and Bizerta; to
the east Rommel, the wily desert fox, had met his match in
General Montgomery and retreated more than seven hundred
miles from El Alamein; and on the Eastern Front the Russians
were achieving big successes with their first winter offensive.
Hitler's blind attack on Stalingrad—he was more concerned
with the propaganda than the tactical victory—had been

stopped and the Russians had encircled General von Paulus's 6th Army and were preparing to annihilate it.

Hitler had just sacked his Army Chief of Staff, General Halder, who had dared to urge that the Stalingrad attack should be abandoned. Since at this time Halder had as much to do with Hitler as anyone, his verdict is interesting:[1]

'His decisions had ceased to have anything in common with the principles of strategy and operations as they have been recognized for generations past. They were the product of a violent nature following its momentary impulses, a nature which acknowledged no bounds to possibility and which made its wish the father of its deed.'

In the Pacific the Japanese had been decisively defeated by the Americans at Guadalcanal and the Americans had made the first move which was to lead them victoriously to Tokyo.

From now on Hitler was never to seize the strategic initiative again. From the Allied point of view the North Africa landing was the beginning of a long, bitter struggle which was to lead on to Sicily and the severe fighting of Italy, then the invasion of Normandy. Some of the more far-seeing Germans knew they could no longer count on victory.

This we know now as history; but cast your mind back to the hopes and fears of 1942, when to the average person of the Allied nations victory was not even to be thought of. It had the same distant appearance that old age has to youth.

With the successful Allied landings in North Africa completed, Admiral Tovey's Home Fleet was brought up to strength by the return of the ships which had left to help protect the great armada, and planning was resumed so that the Russian convoys could sail again. It has been mentioned earlier that the long hours of darkness would give some protection to the merchant-men. On the other hand, far larger German forces were now in northern waters: the great battleship *Tirpitz* and destroyers were at Trondheim, the cruisers *Hipper* and *Köln* and five destroyers were in Altenfiord, almost astride the convoy routes,

[1] General Franz Halder, *Hitler as Warlord* (Putnam).

and the *Lützow* was shortly to join them. The cruiser *Nürnberg* was at Narvik and the battle-cruiser *Scharnhorst*, the cruiser *Prinz Eugen* and five destroyers would be ready to move up from the Baltic in four weeks.

The first convoy to sail was in fact from Russia, QP 15. Admiral Tovey had asked that it should be limited in size to twenty ships, but the Admiralty overruled him and sailed twenty-eight from the White Sea on 17th November. Almost at the beginning of its voyage the convoy ran into a series of heavy gales and what Admiral Tovey had feared actually happened: the convoy could not keep station and scattered before the heavy wind and seas. The destroyers due to join it could not make contact. The merchantmen, unguarded and out of touch with each other, had to make their own way to their destinations in Iceland, and two were sunk by U-boats.

However, 'In the absence of air reconnaissance, for which the weather was quite unsuitable,' commented Admiral Tovey, 'the enemy was presumably even more lacking in knowledge of the situation than ourselves.'

The ships returning from Russia had no cargoes to steady them. Ships in ballast are particularly hard to control in heavy weather and any reasonable station keeping is often impossible. Some of these ships had their propellers half out of the water and their rudders were largely ineffective.

One homeward-bound convoy battling with winds of storm force in the Greenland Sea made good only forty-seven miles 'over the ground' in twenty-four hours—a speed of advance of barely two knots. In the same convoy a Liberty ship broke in half. The destroyers set to work to salvage the two pieces and towed them into harbour.

Tovey had asked that a convoy of six merchantmen should be ready to sail from Iceland shortly before the west-bound QP 15 arrived, but the Admiralty did not approve: instead, the First Sea Lord proposed waiting until 22nd December and sailing thirty-one ships together or three smaller, closely-spaced groups so that the covering forces could screen all three.

But Admiral Tovey disagreed: he had had enough of big convoys with QP 15, where nature, not the Germans, had proved the greatest enemy. He requested instead that ten-ship convoys be sailed with an escort of four destroyers and other small ships available.

'After further discussions,' wrote Tovey, 'including a visit to London by my Chief of Staff, I was directed to sail the convoy in two parts of sixteen ships each, escorted by seven destroyers and some smaller craft; and the Home Fleet was reinforced by two 6-inch cruisers to allow of cruiser cover in the Barents Sea.'

During the winter, he said, a convoy, provided that it was of such a size that it could be handled and kept together, stood an excellent chance of evading both U-boats and surface attack. A large convoy, on the other hand, was likely to get split up (as was QP 15) into a large number of small groups, each of which was more liable to detection by U-boats than a single concentrated convoy, and would present enemy surface ships with an ideal opportunity for an offensive sweep.

'Our own forces are always handicapped by having to identify a contact before they are free to attack; the enemy need not do so. The splitting of a convoy into a large number of scattered units would greatly add to this handicap,' he added.

The convoys had their designation changed. From now on the PQ (outward-bound) convoys would be called JW, and the QP (homeward-bound) were styled RA.

As the thirty ships were being sent out in this operation in two sections, the first half was designated JW 51A, due to sail from Loch Ewe on 18th December, and the other JW 51B, on 22nd December. A homeward-bound convoy, RA 51, would sail from Murmansk on 30th December, its escorts being those that had arrived there with JW 51A.

Admiral Tovey knew that earlier convoys had twelve or more U-boats operating against them. Reviewing the difficulties of operating the covering force he wrote: 'In providing a force of cruisers to protect the convoys, whose maximum speed is about eight knots, against surface attack the difficulty has been to place the cruisers in a suitable position.

'If they manœuvre within thirty miles of the convoy, especially after it has been located by the enemy, they are inevitably in an area where they are exposed to grave risk of attack by U-boats, and it is largely a matter of time and luck when they give an easy target as happened in the case of the *Edinburgh*.[1]

'The Senior Officer of the cruiser force must always be handicapped by the uncertainty of the convoy's position—the estimate of which might well be fifty miles out.

'It is for these reasons that my instructions for the cruiser force are not to close within fifty miles of the convoy. In considering protection for these particular convoys I intended the cruisers should not operate east of 25° or 30° [east longitude] and should not proceed to Kola Inlet unless shortage of fuel necessitated it.'

However, the First Sea Lord insisted that the cruisers cover the convoys right through to Kola. This was justified, Admiral Tovey commented later, 'for otherwise the cruiser force would probably not have been present at the action on New Year's Eve'.

---

[1] Torpedoed by *U-456* while escorting QP 11. Her stern was blown off. She was later sunk after an action with German destroyers.

6

Turkey Time

AFTER the decision to sail the two convoys to Russia had been taken at high level (in this case it had been at the highest level, since both Mr Churchill and President Roosevelt had been involved), the detailed planning began.

To get some idea of what staff work goes into sailing even a small convoy like this (fourteen merchant ships, against the thirty-three of PQ 17), let us follow some of the opening moves.

On 3rd December 1942, the Commander-in-Chief, Western Approaches, responsible for providing some of the escort, signalled to the Naval Officer in Charge at Belfast, and the Captain (D) at Greenock (responsible for the Clyde destroyers) that for JW 51A, the first convoy, two corvettes and two trawlers were to arrive at Loch Ewe on the afternoon of the 14th, and two destroyers at Seidisfiord, Iceland, on the afternoon of the 16th. For JW 51B, the second convoy, the same number of ships were required, the smaller vessels to arrive at Loch Ewe on the 21st and the destroyers at Seidisfiord on the 23rd.

Then there was the question of having submarines watching the German Fleet bases in Norway, and Admiral Tovey signalled on the 4th December what he wanted done. The Flag Officer, Submarines, replied that he appreciated the danger and was arranging patrols—but they would have to enter two Russian zones. The Admiralty signalled to the Senior British Naval Officer (SBNO), North Russia, and the Russian naval authorities were duly informed.

Next the Admiralty warned the headquarters of Coastal Command on 7th December: 'Convoys JW 51A and JW 51B: air co-operation during the passage of both convoys is requested as follows (A) Anti-submarine air escort from United Kingdom and Iceland to limit of endurance. (B) Long-range fighter escort while within range. (C) Photographic reconnaissance of Trondheim when practicable.'

As the days slipped by, orders went to the two cruisers which were to cover the convoy. Admiral Tovey planned to take the battleship *King George V*, the cruiser *Berwick*, and destroyers *Musketeer*, *Raider* and *Quadrant* to sea on the 19th to cover the area to the south-west of the first convoy, JW 51A, and plans had to be made for them to sail.

On 13th December orders went out to Captain R. StVincent Sherbrooke, commanding HMS *Onslow* and the 17th Destroyer Flotilla, that he was to escort JW 51B to Russia, actually joining it from Iceland to save precious fuel.

By the 19th December the Admiralty wanted plenty of warning of German warship movements, and the Air Officer Commanding Coastal Command was told: 'Enemy activity may develop in Northern waters. Special Fleet reconnaissance must now take place over trade protection.'

Meanwhile the sixteen merchant ships (only fourteen of which were eventually to sail) had been loaded, five of them in Britain and the rest in the United States. This in itself was a complicated process. Tanks, aircraft, lorries, guns and many thousands of tons of various other items had to be earmarked from factories and stores and sent overland to the ports, arriving at the right time and at the right quays. In Britain depots, railways, roads and quays were constantly being bombed.

Plans also had to be made for the rendezvous at Loch Ewe, the sailing of the convoy, the return of local escorts which would not go through to the Arctic, the sailing and rendezvous of ocean escorts after they had fuelled at Seidisfiord, and many other allied matters. All signals and orders had to be covered by the highest security grading—at that time it was the British 'Most Secret'. Every single detail had to be handled on a strict need-to-know basis.

Now, having seen some of the over-all planning required let us see how it affected the individual ships: the two cruisers which were to provide the distant escort, for instance. The ships detailed for this duty were the *Sheffield* and *Jamaica*.

71

The *Sheffield* of 9,000 tons, was one of the five *Newcastle*-class cruisers. They were built in answer to the Japanese *Mogami*-class and were handsome ships. The *Sheffield* had two funnels, both heavily raked, and she looked capable of her designed speed of thirty-two knots.

She had twelve 6-inch guns in four turrets of three guns each. Two turrets (A and B) were forward, and two (X and Y) aft. She also had eight 4-inch anti-aircraft guns, smaller light weapons, and six torpedo tubes—three either side. Built by Vickers Armstrong at Barrow, she had a thin belt of armour—between three and four inches—covering her engine-rooms and magazines. She was within a few weeks of her eighth 'birth-day', having been launched on 31st January 1935.

Her consort for the voyage, the *Jamaica*, was in many ways a similar ship, one of the *Mauritius*-class, ordered in 1937 (when, with reluctant slowness, Britain began to rearm) and completed in 1940 by the same builders as the *Sheffield*.

She had the same main armament, and was designed for thirty-three knots, a knot faster than the *Sheffield*. With twin funnels and masts, she too looked the part of a fast, powerful cruiser, designed to safeguard our sea lanes and now carrying out the classic concept of a cruiser's role.

From the 20th November until the 14th December the *Sheffield* and *Jamaica* were at the Fleet Base at Scapa Flow, the anchorage formed by the mainland of Orkney and several small islands, protected by booms and anti-submarine nets. As a base it was well placed, for the Home Fleet could easily sail should any German warships attempt to break out into the Atlantic. But it was a dreary and lonely outpost of the British homeland. During the winter massive low clouds, driven by high winds, covered the hills for days on end. The bleak islands were almost devoid of recreational facilities (except cross-country running) and there were long periods of stormy weather when ship's boats could not safely be used.

Mails and newspapers crossed the swirling waters of the Pentland Firth only when the ferries from Thurso could get through. And the sun, when it could be seen at all, rose only a few degrees above the horizon during the forenoon. Having taken a quick look at Scapa Flow it then slipped away in the south-west to light up more worthy places. Clearly, men of the Home Fleet believed, the Orkneys were never part of Shakespeare's 'other Eden . . . set in the silver sea'.

The *Sheffield* had to repair some damage caused by a minor collision with the *Cadmus*, and then Captain A. W. Clarke, who commanded her, was given time to refresh the ships technically and tactically. 'Particularly,' wrote Captain Clarke later, 'I was advised, in the fields of main armament firing and night encounter exercises. The inference was clear enough.'

For the next ten days the *Sheffield*'s crew—700 men—worked hard. The 'refreshing' operation was inevitably interrupted by one of the famous Scapa gales, which meant both anchors down, and steam for slow speed. A sudden wind shift at 0200 one morning set the anchors dragging and an embarrassed *Sheffield* found herself spending the rest of the night and half the next day entangled by the rudder in the nearby anti-torpedo net.

On 13th December Captain Clarke was ordered to land the *Sheffield*'s aircraft, stock right up to the limit with provisions and fuel, and embark Rear-admiral Robert L. Burnett and his personal staff.

'Evidently,' noted Captain Clarke, 'our destiny was North Russia; and I doubted the operation was likely to be a simple one. The presence of the Admiral, already notable for his outstanding handling of the summer convoy operations against the enemy's maximum effort with shore-based air attacks, indicated trouble for someone.'

And Captain Clarke's guess had been right: five days earlier Admiral Burnett—who was referred to as 'Rear-admiral, Destroyers', received a signal from Admiral Tovey which said:

Sheffield, flying the flag of Rear-admiral, Destroyers, with *Jamaica* [and destroyers] *Musketeer*[1] and *Matchless* is to form Force R to provide cover for convoys JW 51A, JW 51B, RA 51, RA 52.

Submarine patrols will be maintained off the North Norwegian coast.

[1] Subsequently the *Opportune* took her place.

Force R should not normally approach the convoy within 50 miles unless acting on intelligence of enemy surface forces.

Preliminary movements:

(a) Request you attend the JW 51A convoy conference at Loch Ewe a.m. 15th December.

(b) Force R is to proceed to Seidisfiord adjusting passage so as to provide cover to JW 51A over the route between Færöes and position C. . . .

It is probable that weather will not permit cruisers to fuel destroyers at sea, consequently destroyers may be detached to fuel at Kola Inlet as necessary.

Admiral Burnett replied, suggesting that when the *Jamaica* and two destroyers met at sea they should bring mail for the *Sheffield* with them. They did better than that, as will be seen later.

At 0600 on the 14th the *Sheffield* sailed from Scapa west round the north of Scotland and then down to Loch Ewe, the convoy assembly base opposite Stornoway, for the JW 51A convoy conference. As soon as that was done, she sailed again, met the *Jamaica* and two destroyers, and shaped course for Seidisfiord.

From Intelligence sources Admiral Burnett knew that the Germans had recently reinforced their heavy ships in the far north; and although the darkness would reduce the danger from German air reconnaissance, the enemy had plenty of U-boats to place across the path of the convoys. Because of the extent of the Polar icefields the convoys would have to pass south of Bear Island, and in turn that meant the Germans did not have a very large area to search.

In addition, the German surface ships, operating so close to their base at Altenfiord, did not have to worry about fuel. Although they had serious supply troubles, once the ships had it on board and the Führer permitted them to sail, they had a long effective range. They could also afford to keep steam in all boilers whilst at sea and steam at maximum speed for as long as they required. Owing to the distances involved our ships could not do likewise except for very brief periods.

The British ships had to steam between 1,500 and 2,000 miles to get into position. The *Sheffield*, for instance, carried 1,800 tons of fuel, but at seventeen knots burned up eight tons an hour. That consumption rose rapidly as she increased speed—at thirty knots she used 30 tons an hour. So while she was at cruising speed she had a fair radius of action; if she used higher speeds her radius was drastically reduced.

However, when the two cruisers and two destroyers arrived off Iceland they ran into thick fog. It was impossible to detect land, let alone the entrance of Seidisfiord, and Admiral Burnett had to give up the idea of topping up the cruisers' tanks. As the destroyers would soon be short of fuel, he ordered them to wait until the fog cleared and then go into Seidisfiord. After topping up they could join the convoy to help the escorts.

The first convoy, JW 51A, had sailed from Loch Ewe on the 15th and was now well on its way, approaching the danger area.

On 22nd December (the day that Captain Sherbrooke was holding his conference at Loch Ewe with the masters of the fourteen ships of the second convoy, JW 51B, he was to escort to Russia) the first convoy was reckoned by Admiral Burnett to be abreast of Bear Island.

For the next twenty-four hours, while his force patrolled to and fro between the meridians of 10° and 30° east longitude— the 'open gate' to the German warships—he was also keeping fifty miles south of the convoy route as ordered. The men in the cruisers kept their fingers crossed.

On 23rd December the first convoy was well past the most sensitive area and the *Sheffield* and *Jamaica* were getting short of fuel, so Admiral Burnett altered course for Kola Inlet, and at noon on Christmas Eve both ships dropped anchor in Varenga Bay.

That night a heavy gale blew up to add noise and fury to Christmas Eve, and celebrations were cut short by the *Sheffield* dragging her anchors off the ledge on which they were perched, drifting across the bay, and finishing up safely with them holding on to a companion ledge on the opposite shore.

Christmas Day in HM ships is usually something of a riot;

and this Christmas was no exception. There was no time for shore leave—and Murmansk was a dreary place, even apart from the extreme surliness and inhospitable mood of the Russians. The few items on sale in the shops were a fantastic price.

However, the *Sheffield* and *Jamaica* were well provided: the Captain of the Fleet had had the forethought to stock the ships with turkeys (*Sheffield* had received hers via the *Jamaica*). And there was beer for all aboard *Sheffield*, by a special dispensation. It was a bit muddy, admittedly, but loving hands had stowed it with care in the starboard hangar, now empty of aircraft, and even muddy beer, laced with rum, does wonders.

The mess-decks had been decorated in a matter of hours. Admiral Burnett went with Captain Clarke on the traditional rounds of the ship and everyone settled down to an enormous lunch. All those that could were sleeping off its pleasant effects when the alarm rattlers sounded off: an air attack. Clearly the Germans were not gentlemen.

Murmansk, less than ninety miles from the German air bases at Petsamo and Kirkenes, had one of its frequent and usually ineffective air raids. Force R's shooting was, perhaps, a bit wild, Captain Clarke admits, 'and more in keeping with Guy Fawkes' day', but anyway it was Christmas. Then convoy JW 51A arrived unscathed, as an additional Christmas bonus, and with it the destroyers *Opportune* and *Matchless*.

In the evening the unpredictable Russians, in the shape of the Soviet Naval Commander-in-Chief, sent his Russian naval male choir aboard. They sang and sang: two concerts for the ratings, a further one for the wardroom after the evening meal, and a concluding one at an hour after midnight with the two destroyers secured alongside.

Boxing Day passed rather more quietly and next day the four ships of Force R sailed to get into position for our particular convoy, JW 51B, which was by then passing Jan Mayen Island. In Murmansk, as the cruisers left, Captain Scott-Moncrieff, D.S.O. and Bar, was assembling the ships and escorts of the homeward-bound convoy, RA 52, due to sail in a few hours.

The heavy units of the Home Fleet covering the convoy farther west—the battleship *Anson*, with Admiral Fraser on board, the cruiser *Cumberland*[1] and destroyers *Forester* and *Impulsive*—had sailed on Boxing Day to their patrol line between Jan Mayen and Bear Island, some three hundred to four hundred miles from the German base at Altenfiord, which they reached on the 27th.

There were also the lines of British submarines waiting and watching off Northern Norway while the convoys were at sea. Perhaps they had the worst job of all. If German heavy ships left, they had to report them and attack if they could. But most —if not all—of the time it was a question of watching in the merciless gales raging off the coast, men being soaking wet if on the surface, half frozen and dead tired, the conning-tower affording as much protection as a motor-cyclist's wind shield fitted on a half-submerged log. The submarines on patrol were the Polish *Sokol*, the *P 339*, *P 223*, *Torbay*, the Dutch *O 14*, *Graph*, *P 49*, *P 312* and *P 216*.

No one can leave Kola Inlet in its winter coat of snow, ice and slush with many regrets; but none of the four ships of Force R enjoyed the next four days at sea. They ran into severe gales with swirling snowstorms and below-zero temperatures which froze spray on the ships, encasing them in a dangerous sheath of ice.

Plunging north-westwards, rolling wildly, the cruisers had to reduce to ten knots at times in the tremendous seas: although the *Sheffield* was 584 feet long, and the *Jamaica* 549 feet, and both weighed more than 9,000 tons, they climbed up one great wave to its crest, poised a moment, then slammed violently into the trough. From each bridge it seemed the bow would never have enough buoyancy to stop the ship plunging under, but she would recover, flinging away spray high and wide over her whole length. Tons of water would stream off the foredeck as she rose just in time to plunge into the next sea rolling relentlessly on.

These great seas were built up by winds howling right across the Atlantic, through the gap between Scotland and Iceland,

[1] Previously she had been in the South Atlantic, at times near the Antarctic Circle. She had taken part in the chase after the *Admiral Graf Spee*.

and on into the Greenland Sea—an unbroken 'fetch' of anything up to 2,000 miles. The great danger was that if the ship was suspended only by the crest of a wave, or if she plunged too heavily into a sea, she would break her back. As a result each ship's captain stayed on the bridge most of the time. Just the right speed had to be found—not so slow that the ship became impossible to steer, and not so fast that she pounded badly.

Now the water swirling over the ships was gradually freezing: soon it was inches thick over the decks and superstructure. The weather most of the time was so bad that to venture on deck to clear it would have been suicide—but there was always the danger that, with the sheer weight of ice, the stability of the ship would be jeopardized.

The gun turrets, torpedo tubes and radar aerials had to be kept constantly on the move to prevent them freezing up: in particularly heavy weather the most forward turrets (A and B) were trained round on the beam to avoid them being damaged by particularly big seas.

Heating gear was fitted to certain parts of the torpedo tubes because of the constant danger that they would freeze solid; and special precautions had to be taken to avoid any water getting into the barrels of the guns and then freezing—causing the guns to burst if a shell was fired.

The usual tompions—metal caps which screwed on the mouths of the barrels—could not be used: they would freeze solid, and in bad weather it would be impossible for men to remove them. Instead, the ends of cartridge-cases, made of thick cardboard, were used. Thick grease was smeared on and they were stuck on to the muzzles. They were simple to remove: a tube, normally used to explode the cordite charge, was fired. It was sufficient to blow the covers off.

Down below the crew's quarters in those conditions were extremely unpleasant. With all hatches battened down, scuttles secured with deadlights and nowhere for fresh air to enter, the atmosphere was fetid, an unappetizing mixture of stale breath, cigarette smoke and the vomit of those unfortunate men still suffering from seasickness.

The men were usually so dead tired that they could not clean their quarters. If they had been able to, it would have been just as bad in an hour or so. And there was the clammy unpleasantness of condensation collecting on the bulkheads and deckheads, making everything below decks that was not already soaked completely damp and providing a fine breeding-ground for mildew. In cold conditions the condensation froze; at this time the interior bulkheads of Captain Clarke's sea cabin were a sheet of ice.

The men wore special Arctic clothing which did something to keep them warm: heavy woollen underwear under two, three and four jerseys, mittens, sheepskin-lined coats, fur-lined balaclava helmets, seaboots and thick woollen stockings. But often this was not enough to keep out the cold, especially when men could not eat regularly, get hot drinks or were seasick.

Added to this was the fact that they had to sleep—if they were able—at night action stations. The four turrets of the cruisers, for instance, would have men huddled on the decks, ready to go into action in a few seconds should they suddenly encounter an enemy in the darkness. Men's lives were reduced to three essentials: keeping watch, sleeping and eating: there was not time or energy for anything else. The vicious elements and exhaustion took their toll.

Those on the bridge were no better off. The bridge was completely open, with no shelter at all except low armour plate glass screens which deflected some of the wind and spray.

On the second day out from Kola Inlet, two days before the end of the year and now to the southward of Bear Island, Admiral Burnett turned about. He reckoned they had reached some sixty miles south-west of the convoy JW 51B—i.e. between the German base at Altenfiord and the merchantmen. He then swept across the danger zone, watching, waiting and wondering.

He was not the only one doing that. One of the most anxious men aboard was Lt Cdr E. F. S. Back, the *Sheffield*'s navigator. Since leaving Kola Inlet he had been unable to fix his position from any source. There was no sun, no stars and no horizon. It was pure dead reckoning. But upon him rested the task of keeping the plot up to date, with uncertain rates of drift, compasses unsteady in these high latitudes, and the ship battling in

79

heavy seas with steering very difficult. Dozens of errors were possible.

Fortunately during the night of 29th December the gale eased and within a short time conditions were improving. Admiral Burnett appreciated that the convoy might well have been blown south of its course by the gale and, with the anticipated clearing sky, he did not want to be spotted by casual reconnaissance aircraft, so he hauled the cruisers round to the southward.

As the 30th was a comparatively clear day, with moderate winds, the crew of the cruisers were busy chipping away ice with hammers, picks and shovels from the decks, armament and anywhere it was accessible.

Admiral Burnett decided that the destroyers, already very low in fuel, would soon be so short that they would be no tactical use in an action, and sent them back to Kola Inlet.

By now he knew, from an Admiralty signal, that there was a suspicion the convoy had been detected by a U-boat while passing Bear Island. However, his two cruisers were in position. All he could do was to wait and see, keeping the two ships steaming back and forth along their patrol line.

But we must now go back a few days, to pick up the thread of the convoy JW 51B.

7

'By Hand of Officer'

IN HMS *Tyne*, the depot ship moored in Gutter Sound, the destroyers' anchorage under the lee of Hoy in the Fleet Base of Scapa Flow, the teleprinter chattered monotonously, its keys printing an apparently meaningless jumble of figures. It was in fact a signal in cipher, an order which was to lead to the defeat of an enemy fleet in circumstances unparalleled in history.

The signal was addressed to eight people, indicated by a variety of initials at the beginning. One of them was D 17, the abbreviation for the Captain (D) commanding the 17th Destroyer Flotilla.

It was deciphered and typed out. On 21st December a copy was taken 'By Hand of Officer' to the cabin of D 17, Captain Sherbrooke, aboard the *Onslow*. Opening the sealed envelope he read the orders which, although he was unaware of it, were to change his life so radically. They were from Admiral Tovey and said:

'Convoy JW 51B 16 ships. Sail from Loch Ewe 22nd December. Speed of advance $7\frac{1}{2}$ knots routed as follows. . . . Escort Loch Ewe, HMS *Bramble* (S.O. M/S Flotilla) *Blankney, Ledbury, Chiddingfold, Rhododendron, Honeysuckle, Northern Gem, Vizalma.*

'Conference a.m. 22nd December which Captain D 17 will also attend, subsequently proceeding independently in HMS *Onslow* to Seidisfiord. *Oribi, Obedient, Obdurate, Orwell, Bulldog, Achates*, to arrive Seidisfiord p.m. 23rd December.

'Captain D 17 is to sail with these destroyers to join convoy in Position C. When destroyers join Hunts[1] are to remain with convoy to prudent limit of endurance and then return to Seidisfiord. . . .'

[1] The 'Hunt' class destroyers *Blankney, Ledbury* and *Chiddingfold*.

The man reading these orders was tall and slim. His features were finely cut and his hair, prematurely white, was combed back from a high brow. Robert StVincent Sherbrooke—known as Rupert to avoid being confused with an uncle—was the son and grandson of naval officers. The Sherbrookes had lived at Oxton Hall, at Newark, in Nottinghamshire, since the fifteenth century.

He had been Captain (D) of the 17th Destroyer Flotilla and in command of HMS *Onslow* only four weeks. His staff, young naval officers who were already veterans of the Russian convoys, were still trying to size him up and get to know him. They were inclined, at that stage, to be critical in their estimation. In their opinion he appeared the complete opposite to Captain H. T. Armstrong, his predecessor, who had been a man with an infectious and very forceful personality, and whom his staff had almost worshipped. Sherbrooke was reserved, quietly spoken and little given to small talk. He had none of the artificial *bonhomie* which wardroom life tends to force on a naval officer, yet he was not the dour man that his maternal ancester had been, the grim Admiral Sir John Jervis, who became Earl St Vincent after his great victory off Cape St Vincent in 1797. He was too withdrawn, too reserved, ever to be able to say, as 'old Jarvie' did while going into action on that St Valentine's Day, 'A victory is very essential to England at this moment'. He might have known and believed it, and would have given his life to achieve it, but he could never have brought himself to say it aloud.

Nor did Sherbrook look every man's idea of a sailor: gentle mannered, thoughtful, with the fine hands and fingers of an artist, anyone meeting him for the first time would find it hard to place him. One of our better authors perhaps; a classical don in a quiet Oxford college; maybe even an expert on ceramics.

Sherbrooke read through the orders once again and then passed the word that there would be a staff meeting in his cabin after dinner that night. He was lucky with his staff, and although he had never been on the Russian run, they had— many times. They lived Arctic convoys. Life beyond the Arctic Circle had become natural to them; their small talk was a personalized history of those hard-fought convoys. They were young and skilled in their respective jobs and they carried out their dutes with the air of confidence and superiority that is the stamp which the centuries-old tradition of the Royal Navy can impart on men big enough to take it.

Sherbrooke had been fortunate in taking over from Armstrong, who had, by the strength of his character and the power of his personality, brought the *Onslow*—and indeed the whole flotilla—to a high state of efficiency. He had achieved that without bullying or hectoring; the officers and ratings had given him of their best because they wanted to, not because they were frightened of the consequences if they failed the man they had dubbed—because of the shape of his nose—'Beaky'.

While his officers dined as usual in the wardroom that night Sherbrooke, as all captains do, ate in his cabin, alone with his thoughts. He was an experienced officer and a good seaman; and now he faced the biggest test of his tactical and professional ability, and the enforced solitude did not disturb him. All the men who served with him remarked on his quietness. He never joined in the joking and gossiping on the bridge, rarely started a conversation, and spoke quietly when words were necessary. Yet behind that apparently impassive manner a quick and questing brain was at work.

His destroyers might be screening one of the big ships of the fleet, but in his imagination they would become a convoy. What would he do if a German battleship and attendant destroyers appeared there—just below that patch of cloud? As quickly as possible he would answer himself—and then ruthlessly analyse that answer, perhaps rejecting it and substituting another. A sudden air attack from that direction . . . what then? Question and answer, criticism and analysis, followed each other in quick succession through his brain.

And the young officers round him in the *Onslow* during those first few weeks thought to themselves that 'Beaky' Armstrong had been right when he gently warned them that they'd find his relief a vastly different sort of man. They weren't judging him as a naval officer, since the quiet man in an emergency is likely to be as effective as the man with a forceful personality. (The mercurial, temperamental, and egocentric Nelson . . . the dour, silent, extremely grim Earl St Vincent: both fighting the same odds in the same war. Two diametrically-opposed personalities who produced the same result—victory.) They were simply judging him as a man, with a definite yardstick in their mind.

As Europe moved towards war in August 1939, the Navy had been looking for efficient officers with command experience. They gave Sherbrooke—then a commander—a destroyer. In December he was given the *Cossack*, one of the famous Tribal class destroyers. In his flotilla two ships were fitted as leaders. Captain Vian, the Senior Officer, commanded one, the *Afridi*, and Sherbrooke had the other, the *Cossack*. During the disastrous Norwegian campaign Vian had come in for a refit with *Afridi* and, as the Senior Officer, taken the *Cossack*, leaving Sherbrooke with *Afridi* in a dockyard. In that way Sherbrooke missed the *Altmark* episode, when Vian and the *Cossack* had put new life and verve into the cry 'The Navy's here'.

Sherbrooke had won the D.S.O., after getting the *Cossack* back, in the Second Battle of Narvik, when his ship was badly hit. After taking her back to Southampton for battle repairs, he was given the *Matabele*, another of the 'Tribals', and for a year was engaged in the usual tasks that fall to the lot of a Home Fleet destroyer.

Then he was given a fourth stripe and appointed to be one of the Duty Captains at the Admiralty—in effect one of the Admiralty's 'officers of the watch', and a job which gave him a good picture of the war as a whole. It was, however, a depressing one at that time.

Then he had been sent out to Freetown for a year, because of the heavy sinkings by U-boats off North Africa, with the task of hotting up the anti-submarine warfare. Finally, in November 1942 he had been appointed Captain (D) of the 17th Destroyer Flotilla.

After dinner Sherbrooke's five staff officers came to his cabin, which covered the full beam of the ship. There was a door in the middle of the forward bulkhead, with a settee to one side of it and a bookcase on the other. On the port side of the cabin was the inevitable green baize table with chairs round, while on the starboard side there were a desk and an arm-chair. At the after end the equally inevitable fireplace, complete with mantelpiece and electric fire, did what it could to lessen the air of austerity.

The senior staff officer was Lt Cdr Tom Marchant, tall, talkative, with dark wavy hair rounding off a cheerful face. He gesticulated as he talked; he had the air of not taking life too seriously, except where his job was concerned. He was the Flotilla Torpedo Officer and the senior executive specialist officer on Captain Sherbrooke's staff, and therefore second in command. He had served in the battleship *Royal Sovereign* from 1938–41 and for the first two years of the war was covering the United Kingdom–Halifax Transatlantic convoys, and was also present at the reduction of the French Fleet at Alexandria. He was appointed to the *Onslow* while she was still building, one of the officers 'standing by' in the shipyard during September and October 1941.

Next came Lt Peter Wyatt, the Flotilla Navigating Officer. He, in a like manner, was responsible for the navigation duties in the ship and was usually known as 'Pilot'. A large, tall man with a black beard to match, he had a forceful personality. Uniform seemed the wrong dress for him; one felt a pirate's rig, sword in the belt, knife between the teeth and eyes on a fair lady were more in keeping. Before the war he had served on the China Station (his wife had remained in Hong Kong when he was sent to the Persian Gulf and she was taken prisoner by the Japanese when they captured the island). He had spent the first few months of the war on East Coast convoys, went on to the Red Sea for the Italian war, and ended up in Mediterranean convoys before joining the *Onslow*.

The specialist gunnery officer in the ship was Lt J. M. A. Wilson, known either as 'Guns' or Macro, his unlikely-sounding second name. He also had a title, bestowed by the irrepressible Captain Armstrong a year earlier. During the Vaagso raid he had shot down a very high-flying German aircraft with two shells from the ancient 4-inch gun fitted as additional AA armament in place of a set of torpedo tubes.

This had so impressed Armstrong that he promptly dubbed the unbelieving gunner 'Sir Macro Wilson, Baronet, Governor of the Leeward Islands'.

Those serving with him regarded Wilson as a typical gunnery officer; average height, well-built and with a ready and engaging smile, very correct as far as the Navy was concerned, and well able to stand up to the high-spirited ragging of Wyatt and Marchant.

The only RNVR officer on the staff was Lt R. Bird, the specialist in anti-submarine warfare. Known either as Dickie from his name or 'Ping' from the noise his Asdics made, he was round and chubby, with a renowned sense of humour. While serving in the *Berwick* he had, on Christmas Day 1940, been in action against the *Hipper*. Two years and six days later he was to repeat it.

Lt Foster, the Staff Communications Officer, invariably known as 'Flags', could also be described as a typical signals officer: apparently lazy and lackadaisical, but in fact very determined and efficient. He viewed life with a humorous, critical air.

Captain Sherbrooke remained standing while his staff sat at the table facing him. He said: 'I've asked you along to discuss this operation. . . .'

The five men waited, two of them with pencils and paper ready to take notes so that they could later turn his words into written orders. One of them subsequently wrote: 'I remember well our surprise when D 17, who had not been with us long, and who hadn't been with us to Russia, started the meeting and, walking up and down, expounded on his theory on combating the surface threat. He gave the appearance of having studied this aspect for some time, and of being quite clear on what his orders would be. . . . It was during this meeting that most of us first really got to know Captain (D), and I know I for one was very impressed with his pronounced views, and his general air of decision.'

Hands clasped behind his back, white hair combed back, face slightly flushed because of his unavoidable but now necessary loquacity, Sherbrooke walked the width of the cabin, facing his staff as he paced in one direction, his back to them in the other. No gestures, just words spoken against a background hum from the ship's generators, occasional clatter of feet in the distance, or a hail from the Quartermaster overhead to a passing boat.

He argued first from the German point of view, discussing the different types of attack they were most likely to make. With almost total darkness it would be from surface ships rather than U-boats, while aircraft could be almost entirely ruled out. Then he went on to the most likely type.

Incisively, with a complete economy of words, he finally got to the crux of his plan for defending the convoy. He assumed the attack would come from only one sector at a time and therefore, he said, at the first sign of the attack:

(1) The five destroyers of the 17th Flotilla (*Onslow, Obedient, Oribi, Obdurate,* and *Orwell*) would, without orders, leave their positions all round the convoy and join on the threatened side in line ahead;

(2) The convoy would turn away from that direction, the rear merchant ships dropping smoke floats;

(3) The other two destroyers, *Achates* and *Bulldog*,[1] would lay a smoke-screen between the convoy and the enemy;

(4) The remaining escorts (the minesweeper *Bramble*, corvettes *Hyderabad* and *Rhododendron*, and the trawlers *Northern Gem* and *Vizalma*) re-form the escort screen on the convoy.

(5) The convoy to continue to alter course to keep the enemy astern.

While Sherbrooke talked, Peter Wyatt, the navigator, and Bird, the anti-submarine officer, jotted down notes. Then the staff and Sherbrooke discussed the rest of the details of the escort orders, much of which was routine.

The time was now nearly midnight: soon the *Onslow* would have to get under way from Scapa and steam round to Loch Ewe, about one hundred and fifty miles away. Before then, the escort and convoy orders, with diagrams, had to be prepared.

The quintet adjourned to the wardroom; Groves, the Petty Officer writer was summoned to man the typewriter; Lt

---

[1] The latter did not eventually join the convoy.

Henderson, the Captain's Secretary and Sub-lt D. Williams, the Assistant Secretary, arrived to help; and a bottle of Johnny Walker whisky was put by ready to give its 70 per cent proof assistance. Wyatt, who had the facility for putting ideas into words, dictated while Bird worked on the anti-submarine diagrams; Tom Marchant produced the jelly for the old-fashioned schoolroom duplicator and many-coloured copying inks. Wonderfully-coloured escort diagrams were drawn up on the wardroom table, slapped on the jelly in the tray, and copies run off. As one of them wrote later, 'Foster, as usual, kept up his impeccable signal school style of casual critic, Bird kept up a flow of unrepeatable comment, and Tom conducted the whole affair like Toscanini. The resulting orders, in our estimation at least, were a perfect example of clarity coupled with brevity and we were proud of them!'

There was, as usual, the fun of picking code names for the individual ships and groups for use on the voice radio. Thus *Bramble* became 'Prickles', *Northern Gem* 'Rinso', *Rhododendron* 'Pansy', and *Bulldog* 'Growler'. Some of the names for the ships were suggested by their commanding officers' names or personalities—*Orwell*, for instance, commanded by Nigel Austen, became 'Bunny'. Captain (D), for a reason no one could later fathom, became 'Custard'.

It was three o'clock in the morning before the orders were finally completed and clipped together—orders for the seven Fleet destroyers and five small escorts going all the way to Russia, and for the three Hunts going as far as the latitude of Iceland.

The *Onslow* then sailed for Loch Ewe, where the merchantmen were waiting. At 1700 the previous day no one had known what his next job was to be; ten hours later they were on their way, with a mass of paper work and planning completed. It was the way the Navy had to work in wartime.

At Loch Ewe the convoy and escort conferences on Tuesday, 22nd December were held in a wooden hut, and a strong wind was blowing as if to remind all present that it was a bleak

Scottish winter. In fact it was the precursor of a vicious gale in which three of the destroyers were shortly to be immersed.

At the time set for the convoy conference the captains of merchantmen filed into the room, most of them dressed in civilian clothes. Four of them were obviously British; the other ten, from the cut of their suits, were obviously American. To a stranger unused to the ways of such people the fourteen men would seem far from being seafarers—except that their faces were weathered. Most of them carried brief-cases or small attaché-cases, and almost all had a certain air of ponderous shyness. For centuries there had always been a certain amount of rivalry between the fighting and mercantile navies; and it was on occasions like these that the masters of the merchant-men had a wary alertness, a guarded reserve.

Each captain took a seat round the trestled table and then filled in a small slip of paper giving the number of officers, ratings and DEMS gunners in his ship. Each was issued with a copy of the convoy orders which told him the convoy formation number allocated to his ship and the position it would occupy, the evolutions his ship was to perform on given signals from the Commodore (in the *Empire Archer*), the distance between each column of ships and between individual ships in column.

The Senior Naval Officer at Loch Ewe then introduced Captain Melhuish, their Commodore. He spoke to them briefly, outlining the convoy orders, and emphasizing the absolute necessity of keeping their correct stations and not straggling. It was vital, he added, not to make any more smoke than was necessary.

When he had finished, the SNO introduced Captain Sherbrooke, who quietly outlined his plans for the convoy and the escort. He told them that the convoy would turn away from any surface raider while the destroyers would concentrate to beat off the attack. The merchant ships at the rear of the convoy would drop smoke floats.

He also emphasized—since few of the masters of the merchant men had any illusions about Russian convoys, and tended to base their ideas on the many ships sunk during the prolonged daylight of the summer convoys—that this time darkness would be their greatest ally. Attacks by the *Luftwaffe* would be unlikely Sherbrooke said, and U-boats would have a good deal of trouble finding the convoy. The only likely form of attack would be from surface ships. Bad weather, he said, would also help hide the convoy, though it would make station-keeping harder.

'The atmosphere,' one of his staff officers wrote later, 'was one of a lecture on agriculture in a village hall rather than on war. At the end, although one had the impression that the Merchant Navy had not yet fully forgiven the Navy for PQ 17 and was still reserving judgment, one or two of the Masters did give me an encouraging word of confidence!'

During the conference there was much talk on when smoke floats should be dropped. It was finally agreed that as many ships as possible should drop them as soon as the initial turn away from an enemy surface ship had been made. There was also a discussion on how far the convoy should steam in an unfavourable direction in the event of a surface attack from ahead. The decision was left to the Commodore, Captain Melhuish, based on estimates of the situation provided by Captain Sherbrooke. It was to prove significant later on.

The conference ended with the usual 'I hope we have a good trip, gentlemen', and the merchant ship masters put their orders in their brief-cases and a launch took them across the windswept waters of the loch to their ships. They had only three or four hours to digest their instructions before leaving.

After that Sherbrooke held an escort conference giving his orders to the escorts—under Cdr H. T. Rust, D.S.O., in the minesweeper *Bramble*—which would take the convoy up to position 'C', off Iceland, where Sherbrooke and his destroyers would meet it and take over. Rust was an old friend—the two men had been in the same term at Dartmouth and each had a complete trust in the other.

The merchantmen sailed that Tuesday afternoon, 22nd December, as described in the first chapter, and the *Onslow* followed at 1500, quickly passing them as she headed for Seidisfiord to join the other four 'O' class destroyers of the 17th Flotilla—

which had arrived there independently—and also the *Achates* and *Bulldog*, which had sailed together from Greenock at 0900 the previous day.

Knowing that lack of sleep would be one of the big enemies once the ocean escorts joined the convoy on Christmas Day, Sherbrooke was determined to get to Seidisfiord as quickly as possible so that the men should get a good night's sleep on the 23rd. *Onslow* therefore steamed out through the North Minch at twenty-five knots.

But his luck was out: the glass was falling and very soon the wind had risen to fifty knots, a fresh gale. *Onslow* pressed on, plunging her bow into the heavy seas and scooping tons of water on to the foredeck, but both Sherbrooke and Wyatt, the navigator, were watching constantly to make sure her speed was kept at a safe level. The wind increased by 0500 next day, Wednesday, to a full gale, and thick grey clouds, harried by the high winds, seemed to reach down to the sea. Soon the ship was pounding badly: as she lifted to the crest of a wave her bow slammed down so hard into the trough that there was the danger that she might break her back. Down below it seemed as if one was in a steel box which was constantly being dropped on to a hard road. Reluctantly Sherbrooke reduced speed, a few revolutions at a time, until he found that, carefully watched, she would make twenty knots without thumping everyone's teeth out.

Long years of experience by commanding officers and navigation specialists are needed at such times as this to avoid serious damage and yet still make good time on a passage. The fastest possible speed for a ship in heavy weather depends on her dimensions—primarily her length—in relation to the existing sea and swell waves. There are many other factors to be considered too, such as the angle the ship's course is making with the seas that are running; the shape, length and height of swell waves and their rate of advance; and whether the ship is deep-loaded or light in the water. However, it is not always just a case of reducing speed to avoid damage. On the contrary, when a gale first springs up the swell waves are fairly steep, but they run close together. It is then often best to steam at high speed so that the sharp bows of a destroyer will cut swiftly through the young waves, and the ship has no time to plunge into successive troughs. There will be a great deal of spray flung around; but so long as the air temperature is above freezing point, there will be no danger of ice forming on board.

Sherbrooke's fast passage to Seidisfiord paid off, for he missed the worst of the gale. Although the *Onslow* had to fight her way through the winds of forty-eight to fifty-five knots, the *Bulldog* and *Achates* ran into such heavy weather that, on the Tuesday afternoon, when the convoy and *Onslow* sailed, both those destroyers were forced to heave to. Nearly twenty-four hours later, with the deadline of Tuesday for arriving at Seidisfiord fast approaching, the Captain of *Bulldog* had to signal:

Hove to in position 180 degrees Stokkness Light 8 miles, Achates *in company. Southerly gale, force 12. . . .*

Force 12 was the highest classification for wind velocity on the Beaufort Scale. This scale, drawn up by Admiral Sir Francis Beaufort in sailing-ship days (1808), is still in use for weather observations and forecasting. It meant winds of hurricane force—more than sixty-five knots—and, in terms of the pressure the wind exerted, that was over seventeen pounds per square foot.

Before long *Bulldog* was so badly damaged by the heavy seas that it was useless for her to go on to Iceland when the weather eased, and she had to return to the United Kingdom for repairs. The *Achates* sprang her new topmast, but she was able to carry on to Seidisfiord, where it was re-stayed.

Meanwhile the *Onslow* arrived in Seidisfiord on Wednesday evening. Near the fiord entrance the wind was still blowing forty knots and Sherbrooke found that *Oribi, Obedient, Obdurate* and *Orwell* were at anchor, having already fuelled from a tanker.

Even at the best of times Seidisfiord was a treacherous spot for anchoring. It was simply a typical fiord enclosed by steep cliffs and barren mountains. Almost everywhere, except near the head of the fiord, the water was too deep for ships to anchor, forcing them to use the part where it was very narrow. As a result, when they swung at anchor their sterns passed uncomfortably close to the shore.

That, however, was the least of their worries: sudden violent wind squalls of near hurricane force would frequently roar down the fiord with no warning, snapping wires, dragging anchors and threatening to blow the ships ashore. At least one warship had been swept right out of the fiord, the anchor dragging beneath her like the hook on the end of an optimistic angler's fishing line. The squalls were caused by cold air trapped in the glacier valleys being sucked out by the higher winds and sent howling down the fiords. The first warning the ships had would be the sight of spindrift approaching very fast. Then, seeming as if it was solid, it would strike them. Ships had to maintain steam all the time for working their main engines and a most careful anchor watch had to be kept. Oiling from the tanker was a nightmare because if one of these squalls arrived on the scene when the destroyer was secured alongside, it would snap the wires like string and the fiord was so narrow at this point that there was barely room to manœuvre.

That Wednesday night was a wild one, with almost every one of the destroyers, both anchors down, using their engines while trying to stop dragging about in the fiord, a danger to themselves and everyone else. All thoughts of a good night's rest before sailing to join the convoy vanished.

8

Christmas Eve, 1942

AT 1130 next day, Thursday, the battered *Achates* arrived, so that Sherbrooke had the ships of the ocean escort present in the fiord. Even before the force sailed to join the convoy—which by now was fighting its way north in heavy weather—he was short of a destroyer. It was not a very promising start. However, he ordered all commanding officers to report on board the *Onslow* to receive their orders. He had met only one of them before.

Together the stories of the six destroyers' activities up to then provide a good indication of the way the smaller ships of the Royal Navy had to be used so that the maximum usefulness was squeezed from them. We can take *Achates*, since this was destined to be her last voyage, as an example. She had recommissioned in April after a long refit at Swan Hunter's yard on the Tyne. There she had been provided with a new bow after the original one had been blown off by a mine in Icelandic waters the previous year. She was assigned to the Clyde Special Escort Force, formed as a small reserve of ships which could be used when necessary to reinforce the escort groups employed on the regular convoy cycles.

Thus it was from the friendly shores of Gourock, on the Clyde, that she was to operate for the final busy months of her career. Her first real job was to help escort PQ 16 to North Russia, and the seemingly continuous air attacks on the convoy during the last week of a brilliant May had been a real test for her officers and crew. After a short spell in Murmansk, an uneventful return convoy and a short period of boiler-cleaning leave, *Achates* was off again to Russia, this time with PQ 18, and had another tough battle with the *Luftwaffe* and U-boats. The voyage was memorable for the number of abortive U-boat hunts in the difficult Asdic conditions that exist in northern waters. Her stay in Archangel was remarkable if only for the number of nights in which parties of seamen had to be landed to put out fires started among wooden buildings ashore by the *Luftwaffe*'s incendiary bombs.

Just before sailing with PQ 18, a new commanding officer, Lt Cdr A. H. T. Johns, had been appointed. After bringing the *Achates* home to the Clyde—at a pleasant eighteen knots all the way—he took her southwards to Gibraltar, where they found the largest assembly of escort ships that any of them had ever seen. After a week of conferences and preparation they sailed to escort the vast array of ships (which had been appearing as if by magic from the wastes of the Atlantic) to the beaches of North Africa for the great landings.

For the next ten days the *Achates* had been involved in some desultory bombardment and a lot of patrolling off-shore. When screening some large ships on the way back to Gibraltar, however, they detected a submarine and after several attacks were thought to have sunk it.

Not so successful were their efforts on the homeward voyage when, in a rising gale in the Bay of Biscay, the troopship *Warwick Castle* was torpedoed and sunk. Fortunately there were no troops on board but, as one of the *Achates* officers wrote later, 'It gave us our first taste of the pitiful task of picking up survivors, of getting weakened, frightened men on to our slippery steel decks, of resuscitating the apparently drowned, of burying the dead, and of accommodating the living in our already overcrowded mess-decks.'

The end of November, as the first plans for convoys JW 51A and JW 51B were being made, found the *Achates* back in Gourock for well-deserved leave. Then the orders arrived which brought her to Seidisfiord on Christmas Eve 1942 for her last and bravest voyage.

Lt Cdr Johns was one of the youngest of the destroyers' commanding officers. His second-in-command was a twenty-four-year-old Channel Islander, Lt Loftus Peyton-Jones, whose father, a well-known Jersey yachtsman, had commanded a destroyer in the First World War. The next senior was an

RNVR lieutenant, Eric Marland, D.S.C. and Bar (the latter for sinking the submarine in the Mediterranean). A brilliant graduate of Magdalen College, Oxford, he was imperturbable and competent, endowed with a modest assurance and quiet cheerfulness, and brave as only those with true faith can be.

The navigator was a young RNR sub-lieutenant, Kenneth Highfield, who had only just completed his apprenticeship with the P & O Line. The doctor was Surgeon-Lt James MacFarlane, who had announced his engagement a few months earlier. A fine doctor, he was perhaps best remembered as a cheerful and willing messmate, ready to turn his hand to any of the hundred-and-one jobs that must be undertaken by some member of a destroyer's wardroom. Another cheerful man was the Chief Engineer, Lt Peter Wright, RNR, who had more seafaring experience than most of the others and delighted in leading them up the garden path. One of the least experienced was a young man from North London, Sub-lt F. R. Barrett, but he made up for his lack of nautical knowledge by his determination.

These officers were all, with the exception of Lt Peyton-Jones, to be killed within a few days. The other members of the wardroom, who survived, were the Gunner (T), Mr E. W. Smith, and Sub-lt A. J. Davidson.

However on this Christmas Eve, knowing they were to sail with the rest of the destroyers before midnight, all the officers were trying to decide the burning question of whether to have the traditional Christmas dinner before they sailed or wait until they arrived in Murmansk. No compromise, they declared, could be allowed to spoil their enjoyment of the excellent turkeys they had embarked at Gourock. In the end they decided to postpone the celebration until they arrived in Murmansk.

The most senior officer among the destroyer captains after Captain Sherbrooke was Cdr J. E. H. McBeath, D.S.O., D.S.C., commanding the *Oribi*, and then came Lt Cdr David Kinloch, commanding the *Obedient*. Lt Cdr C. E. L. Sclater, of the *Obdurate*, was the only commanding officer who actually knew Sherbrooke, having served with him a few months earlier at Freetown while commanding *Wild Swan*.

The *Obdurate* had, like *Obedient*, been completed at Denny's yard at Dumbarton only a few weeks earlier and had gone straight to Scapa Flow to 'work up' her ship's company, who came from Devonport. Because the weather was so bad they did not even succeed in carrying out a proper shoot with a target before going off to escort the *Argonaut* taking stores to Spitzbergen and bringing back RAF personnel from Murmansk. The voyage about to begin would be the ship's first convoy operation, and in addition Sclater had had three different First Lieutenants, two of whom had gone sick.

The last of the flotilla, the *Orwell*, had been commissioned in September after being completed at Thornycroft's Yard at Southampton. Her early days are perhaps best described by one of her radar operators, Dennis H. Mackness, of Foleshill, Coventry:

'When we commissioned *Orwell* in Southampton only one of the six radar operators had ever before served in a warship, and he had spent only a short time in a cruiser. I doubt if any of the others had even seen a destroyer before, least of all viewed the prospect of living in one for a long period of time. But during our training we had heard from any number of instructors (with tales of the far-away China Station and a suspicion of a leer on their faces) that "Destroyers—they were the boats. Wouldn't change 'em for anything. Less discipline, canteen messing . . ."

'So when my draft came through I was pleased to find it was to one of these instructors' paradises. After several train journeys we found ourselves lined up on the jetty alongside the *Orwell*. A fiery little man dashed up and down issuing orders with the speed of a machine-gun, seemingly none too pleased with life or the incoming draft. There were a few muttered warnings from the older hands in the ranks, "He's the G.I." (Gunner's Mate). We could not recall any warnings from our instructors about such a person and hoped it was only a temporary phase.

'With a sudden roar of "Communications go aboard!" he stopped in front of our little party. We politely inquired just what party the Radar Branch was. We should have known better with a man of his vocabulary. Eventually, with a puzzled air, he pushed his hat to the back of his head and strode off, streaming orders at ratings who were unloading the kitbags and hammocks.

'Seeing our chance to escape, we went on board and eventually found out that we did in fact mess with the Communications Branch, a motley collection of signalmen, coders, telegraphists, the Sick Berth Attendant, Writer, cooks and radar operators. We totalled about 25 men, of whom about four had been to sea before.

'Our first job was to secure a locker (a necessity, we had been told, together with a regular place to sling our hammock). How right our informant had been, and how loud were the cries of distress from the unfortunate few when it was found there were not enough to go round. A locker was to prove a most important possession in the future. It was almost impossible to keep things tidy and in order (your No. 1 suit, for instance) when stuffed inside a kitbag, especially as they were slung about all over the place by your messmates or the rolling and pitching of the ship.

'Eventually we settled in and took stock of our surroundings. The mess-deck was spotless and smelled of new paint. The mess lockers were stocked up with all the necessary cups, plates and cutlery. This place was to be our home for a long time. The ship was steady as a rock alongside the quay wall and the prospect did not seem at all too bad.

'At this time the Radar Branch was regarded as something of a mystery and did not work as part of the ship. Two or three of us had the job of officers' servants, which included taking care of the after flats, and were rewarded by having "big eats" in the officers' pantry on duty nights. The remainder of the radar ratings did the mess-deck chores.

'Sleeping was a bit of a problem. There were slings for nearly everyone, but once again the unfortunate few with nowhere for their hammocks had to manage as best they could, sleeping on lockers, on the table—and even under it. Hammocks were slung in all directions, interwoven between the many lengths of piping running along the deckhead. Some were pulled high to miss the fellows slung beneath.

98

'Eventually we left the security of the dockyard and sailed north for Scapa Flow to do our working up before becoming "operational".

'While we were learning our jobs around the ship we were also learning to live together as a team. We had by now realized that if the food was not prepared and taken to the galley there was no dinner, and we were soon able to prepare a decent meal—although the duffs and pastry left much to be desired and there were enough eyes left in the potatoes to see us through many a week.

'So in all innocence we sallied forth after many buzzes [rumours] ranging from Gibraltar to South Africa (someone had even seen pith helmets) on what was to be the first of several Russian convoys. . . .'

We shall return to Mackness later in the narrative. In the meantime the five commanding officers went across to the *Onslow* to meet Sherbrooke and receive their orders. For all of them, with the exception of Sclater, it was their first chance of sizing up their new Captain (D), and their first impression was identical with that of Sherbrooke's staff. There was not much small talk and soon they left the *Onslow*. Later in the day they joined each other for dinner—Nigel Austen, for instance, dining with David Kinloch, who was an old friend from before the war, when the two of them had been instructors at Portsmouth. Each captain went back to his own ship in time for boats to be hoisted in before sailing. All the destroyers had topped up with fuel from the tanker *Scottish American*. For a short while it was peaceful in the fiord.

9

'Anchor Aweigh'

IN Seidisfiord it wanted an hour to midnight on Christmas Eve 1942, and a light but bitter wind funnelled down the striated sides of the mountains and ruffled the water. The air was raw, as if chilled by its passage over the island's glaciers and the snow capping the great ridges of rock; and, in spite of numerous layers of heavy clothing, men shivered in the darkness.

Unlike the previous stormy days and those to follow, it was a fine night. Overhead the fronds of the aurora borealis flickered across the sky in magnificent trailing veils and curtains of changing colours; and near the head of the fiord, just in sight of the anchored destroyers, friendly-looking lights showed in the windows of the houses of the small fishing village, for war and the black-out had not yet come to these northern people. It was, with the snow and the aurora borealis, an almost magic setting for Christmas.

In homes throughout the Christian world it was the time when fathers normally tiptoed round small beds and cots, gently placing Christmas stockings for excited children to find in the morning. However, in many homes, widows, after dreary days searching scantily-stocked toy shops, had the melancholy task; in others wives did it, and wondered and worried about their husbands serving so many miles away.

Husbands, for instance, among those men forming the crews of the six destroyers now at anchor in the fiord, who even now were dragging on thick woollen vests, long pants, shirts, trousers and as many jerseys as would fit, before climbing into heavy stockings, seaboots and finally duffle coats, balaclava helmets and gloves, cursing and grumbling as usual, saying a lot and meaning little of it; apparently envying the soldier with his feet on dry land and his evening out with a girl.

Special sea duty men had been ordered to their stations. Forty minutes before midnight the ships would sail. Reluctantly (for it was warm below, even if the air was fetid because all the scuttles, deadlights and hatches were screwed down tight; and anyway, this was the beginning of it all) the men trooped to their allotted stations, leaving their shipmates asleep in their hammocks.

In each destroyer some of the men went forward to the narrow fo'c'sle to work under the cable officer and weigh anchor, and with them was a stoker petty officer to work the capstan. The chief quartermaster had gone to the wheelhouse—he always took the wheel when the ship was entering or leaving harbour. With him were telegraphmen who, as orders came down the voicepipes from the bridge, would work the telegraphs which relayed orders to the engine-room.

A seaman had gone to the bridge to act as messenger; others went as look-outs. The yeoman of signals was there too. The navigator came up from the charthouse to speak to the officer of the watch. Finally, the captain came up from his sea cabin.

In the *Onslow* the tall figure of Captain Sherbrooke, muffled in a duffle coat, thick scarf and cap, was standing at the forward part of the bridge with his navigator, Lt Peter Wyatt, and the officer of the watch.

In the *Orwell*, Lt Cdr Nigel Austen was looking at his watch and talking to his navigator, Lt Patrick Satow, a man 6 ft. 4 in. tall and with an almost encyclopaedic memory. Each captain had planned his ship's role; each navigator had gone over the proposed course. Since they were officers with bitter experience of Russian convoys, they had no need to study the authorities on the waters ahead of them—the *Arctic Pilot Volume III*, and the *Norway Pilot Volume III*.

The minutes ticked by. The steep sides of the fiord, thanks to the unreal light of aurora borealis, could just be distinguished in the darkness. From each bridge eyes strained to see the position of *Onslow*, the flotilla leader.

In *Orwell*—as in the other destroyers—the engineer came up to the bridge and reported.

'Main engines ready for sea,' Lt Tribe told Lt Cdr Austen.

101

'Very good, Chief.'

The two Admiralty-pattern, three-drum boilers were ready. Although only one would be connected up for the time being to save fuel, together they could develop 40,000 shaft horsepower.

But first there was the job of heaving up the anchor, which alone weighed a ton and three-quarters, apart from the forged-steel chain cable.

Austen picked up the telephone linking the bridge with the fo'c'sle and spoke to the cable officer.

'Shorten in to three shackles.'

The cable officer passed the word to the stoker petty officer who started the capstan revolving, hauling in the chain cable. It took some time before the cable officer could report that he had shortened in to three shackles—more than 200 feet—because so much cable had been veered in the deep waters of the fiord.

Then five of the destroyers waited for the signal from the *Onslow*. Suddenly a light flickered, the yeomen of signals read it, mentally changing its Morse into words, and passed the signal to their captains.

In *Orwell* Austen gave the order 'Weigh'.

A quick word from the cable officer and the capstan started its clanking again. He was watching the angle of the cable as it led away from the ship to the anchor deep down in the cold, dark waters of the fiord. The ship was slowly being pulled over the anchor and the angle became steeper. Soon the cable was hanging vertically.

He spoke into the telephone again: 'Up and down.'

The capstan became less laboured.

'Anchor aweigh.'

With the anchor clear of the sea-bed the last tenuous link with the land had been severed. The cable officer watched until the anchor broke surface, saw there were no underwater cables or bits of wreckage hooked on to it, and reported: 'Clear anchor.'

Austen gave his first order to the engine-room. It was repeated down the voicepipe to the wheelhouse, where a rating swung over the telegraphs, one for each engine.

The ship shuddered quite gently. The water round the stern boiled and swirled as the two propellers started to spin, one one way, one the other, as Austen turned the ship to point her bows eastwards down the fiord.

Then, as she swung round, both propellers started to push her ahead, and the quartermaster at the wheel obeyed each helm order and repeated it back up the voicepipe. Dimmed navigation lights were switched on to help the five destroyers take station on the *Onslow*.

Slowly, now hidden from the shore by the blackness, they nosed their way down to the entrance of the fiord. The special sea duty men handed over to the sea duty men of the watch, and the destroyers began to pitch slightly as they met swell waves from the open sea.

The pitching and rolling increased, and at 2320 they were past the boom and at sea, a single line of five destroyers 'following father', in this case the *Onslow*. Station keeping at night was always difficult, dangerous and tiring. It said three cables distant in the book—six hundred yards. At that range in darkness the stern of the next ahead was at best merely a small slightly darker blob in an all-enveloping black blanket. The wake was something of a help, but whatever happened that black blob must not be lost to sight. However tired a man was, however much the ship rolled, pitched and yawed, the next ahead must be seen and followed.

If she were lost, then an increase in speed might mean a collision—six hundred yards at twenty knots took less than a minute to cover. Five degrees difference in course, and the chance of finding the ship again was negligible until daylight and even then it would by no means be certain.

Within a few minutes the order went round each destroyer to clear the lower mess-decks and flats as they steamed through the minefield off the entrance to Seidisfiord. Although they knew the way through there was always a chance that a mine might have drifted.

The watches changed: midnight came and passed, bringing Christmas Day, and the ships, still in line ahead, steered east-south-east. Just after 0200, when *Onslow* had signalled the ships to form line abreast, wireless operators heard a signal coming over addressed to Captain Sherbrooke. It was from Admiral Tovey, the first he had received at sea on this operation, and said briefly:

I estimate position of main body JW 51B at 0800 25th based on escort aircraft report as 065° 14' north, 008° 31' west, speed 7 knots. One or two groups of stragglers about 15 miles astern overtaking.

The position put the convoy about one hundred and fifty miles east of Seidisfiord. It had already travelled a distance equal to that from John o' Groat's to Land's End, and yet it had hardly started on its voyage.

Already it might have been spotted by the enemy. Admiral Tovey had signalled earlier the day before that a westbound U-boat was nearby, and its course must have taken it within a short distance of the convoy. Had it sighted the merchantmen? Probably not, since the Navy's wireless stations would almost certainly have intercepted its sighting report and warned Captain Sherbrooke. On the other hand, the U-boat was westbound—going out on patrol: it might be shadowing. . . . Still, Cdr Rust, the SO of the close escort, in *Bramble*, would have also received Admiral Tovey's signal and his ships would be watching and waiting, their Asdics pinging away.

And just after the U-boat signal the Admiral had wirelessed to Rust: *Your position was probably reported by a FW aircraft at 1315.*

At that time the convoy was in such a position that it could only be heading for Russia: it was too far to the north-east for it to be going to Iceland. Sherbrooke, to whom the signal had been repeated, had speculated on the probable reaction to the aircraft's signal in I/SKL, the Operations Department of the German Naval Staff. Would U-boats now be assembling across the path of the convoy? Were the surface ships waiting for the convoy to get a good deal nearer? As usual, for officers carrying such responsibilities, there were plenty of questions and no answers.[1]

Because the convoy was a mere speck in the ocean and would

[1] In fact the aircraft did not report the convoy.

be hard to find, Captain Sherbrooke took his six destroyers to a position ahead of the convoy and then turned to steam down its track, his course being the reciprocal to that of the merchantmen. Visibility was just over three miles, so he spread out the destroyers, which were still in line abreast, so that each was three miles from the next, thus forming a front fifteen miles wide and able to search over a width of twenty-one miles.

Look-outs were watching their prc-ordained arcs of the horizon, officers of the watch searched ahead with binoculars; but noon came and passed without any sign of the convoy. Was it more than twenty-one miles off its track? Had it passed them to one side or the other, just a short distance out of sight of the destroyer on each wing?

The weather had been good since Admiral Tovey's signal, so this was unlikely. Probably they had been slowed down—particularly if whipping up stragglers; and the aircraft may have given an inaccurate position in the first place.[1]

Fortunately the convoy would be against the lighter southern sky—although in this latitude the sun rose only one degree above the horizon at noon. Then at 1430 a lookout in the destroyer at the western end of the line sighted the convoy to the south-west. Signal lamps flickered across the line of destroyers and Sherbrooke swung his force round to meet them. The convoy was fifteen miles to the westward of its intended track.

The merchantmen were in four columns but some of them had straggled, unable to keep up with the convoy despite all efforts by the escort. Rather than use his own destroyers to rush around using up their precious fuel, Captain Sherbrooke decided to keep the *Blankney*, *Chiddingfold*, *Ledbury* and *Circe* to chase up the stragglers until darkness.

Soon the convoy was sorted out, the stragglers urged back in position, and the six destroyers took up their screening positions —*Achates* on the port quarter, *Orwell* and *Oribi* on the port side, *Onslow* ahead, *Obedient* and *Obdurate* on the starboard

[1] The navigator of one of the destroyers kept a 'Black List' of individual convoy commodores, particularly those who, for no proper reason, did not worry overmuch about navigation. On many occasions he had, through knowing that a certain commodore was commanding a convoy with which his ship was to rendezvous, saved a lot of time and valuable fuel by looking first where the commodore might be, rather than should be.

side, with the two trawlers *Vizalma* and *Northern Gem* astern with the corvette *Rhododendron*, ready to pick up survivors if any ship should be torpedoed. The *Bramble*, with her better radar, and the *Hyderabad* were placed well ahead.

As darkness fell the three Hunts and the corvette *Circe* were ordered to detach from the convoy: their part of the job was done. They already had their orders and only *Blankney* had anything to be cheerful about, since for her they meant a few hours' rest. Six days earlier the omnipresent Admiral Tovey had signalled: *After leaving convoy HMS* Blankney *return Scapa for repairs to compass. HMS* Ledbury *and HMS* Chiddingfold *to Loch Ewe.*

Blankney led the ships away. The usual 'Good Luck' signals were passed, and the fourteen merchantmen were alone with their new and final escort. Once he was well away from the convoy and so near Seidisfiord that it would not matter if the enemy did fix his position by direction-finder, the commanding officer of the *Blankney* signalled to Admiral Burnett, commanding Force R, the position of the convoy at 1700, the course it was steering and its speed. That would give Admiral Burnett something to work on, although a lot could—and did—happen in the next six days.

Slowly, at eight knots, the merchantmen crawled north. The escorts, in a watchful ring, weaved round and about them, Asdics pinging, watering eyes watching—both for a probable enemy or a possible friend.

Matthews, the Commodore's Yeoman of Signals, smoked a cigar as a gesture to Christmas on the bridge of the *Empire Archer* and thought about life in general. Exactly a year earlier he had been in the English Channel aboard a small collier in a convoy bound for Southampton. Twenty-three 16-inch shells from the German batteries along the French coast near Cap Gris Nez had splashed around them. Now, on Christmas Day 1942, the temperature was starting to drop as they steamed towards the Arctic Circle. However, Matthews thought, he had plenty of books to read—ranging from *Russia* by Bernard Pares to H. G. Wells's *Mr. Polly* by way of *Why France Fell* by André Maurois.

All through the convoy men's thoughts turned to home: home in some United States or British town or village where tonight, especially, they would be missed more than usual.

The convoy continued its zigzag course. Every now and again in the darkness one of the destroyers, afraid it had weaved too far, would nose her way in carefully to find a column of merchantmen then, reassured, take up her position again. Watches changed. At present the two watches, port and starboard, were each split into two, the first part and the second. With the ship at cruising stations, only one part of the watch was on duty. That meant three parts were resting, the idea being that they should have as much sleep as possible before the ship went to defence stations, where the whole of one watch was on duty, and the men got little rest.

Huddled round a gun mounting, at a searchlight platform, at torpedo tubes, the men tried to keep warm and if possible to doze. Lucky ones found a few feet of flat surface—a ready-use ammunition locker for instance—to lie on; others crouched in the lee of something, trying to keep out of the bitter wind. Except for when there was a following wind, the ship's forward speed increased the actual wind so it was always very breezy on deck.

As always it seemed that night would never end; but somehow it did, giving way almost imperceptibly to an unreal and eerie greyness. It always seemed colder at this time of the day; but men's morale and physical resistance were lower.

As the blackness was slowly rolled back and ships could gradually be distinguished in what, in these latitudes, passed for daylight, anxious men counted them. Commodore Melhuish, from the bridge of the *Empire Archer*, Captain Sherbrooke from the *Onslow*, Lt Cdr Kinloch from the *Obedient* . . . all eyes ranged down the four columns of merchantmen. Three . . . seven . . . ten . . . fourteen. All there, and no stragglers. It was as it should be, but how it so seldom was.

Boxing Day . . . by now tiredness was setting in. Captains and navigators, who rarely left the bridge, snatched what sleep they could, and were beginning to feel weary although they knew this was only the beginning. The weather had let up temporarily but there was another week at sea. At noon the convoy's latitude was 68° north—they were now inside the Arctic Circle.

Away in Iceland, Admiral Sir Bruce Fraser, second-in-command of the Home Fleet, had ordered his force—the battleship *Anson*, the 8-inch gun cruiser *Cumberland* with three screening destroyers—to raise steam. Later in the day they sailed from Akureyri to carry out Admiral Tovey's orders, received ten days earlier, 'to cover convoy JW 51B while convoy is between approximate longitude 001° E and 015° E . . .'

The other covering ships, the *Sheffield* and *Jamaica* of Force R, were by now in Kola Inlet, having seen the earlier convoy, JW 51A, arrive safely. As mentioned earlier, they had had a good Christmas Day, and Boxing Day was being used to sleep it off. Next day they would sail to cover JW 51B, now slowly approaching them.

In the afternoon a Liberator bomber of Coastal Command found the convoy and slowly circled it. Previously Peter Wyatt had worked out what he thought was the convoy's exact position and as the plane came round the *Onslow*'s Yeoman called it up with a signal lamp and passed the latitude and longitude as well as the speed of the convoy. Later in the afternoon the plane would land in Iceland and report the convoy's position to the Admiralty, who would be able to see how far behind or ahead of schedule it was, in turn warning both Admiral Burnett in the *Sheffield* and Admiral Fraser in the *Anson*, if necessary.

By using the aircraft as a messenger Captain Sherbrooke avoided breaking wireless silence. In fact, he would use his wireless only in an absolute emergency—sighting an enemy ship for instance. For signalling between ships wireless could be used if absolutely necessary. In that case a ship would use a certain agreed wavelength with her transmitter turned down to low power, giving a very limited range. It could be picked up by a U-boat if it was nearby, but could not reach land from their present position.

Shortly after the Liberator had turned back for its base, the convoy's latitude and longitude noted down, a Catalina flying boat joined and circled.

By this time the merchantmen were steaming along at eight

and a half knots and in good order. Things were going well. The Commodore, however, was suffering from the *Empire Archer*'s tendency to be a 'smoker'. She was coal-fired and had a low funnel, and in a following wind the smoke blew forward over the bridge, setting the men coughing and making their eyes stream. Far worse, as Commodore Melhuish reported later, 'it was at times positively dangerous as the view ahead was entirely obscured'. In addition, smoke was likely to reveal the convoy's position because it could be seen much farther away than masts or the outlines of ships. But there was nothing the *Empire Archer*'s Chief Engineer could do: the quality of the coal was to blame.

Apart from a mine which was sighted very close to the Commodore and was sunk by the *Rhododendron*, Boxing Day was quiet, and so was the long night that followed. Next day the battleship *Anson* and the cruiser *Cumberland*, with their destroyers, reached their covering position and passed south of the convoy so that they could now screen it from German surface ships which might be trying to approach from the south.

They could not cover it against enemy warships sailing from Altenfiord, or from any that sailed from Trondheim and hugged the coast until they reached North Cape. It was Force R's job to plug this gap; and, as narrated earlier, Admiral Burnett sailed on this day, 27th December, to take up his covering position.

Meanwhile the submarines—six British, including the *Graph*, the Dutch *O 14*, and the Polish *Sokol*—were patrolling closer inshore, forming the full-back line through which the German ships would have to pass if they left Trondheim or Altenfiord to attack the convoy.

Slowly the latitude noted in the ships' logs increased—70° north on the 27th, 72° north the day after; slowly the longitude moved eastwards—from 6° west on the 26th, to the meridian of Greenwich on the 27th, and 4° east on the 28th.

Slowly the pencilled line of their track moved north-east up the chart, climbing far beyond the Arctic Circle, then moving east to begin at long last to steer towards Murmansk itself. But from now on, every mile they steamed brought them nearer to the German main fleet bases in Norway. Vest Fiord, with

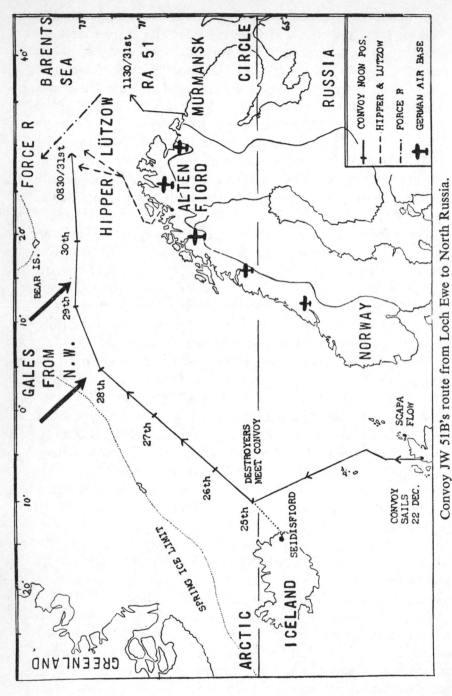

Convoy JW 51B's route from Loch Ewe to North Russia.

Narvik at its head, was less than four hundred miles way—a bare eighteen hours' steaming for a German pocket battleship or cruiser—while farther north, at the moment five hundred and fifty miles away but every minute drawing closer, was Altenfiord, just short of the hump which is North Cape. From this lair the Germans could act as sentinel or as ambusher: their ships would have to steam less than two hundred miles to attack a convoy, and with their home base so near, there was no risk of being cut off and forced into battle.

10

The Row Begins

WE must follow the German side of the story for the past few days. On the very day that the convoy had sailed from Loch Ewe, Hitler was holding a naval conference at Fort Wolf—the first for more than a month. Admiral Raeder had flown in from Berlin and Field-Marshal Keitel was there, as well as Vice-admiral Krancke (Raeder's representative at the Führer's headquarters) and Captain von Puttkamer, Hitler's naval aide.

The meeting was held in a concrete bunker several feet below the ground. The room, although it had a form of air conditioning, smelled damp. Hitler, as always, wore a grey semi-uniform jacket with very wide lapels, plain except for six brass buttons, the Nazi Party's vulture-like emblem on the left sleeve, and the Iron Cross pinned to his left breast.

Keitel and Raeder were complete members of the Officer Corps in matter of dress: Keitel wore a tunic with a high collar, an Iron Cross hanging between its points; Raeder always affected a stiffly-starched winged collar and black bow tie, one of the few naval officers to do so all the time.

When the heel-clickings, salutations and greetings were over Raeder started making his report, beginning, because it was the Führer's 'Zone of Destiny', with Norway. The heavy cruiser *Hipper*, pocket battleship *Lützow*, cruiser *Köln* and five destroyers were at Altenfiord; the cruiser *Nürnberg* and a destroyer at Narvik; and the *Tirpitz* was at Trondheim with three destroyers. The *Scharnhorst*, *Prinze Eugen* and five destroyers would be ready to transfer from the Baltic next month, he added.

He had a plan for the *Lützow*, he told Hitler: it had been assigned to cruiser warfare in the Arctic 'since supplies are apparently being carried to Northern Russia in unescorted vessels at the present time, and submarines are not very effective during the dark months of winter for patrolling the northern supply routes'.

Next he turned to fuel oil: the situation 'is going to become more difficult in the near future because the Italians need large additional supplies. . . . Even now our fuel oil situation is such that the large vessels cannot be refuelled in the main harbours unless allocations are made far in advance, since we are unable to keep sufficient supplies on hand'.

To this, Hitler made a curious reply. He considered that 'the danger of a possible Allied invasion of Northern Norway is greatest in January. Anti-aircraft defences are helpless because of the darkness'.

After listening to Raeder for another ten minutes, Hitler broke off the conference and told him to join him for dinner. The conference went on afterwards. It was destined to be the last ever attended by Raeder as Commander-in-Chief of the Navy due to the circumstances surrounding convoy JW 51B, which—by the time the conference ended—had sailed out into the Minch and was beginning to feel the swell from the Atlantic.

While the Germans argued, the convoy, now steering a more easterly course, made good progress and averaged about eight knots. It was not fast; indeed, it was lamentably slow in terms of getting through the danger area quickly.

On the Sunday evening of 27th December one of the wireless officers in the British tanker *Empire Emerald* was listening in on 434 kcs when he heard homing signals being transmitted on a bearing of 056°—on the port bow of the convoy.

The Commodore was told and he passed the message on to the *Onslow*. 'Flags', Lt Foster, was told and he reported that *Obdurate* was guarding that frequency. Captain Sherbrooke ordered her to be called up to see if she had heard anything. However, her captain replied that nothing had been received, and Sherbrooke 'considered it unlikely that the signals referred to the convoy or necessarily emanated from a U-boat'.

That night the barometer started falling slowly but with an

ominous steadiness: another big depression was rolling across the North Atlantic towards them. Then the wind got up, first just whining in the rigging and wireless aerials. Within an hour it was beginning to howl with high-pitched urgency, bringing fair-sized seas in its train and snow squalls which blanketed off what little visibility there was in the darkness. It was now that station-keeping became a real nightmare.

On the bridges of the merchantmen, officers and look-outs strained their eyes streaming from the wind, trying to see the ship ahead and keep station on it, but also keeping a sharp look-out for those on either beam and the one astern: more than one officer of the watch was startled to find the bows of the ship next in station astern almost alongside his bridge and only a few yards off.

Then, for long agonizing seconds—sometimes minutes—the fate of the two ships would hang in the balance: had the other ship seen him? Would she reduce speed and drop back into her rightful position? Or would someone panic, order the quarter-master to put the wheel hard over, and sideswipe him with her stern as she swung wildly away?

It was worse in the destroyers—even in good weather it was hard to keep any sort of control over the ship at the slow speed of the convoy; and as the wind piped up and the seas increased it became almost impossible, with the bow falling away under the pressure of the wind. Increasing speed to regain control meant zigzagging to keep with the convoy, for each escort had its own definite position: a few hundred yards out of station could mean a collision or the convoy lost from sight altogether.

The two trawlers *Northern Gem* and *Vizalma*, and the corvettes *Hyderabad* and *Rhododendron*, were like half-tide rocks, with seas breaking over the fo'c'sle and the ships rolling violently.

At first the wind was north-west, on the convoy's beam. The merchant ships carrying huge crated aircraft on their decks were rolling heavily, the sides of the crates acting as sails and pressing them over. They would roll slowly to leeward and stay there for a few uncomfortable and alarming moments as the great gusts of wind thrust against them, then slowly roll back, only to go over again.

114

Soon the wind was screaming at Force 7 on the Beaufort scale—twenty-seven to thirty-three knots and bordering on gale force. Spray blowing over the ships started forming ice on the decks, rails and superstructure. At first it was only a thin sheet, but almost imperceptibly the ice thickened and hardened.

Throughout the rest of the night the watches changed and weary men tried to sleep. Mackness, one of the *Orwell*'s radar operators, wrote: 'When we hit the bad weather we found out what being in a destroyer really meant. There was the noise of the ship shuddering and creaking as she ploughed through the heavy seas. She would shake on the top of a huge wave and then plunge like a stone dropped over a cliff, hitting the bottom of the trough with a crash. Then she would struggle on to the next wave and repeat the performance, seemingly trying to outdo each effort for noise and violence.

'She would roll wickedly from side to side, making it impossible for a man to stand up unaided. We who were inexperienced were caught unprepared. It did not seem possible that a ship could behave like this.

'The gash bucket, filled with dirty water and greasy oddments upset from its moorings and poured its contents over the mess-deck; the messtraps jumped from their places and clattered backwards and forwards with each roll. They were joined by a flood of potatoes ejected from their sacks. Someone would attempt to empty the washing-up water and the ship would ease up until the man, lulled into a sense of false security, would let go his hand-hold. The ship would then immediately roll violently and with unexpected venom neatly overturn him, adding the washing-up water to the quagmire fast collecting on the deck.

'If there happened to be a heavy following sea the waves would break on board and come racing forward along the flats, through the hatch and cascade down on to the mess-deck like a miniature waterfall. Then it would squelch back and forth with every movement of the ship, taking with it any clothes that fell from the racks, and soaking through the sack of cabbages stowed nearby. Within a very short time they gave off a smell which words could not describe, and were thrown overboard.

115

'Meals were hopeless in such weather, even for those hardy enough to try to eat. After a man staggered from the galley with whatever had been prepared, he tried to share it out. It was laughable. You wedged yourself against the table, held your plate in one hand and, with the other, tried to dish out the food. The table lurched up and down, often with a cork-screw motion, upsetting any efforts you made. Then the ship would give an extra lurch and clear the table, depositing the food either in your lap or on to the deck.

'But worst of all was seasickness. It affected all sorts of people. One torpedoman, for instance, who had spent years in the Service, would turn green at the slightest roll. Another chap, a "Hostilities Only" rating fresh from the country, would not be affected. (There was one seaman who could stand the roughest of seas, but the moment he stepped in a train to go on leave he would be sick.)

'Those who were ill would stagger to and from watch and whenever possible try to sleep it off on lockers or in hammocks. They would lie there with their faces ashen, often moving only to dash to the upper deck to be ill. Often they were too late, and the squalor increased.

'Watch-keeping, too, was trying. We were then at Defence Stations, four hours on and four hours off. Your period off watch would often be disturbed by action stations.

'After four hours on the upper deck, with freezing winds, snow showers and heavy seas breaking on board, men would come down below and almost cry with agony when the warmth of the mess brought circulation back to their frozen limbs. Often their clothing was soaking wet, with little chance of getting it dry before going on watch again.[1]

'Hammocks were often left up, against all regulations, and were a haven of rest where, for a few hours, you could try to

[1] Much of the warm clothing as well as huge food parcels, sweets, tobacco and magazines came from 'Aunty May', Mrs May Hanrahan, of Central Park, New York. The wife of a retired U.S.N. captain, she adopted the famous 'Tribal' class destroyers. When the original sixteen was reduced to three or four, she adopted other ships. In addition she ran a large credit for each ship with a large London store. At the end of the war she was presented with a diamond brooch and a silver model of a 'Tribal' as a token of the gratitude of the destroyers' officers and men.

forget everything in sleep. That is, when you got used to the hammocks swinging so that everyone banged into each other. However, there were times, usually in the darkness, when your hammock was not slung and the nearest locker was as far as you could reach.

'Wet clothes were a special problem and the more fortunate men who kept watch in the dry lent out their duffle coats. Drying the clothes was made more difficult by the condensation on the mess-decks.

'Food was hard to store. We started off well with sacks of bread, potatoes and cabbages, but these were soon ruined by the water swilling about. Before we reached Russia we were rationed quite strictly to the bread the PO Chef could bake and to ship's biscuits. Tins of dehydrated potato became popular. There was also a shortage of crockery and cutlery, the former because we had not secured it properly and the latter because knives, forks and spoons were often not taken out of the mess kettle before it was emptied over the side. At that time it was "Tinkle, tinkle knives and spoon, all the forks will follow soon". It was surprising how a dinner could be eaten with a pair of scissors or a tin opener.

'But although the life was cursed and grumbled at, there was a good deal of humour around, and the daily tot of rum often did much to settle uneasy stomachs (even if only for a couple of hours). Those who could stand the rough weather usually made their presence known in the hope of getting a spare tot from some unfortunate who could not stand the smell of rum in his present condition.'

On board the merchantmen conditions were almost as bad.

Matthews, the Yeoman in the *Empire Archer*, noted tersely in his diary that same day: 'Water pipes frozen. Unable to wash, unable to sleep, unable to keep warm. Inside bulkheads covered with ice. A very uncomfortable night.'

The wind continued blowing at Force 7 and in the late afternoon the following day the *Onslow*'s wireless operators picked up a signal from *Oribi* on Fleet wave, short range. It was in code and was immediately taken to the duty cipher officer, to be decoded. He soon got to work, but it did not make sense: the signal was certainly not in a code of which *Onslow* had the key. The *Onslow*'s operator was told to ask *Oribi* for a check and repeat; but before she answered the snow squalls cleared away and visibility increased, so Sherbrooke ordered her to be called up by signal lamp and told to pass the message visually.

However, within half an hour, before *Oribi* sent the message by lamp, more snow squalls arrived and visibility closed down. *Oribi* was not seen again by *Onslow*.[1]

Just before midnight the American ship *Jefferson Myers*, whose captain was the Rear-commodore (and would take over if the Commodore and Vice-commodore were lost) ran into trouble. She was rolling badly, partly due to the big seas coming in on her port beam and partly because of the enormous windage caused by the four big crates containing bombers which were lashed on top of her hatches. Soon it was seen in the darkness that they would break loose altogether and do a great deal of damage.

Her captain knew that if he kept on the present convoy course of 071° they would certainly come adrift, and from his position leading the starboard column he signalled across to the Commodore that he would have to heave-to. The Commodore agreed, but could do nothing about it. 'It would have been hazardous and probably impossible to heave-to the convoy,' he reported later.

The *Jefferson Myers* left the convoy and then turned into the wind on to a course of 055° where, with her screws turning slowly, she rode the long seas more comfortably and men could work in the darkness on the ice-covered decks putting more lashings round the vast crates.

So Monday the 28th passed—though in the long hours of darkness, snowstorms and Arctic desolation days meant very little except to navigators. Tuesday came, and with it even

---

[1] *Oribi* later reported that she lost the convoy because of gyro compass failure and signalled her intentions by wireless. She rejoined for a short while during the night and parted company before daylight. Having searched for the convoy for the next twenty-four hours, she set course for Kola Inlet, arriving on 31st December.

worse weather, the wind backing so that in the early hours it was round to north-north-west, blowing at nearly forty knots.

The gale had been raging more than twenty-four hours now and the wind, tearing down from the Polar icefields, was as bitter as any the convoy crews had yet encountered. It was knocking up waves eighteen feet high and blowing the crests off in spindrift: dense streaks of foam laced the tumbling surface of the waves, which were seven hundred feet apart and travelling at around thirty-five knots.

Within a short while the *Daldorch*, leading the port inner column, signalled that her deck cargo had carried away. She could no longer steer the convoy course and would steer 055° until the weather eased. This probably misled the ships of the port wing column, because at 0200 the trawler *Vizalma*, whose station was the last ship in the port wing column, discovered that she and three other ships were separated from the rest of the convoy. The ships were the *Calobre*, whose captain was Vice-commodore and who led the wing column; the *Chester Valley*, which was third in the column (the *Ballot* was second, but was not among them); and one other ship which the *Vizalma* believed was either the *Daldorch* (which had earlier signalled she was leaving the convoy) or the *John H. Latrobe*—probably the former.

All four merchantmen were finding it impossible to keep on the convoy course of 071° because of the heavy seas and high wind, which forced their bows off, so they hove-to, all on different courses and all drifting off in different directions. *Vizalma*'s skipper decided to stay with one of them and chose the *Chester Valley*. Cautiously she steamed up fairly close and hove-to nearby.

All through the morning the two ships stayed hove-to, one a merchantman loaded with twenty-five tanks, ten fighters, 4,371 tons of miscellaneous cargo and four bombers in crates on her hatches, the other a tiny trawler almost lost from sight in a freezing veil of spindrift and snow, ice smothering her whilst she rolled and pitched violently.

Then at noon the skipper of *Vizalma* thought the weather had eased a bit and signalled to the *Chester Valley* that he was going to try to steer 070° to pick up the convoy again.

The wheel was put over and almost immediately a heavy sea washed right across her, thundering in over the fo'c'sle, smashing a hatch and pouring into her magazine. In a few seconds there was three feet of water in the magazine, and to stay on that course would have been suicide. She hove-to again and the slow job of pumping out the tons of water, slopping about from side to side as she rolled, began.

Then at noon on this vile Tuesday the weather suddenly moderated and visibility in the half-light increased to ten miles. Quickly the anxious escorts looked for the convoy: it hardly existed as such: instead of fourteen ships in four orderly columns, there were only nine merchantmen in sight scattered all over the horizon.

Like patient but persistent sheep-dogs the escorts got the nine back into position again, but it was a slow job because of the heavy seas. None of the merchantmen could turn quickly and they could only steam at slow speeds—not much more than a walking pace.

By this time anything up to three inches of ice had formed on the ships. Wire, normally only as thick as a little finger, was so encased with ice that it was as round as a man's thigh; a curtain of ice joined gun-barrels to the deck; the breeches of the guns themselves were frozen solid, along with the training gear. Depth-charges were frozen in their traps and throwers; the torpedo tubes were stuck. The ships had lost their shape; they looked like models made of icing sugar on top of a special cake. (See pictures 1, 2 and 3.)

As they were, in their sheath of ice, the escorts were no longer fighting machines. The only consolation was that any enemy vessel would be in the same plight.

It was in these bitterly cold conditions that the radar operators realized how lucky they were to have some shelter. The lookouts, bridge personnel and guns' crews were exposed to the full fury of the Arctic, but they were in the two radar offices, one above the other, between the bridge structure and the funnel. An electric fire and the heat from the equipment itself kept the cabins warm; but the strange assortment of smells, coupled with the rolling of the ship, made it necessary for most of the youngsters to keep a cleaner's bucket within reach.

Captain Sherbrooke's problem was to find the missing ships: five merchantmen, one destroyer, *Oribi*, and a trawler. Since *Oribi* was on the port side, and it was from the port wing column that the ships were missing, it seemed possible to him that they had all gone off in the darkness and murk together and would be away somewhere to the north-westward.

A third of the convoy was missing. It was vitally necessary to round them up as soon as possible, before they straggled too far. Sherbrooke therefore decided to send a ship to search with radar.

In addition the problem of navigation was rearing its ugly head: Peter Wyatt had not had a decent sight for forty-eight hours and during most of that time a gale had been blowing. These powerful and prolonged winds set up a strong drift—the whole surface of the sea moved bodily to leeward. In remote areas where few mariners had previously sailed this drift was difficult to assess and could be anything up to fifty miles a day. In addition, the convoy had been wobbling about on its course while the heavy seas were running.

On dead reckoning—simply the course steered plotted out on the chart with allowances made for leeway due to the wind and the surface drift, which could only be estimates based on experience—the convoy should alter course round more to starboard, from 071° to 090° (due east).

Sherbrooke decided to send the minesweeper *Bramble*, one of the few escorts fitted with an effective surface-search radar set, to look for the missing ships, and at 1230 on 29th December she was called up by signal lamp and told to search to the north-west. Rust, her captain, was warned that the convoy would shortly alter to due east, the time depending on the result of a star sight.

As soon as the final Morse 'R' came from *Bramble*, showing she had received the signal, she turned away, her radar aerials revolving, to begin the hunt. She was never seen again by British eyes.

During the evening the gale blew itself out and with the easement from the howling wind came less wild seas. Life in the ships became more bearable and the senses, previously numbed by the sheer weight and insensate fury of the wind, recovered. But not fully, since few of the men had had any real rest for the past forty-eight hours.

Once again the radar aerials could turn and the search radar could be used to keep an eye on the convoy. However, when looking at it in these early days, before scientists had designed a method of projecting the 'picture' on to a cathode ray tube like today's television, it needed considerable skill to read it intelligently. When looking at the convoy it was difficult to distinguish individual ships, and radar operators found it very different from their initial training when, from a set sited on Douglas Head, in the Isle of Man, they had followed the passenger steamer *Lady of Man* across the Irish Sea.

Both the search and the gunnery radar aerials had to be cranked by hand to search around the horizon; but whereas the gunnery radar transmitted only a narrow beam of radio waves —rather like a spotlight torch—and was intended to feed ranges to the guns, the search set was used, as its name implies, for seeking and tracking surface ships.

As usual the greatest strain of all was on Sherbrooke: the safety of every merchantman and every escorting warship was his responsibility. Now, through the gale, through the wilfulness of Nature herself and not the carelessness or wrongful planning of man, a third of the convoy was missing. No one was to blame —you couldn't blame men for not seeing when a snowstorm in the darkness cut visibility to a few yards, when every quartermaster was fighting to steer his ship to within ten to twenty degrees either side of the proper course.

Even though the gale had gone raging on ahead of them, there was still plenty of trouble. During that Tuesday night—'a night as black as a lion's throat, with intermittent showers of snow and sleet,' as Captain Sherbrooke wrote later, 'I had gone to my sea cabin just below the bridge for a few minutes when suddenly there was a shout down the voicepipe from Foster, my Flotilla Signals Officer, "We are going to hit the *Orwell*".

'You can imagine my feelings—two damaged destroyers, one probably unable to steam, in the Arctic Circle and hundreds of miles from anywhere, and the already insufficient escort further reduced. I think that really *was* the worst moment in my life!

'On the bridge within seconds, I was just in time to see the *Orwell*'s stern pass under *Onslow*'s bow. We were crossing on 90° opposite courses and missed each other by about twenty feet.'

Equally startled was Austen, the *Orwell*'s captain, who had been called to his bridge by a similar and equally alarming report. His relief at having avoided a collision was shortlived: a winking signal lamp from the *Onslow*'s bridge demanded to know why he had endangered the Senior Officer's ship. Both destroyers swore the other was out of position; but Captain (D) was displeased and his signal, couched in traditional, prosaic terms, said 'Reasons for this occurrence are to be rendered in writing on return to harbour. . . .'[1]

The incident, unimportant as it seems since the collision was avoided, shows how the convoy escort can have its main strength halved in a few seconds—for, with *Oribi* gone, only four fleet destroyers remained. It was the knowledge that this sort of thing could all too easily happen that added to the strain of the ordeal for individual captains and for their Senior Officer. Perhaps no less tiring was the prolonged anxiety felt by navigating officers, some of whom were on duty on the open bridge for eighteen hours a day, snatching what sleep they could on a settee or on the deck of the cramped charthouse.

In the early evening of Tuesday, Peter Wyatt, who had been hanging about on the bridge for hours with his sextant, finally managed to get a star sight. He worked it out and found it put the convoy well behind the dead-reckoning position, and because of that the convoy did not alter round to due east until just before midnight.

Wednesday, 30th December, with the convoy eight days out from Loch Ewe, found the weather a good deal better and all ships had every available man on deck chipping off the sheath

---

[1] After the action, when Captain Sherbrooke was very badly wounded, the *Orwell* was very touched by a thoughtful message cancelling this signal.

of ice. Hammers and shovels scaled it off decks and gunnery officers saw to it that it was cleared from round the guns. The canvas bags over the breeches were untied—the drawstrings were like hard wire—and the breeches opened. In several of the ships they had frozen solid and it took a lot of work to get them functioning again.

The convoy was now doing only six knots to give the stragglers a chance to catch up and at 0900 the first of the missing ships arrived and took up her position in the convoy. But as the convoy was well behind its schedule—there was Force R, the cruisers *Sheffield* and *Jamaica* to consider—Captain Sherbrooke and the Commodore decided to increase to nine knots at 1100.

Half an hour later ships were sighted to the south-west of the convoy, on its starboard quarter, and Sherbrooke ordered Sclater, in the *Obdurate*, to go and investigate. She found two more merchantmen and escorted them back to the convoy. Anxious not to lose them again Sherbrooke reduced the convoy speed to eight knots until they were in their proper stations, and then increased to nine knots once again.

Now there were only two merchantmen, *Oribi* and the trawler *Vizalma* missing. There was every hope, however, that *Oribi* had them all under her wing and was taking them on to Kola Inlet by herself. In actual fact the *Vizalma* with her consort, the *Chester Valley*, were at this time making eleven knots and, in their attempts to catch the convoy, had overtaken it and were now ahead and slightly to port of its track.

In the late afternoon, while signalling to the *Chester Valley*, the *Vizalma* saw another ship flashing in the distance. The trawler's skipper decided that, as he did not want to attract attention, since there might well be marauding German surface ships about, he would not investigate.

A little earlier, in the forenoon, a signal from the Admiralty warned Sherbrooke that there was a lot of activity by German wireless stations along the Norwegian coast, which were transmitting alarm reports. There was a good deal of speculation on *Onslow*'s bridge about this—did it mean the convoy had been sighted and the Germans were preparing an attack? Was it in connection with Force R? Or something entirely different?

The convoy would, by next day, be in the most dangerous position of all, Sherbrooke realized. Even now they were less than two hundred miles from Altenfiord. The fact that JW 51A had got through without being attacked was no consolation— it might have been sighted so late that the Germans could not get into a position to attack; and, seeing it was a small convoy, the Germans could have guessed the ships were being sailed in two parts and that the others were coming along later.

The final verdict was that no one could be sure, but the primary task—getting the escorts clear of ice as fast as possible, so that once again they would be efficient fighting machines— must be carried out quickly.

Several tons were thrown over the side by the evening, by which time the gun positions and most of the ship were clear. Ordnance artificers checked their guns and equipment, the Gunner (T) was satisfied with the torpedo tubes and the First Lieutenant was glad he could see the ship again—even if eroding patches of rust were appearing through the grey paint.

Sherbrooke now reckoned the convoy was now entering the main danger area but might well have come so far without being sighted. One could not be sure—nothing was ever sure in sea warfare—but it was reasonable to hope.

By this time the Germans were in fact already planning a heavy attack on the convoy. For earlier that day at 1240, while *Obdurate* was still astern of the convoy shepherding the two stragglers, a German submarine, *U-354*, commanded by Lt Herschleb, passed close to the convoy. Hearing the muffled and rhythmic beat of their propellers underwater, Herschleb had warily come up to periscope depth to have a look round. And even though he had suspected it from the moment his hydrophone operator first reported a contact, he was excited by what he saw: a series of dark shapes moving slowly across the surface of the water—a British convoy, bound for Russia. . . .

The light was bad. Herschleb quickly swung the periscope right round so that he could search the whole horizon: no other

125

enemy ships and no aircraft in sight: it was safe to surface. Ballast tanks were blown and like a vast whale *U-354* slithered to the surface. The hatches were thrown open and the conning-tower manned.

With powerful binoculars, Herschleb inspected the convoy, noting its course and speed and quickly taking a range and bearing. A few minutes later he took another range and bearing. That would give a rough idea of its course and speed.

Down below his navigator took the U-boat's position from the gridded chart and a brief signal was given to the wireless operator to send off to Admiral Dönitz, commanding U-boats from his headquarters at Kerneval, near the French naval base at Lorient. It was also addressed to Admiral Klüber, commanding the northern area at Narvik, and would also be passed on to Berlin.

The signal said: *Convoy in position square AB 6388. Enemy's course 070° speed 12 knots.*

By the time the operator had got the signal away, another was lying on his table: *Convoy 6–10 steamers. Square 6394. Enemy steering 100°. Convoy weakly escorted. Escort several destroyers to one light cruiser.*

Having got a satisfactory—albeit inaccurate—enemy report transmitted, Herschleb then decided to work himself round ahead of the convoy to make a torpedo attack. An ideal position would be on the starboard bow of the ships.

Slowly *U-354* forged ahead in the near-darkness and, as soon as he was in position, Herschleb took the submarine down to periscope depth. The time now was just after 1600 and he waited for the first ships to come into sight. It did not take long. Down rumbled the periscope and three torpedoes left the tubes, speeding towards the convoy. In the U-boat Herschleb and his men counted the seconds on a stop-watch, but there was no noise of the torpedoes detonating against any of the merchantmen. Up went the periscope, and a tense Herschleb saw the convoy had zigzagged at the last moment and the torpedoes had passed astern of the ships.

The convoy soon disappeared into the gloom and there was no chance of getting into a good firing position again for some time, so he surfaced and sent off another signal to Dönitz and Klüber:

Convoy in square AC 4189. The convoy split up. Zigzag of up to 80°. About 10 steamers, several destroyers and one cruiser. Fired three torpedoes but these missed because of zigzag. Weather good apart from snow squalls.

Then he started off on the surface to get ahead of the convoy and make another attack. Time was slipping by, but the darkness gave him confidence. Suddenly at 2015, he saw a destroyer bearing down on him and *U-354* dived hurriedly.

The destroyer was the *Obdurate*, on the starboard wing of the convoy. Her Asdic had been pinging away as usual when the monotonous 'ping, ping, ping' developed an echo: a contact! Quickly the operator gave the bridge a bearing, the *Obdurate* was swung round on to it, and the alarm rattlers sounded.

A minute later, at 2014, they spotted the low dark shape of a U-boat on the surface and the *Obdurate*'s captain, Sclater, prepared to ram. However, before the *Obdurate* could get into position, the U-boat slid down into the obscuring depths of the Arctic. In the meantime a signal was flashed to the *Onslow*.

Sherbrooke was too far away on the other side of the convoy to help, but he ordered *Obedient* to join *Obdurate* in the hunt, and himself moved across the front of the convoy to help fill up the gap in the screen caused by the departure of the two ships.

Both destroyers searched, their Asdics sending sound waves searching through the water, seeking a U-boat's hull to strike and rebound back from it into the receivers. The Asdic operators had lost their first contact and once again were listening to the ping, ping, ping, ping . . . then, faintly at first, there was the echo: ping-ding, ping-ding, ping-ding.

'Contact bearing dead ahead, 1,000 yards. . . .'

In a few moments depth-charges splashed over the side of the *Obedient*, sinking to a depth where the pressure of the water operated hydrostatic valves and detonated them. But after the explosion there was no sign of wreckage or oil. And once the noise of the underwater disturbance had died away the Asdic operators reported:

127

'No contact.'

For nearly two hours the destroyers searched; but they had no luck. The escort orders were quite explicit about the next move—because of the need to conserve fuel, no U-boat hunt was to last more than two hours. The two destroyers left the spot and steamed on to rejoin the convoy.

Kinloch, doubtful if the contact they had depth-charged had in fact been a U-boat, reported to Sherbrooke at 2314: *Four depth-charges dropped on non-submarine contact.*

At 2356 Herschleb, having heard the propeller noises fade into the distance, surfaced warily, took a good look round, and signalled to Admiral Klüber:

From 2030 depth-charged and forced to submerge. Last position of convoy was AC 6451 and mean course about 120°, speed thirteen knots. Weather very good and I am pursuing.[1]

[1] The course was in fact 090° and the speed nine knots.

11

'So Much Old Iron'

'In war events of importance are the result of trivial causes.'—Cæsar, *De Bello Gallico*

THE German Naval Staff had of course been well pleased with their attacks on PQ 17 in June and PQ 18 in September, and ever since then had kept up their U-boat patrols across the probable routes of convoys beyond the Arctic Circle, watching and waiting for the first signs of another one on its way to North Russia. It had been a long wait; for thousands of hours the men of the U-boats had faced foul weather, bitter cold and the storm-swept darkness. All through October, then November and now December it had been the same story: nothing to report. Nothing to report, that is until the closing days of 1942.

The Naval Staff were all ready for the next convoy when it should appear and had a plan, Operation *Regenbogen* (Rainbow), prepared. From the German records it is clear that they had in fact sighted JW 51A, although it was not attacked, because as soon as Herschleb's sighting report concerning JW 51B came through the Germans called it PQ 20. That was the number it would have been under the old PQ designation (i.e. JW 51A would have been PQ 19 under the old title, and JW 51B designated PQ 20).

The German Naval Staff had the *Hipper*, *Lützow* and several destroyers at Altenfiord, as well as other ships farther south. Operation Rainbow provided for an attack by the *Hipper*, *Lützow* and six destroyers, but there was also another plan, Operation Aurora. This provided for the *Lützow* either to sail alone from Altenfiord and break out into the North Atlantic for a commerce-raiding foray, or go off by herself after completing Operation Rainbow with other ships. As the Naval

129

Staff did not know when the British would sail the next convoy, Operation Aurora might come first, in which case another ship would take the *Lützow*'s place for Rainbow.

Both the *Hipper* and the *Lutzow* were powerful ships. The former, whose full name was *Admiral Hipper*, was a heavy cruiser with eight 8-inch guns in four turrets, two placed forward and two aft. A dozen 4.1-inch and a dozen 37-mm. were fitted as anti-aircraft armament and she also had a dozen torpedo-tubes.

Geared turbines (she had diesel engines for cruising) driving four propellers gave her a designed speed of thirty-two knots; and with more than five inches of toughened steel armour plate covering her vitals she was indeed a powerful vessel. She had been launched in 1937 by Admiral Raeder from the Blohm and Voss yards at Hamburg, and he had named her in memory of the commander of the German battle-cruisers at the Battle of Jutland.

Her consort, *Lützow*, was a sister ship of the *Admiral Graf Spee*, which had scuttled herself in 1939. The pocket battleships —known as *panzerschiffe*, armoured ships, by the Germans— were a very interesting and clever design; they were the first ships of that size to have their hulls electrically welded and to be propelled by diesel engines. Costing £3,750,000, they had six 11-inch guns, each of which fired a 670-lb. shell and had a range of fifteen miles. With a speed of twenty-six knots and a range of 20,000 miles, the *Lützow* was protected by a belt of more than four inches of armour plate.

The *Lützow* had been launched somewhat prematurely at Kiel in May 1931. The then Chancellor, Brüning, was in the midst of expounding the meaning of the ship for the German people when suddenly she started to slide down the slipway— released too soon by an over-zealous official. The aged President Hindenburg, who was to have launched her, hastily tried to grab the bottle of champagne dangling from the great ship's bows so that he could break it in the traditional way. It was, however, torn away and fell to the ground. As the ship sped into the water Hindenburg bellowed after her: '*Deutschland* be thy name. Carry this name to the pride and fame of Germany on all seas!' However, as mentioned earlier, Hitler changed her name during the war to *Lützow*, and perhaps that freed her from Hindenburg's hurried injunction.

Both the *Hipper* and the *Lützow* were, because of their armour, almost impervious to any shells less than 8-inch (as was shown in the Battle of the River Plate) and would have little to fear from the guns of British destroyers escorting the Russian convoys, which were either 4.7-inch or 4-inch—the latter of World War I vintage. The only danger would be from torpedoes.

Six destroyers were to escort them: *Z 29*, *Z 30* and *Z 31*, armed with four 5-inch guns, eight torpedo tubes, and capable of more than thirty-five knots, and the *Richard Beitzen*, *Theodor Riedel* and *Friedrich Eckholdt*, which had five 5-inch guns and eight torpedo tubes and could make thirty-six knots. Each of the destroyers was, therefore, more than a match for a British fleet destroyer and considerably more powerful than the Hunt class. All these ships were waiting at Altenfiord, in ambush as it were, for the next British convoy to be sighted.

Now we must turn to another factor which does not, at first sight, appear to have any bearing on JW 51B; but in fact it has. It is a link—and an important one—in the chain of circumstances which led Hitler to make his fateful decision.

For some weeks past a row had been brewing up between Raeder and Göring over the question of transport ships in the Mediterranean. This was one of the frequent inter-Service quarrels which marked the limits of co-operation between the Navy and the *Luftwaffe* and was a direct result of the animosity which existed between the two men.

Although the circumstances were complicated the situation briefly was this: hitherto the transport ships had been under the control of various naval commanders who worked in conjunction with General Kesselring, the Commander-in-Chief, South, and the High Command of the Italian Navy, the *Supermarina*. That much was orthodox and fairly simple.

At this time, December 1942, the Allies had landed in North Africa and were fighting their way towards Tunis, while General Montgomery, with the 8th Army, was battling towards Tunisia

131

from the opposite direction. The main German problem was to keep Rommel supplied in North Africa, where he was fighting a war on two fronts.

However, control of those transport ships was not limited to the Navy: the portly Commander-in-Chief of the *Luftwaffe*, Göring, also had a hand in it. This came about because in peacetime authority over transports rested with the Reich Transport Ministry, and in wartime the Minister acted in matters of a military nature under the Deputy for the Four Year Plan, Göring. To avoid the work involved, he appointed Gauleiter Kaufmann as Reich Commissioner for Shipping.

Early in December, after the Allies landed in North Africa, the two men went on a tour of inspection in Italy, and the result was the appointment of a 'Deputy for German Sea Transport in the Mediterranean', with orders giving him widespread powers—so wide-spread that the Navy woke up on Christmas Eve to find that the Deputy had secured control not only of the transports but of the individual port commanders in Tunisia, and the technical and repair staffs working on U-boats and other warships in various parts of Italy.

In a 'Most Urgent' signal to the Naval Staff in Berlin that day the Naval Command in Italy warned: 'This move restricts the authority and responsibility of the German Naval Command Italy, and in the long run will eliminate it completely.' It concluded: 'I feel bound to report that execution of the order [from Göring] will not reduce the prevailing difficulties over naval transport. On the contrary, it will increase them.'

At the same time Kesselring was complaining about Raeder's alleged interference and one of his officers, in a telephone message to the Naval Staff in Berlin, said: 'The Commander-in-Chief, South, will arrest any admiral who disobeys his orders.'

These were strong words, but when Admiral Krancke was told at Fort Wolf, he said no immediate action was called for and a notation for later action would suffice. The later action came on the 28th when Raeder, Krancke and several staff officers met to discuss the new situation. They all agreed that Kaufmann and Göring were at the bottom of the trouble, and 'it can rightly be assumed that the Führer had no previous knowledge'.

The report added that the C-in-C, Navy, 'is disregarding such all-too-human failures for the sake of the cause', and concludes with the question: 'Our main problem remains: how do we tell the Führer?'

Added to this was a pencilled marginal note: 'Vice-admiral Krancke will be given the "Cripps Mission" of discussing this whole matter as soon as possible at Headquarters.'[1]

Vice-admiral Krancke undertook the Naval Staffs' 'Cripps Mission' on Wednesday, 30th December 1942 at the time Lt Herschleb in *U-354* sighted the convoy. Hitler usually held three 'situation conferences' during the day—in the morning, afternoon and evening. Krancke had resolved to use the morning one to carry out his unpleasant task of trying to square Göring's yards.

Inside the bunkers at Fort Wolf there was an air of unreality, heightened by the constant electric light and lack of daylight, and the ever-present hum of the air-conditioning plant—'A mixture of cloister and concentration camp' according to General Jodl. Outside a thick carpet of snow covered the ground and coated the trees of the gloomy woods. Hitler seldom went outside into the fresh air now, as if he found even the primeval gloom of the forest too much for him, although in the summer he had taken occasional walks among the trees with his Alsatian Blondi. (Eva Braun and the dog, according to Hitler, shared the distinction of being the only two beings that understood him.)

His commanders and foreign visitors had to come all the way to Rastenberg to see him, usually flying to an airfield nearby and then being driven by car through the three concentric rings of barbed-wire entanglements, each with its own guard post, to the huts and concrete bunkers, camouflaged green and grey, which constituted Fort Wolf.

Krancke found that Göring had flown in unexpectedly and was present at the conference, and with Hitler were his usual aides.

---

[1] 'Cripps Mission': a reference to the hostility of the Congress Party after Pearl Harbour, when India was menaced by Japan. Gandhi wanted—especially as the Japs drew near—to be neutral. Sir Stafford Cripps was sent out to try to save the day, form a Constituent Assembly of all parties and religions and offer full independence after the war should the Assembly request it.

The Army and the *Luftwaffe* reported on the war fronts—the Eastern Front being discussed at length, the dull-eyed Hitler wanting to know every detail of the latest German and Russian moves and giving Keitel his instructions.

With that over, he turned to the transport situation in the Mediterranean. First Göring gave his views. His podgy face, many chins, corpulent belly and splendid uniform (cut from the finest materials to his own design), combined with the perfume he used, gave the impression of a degenerate and sensuous Eastern potentate rather than of the leader of the *Luftwaffe* and Hitler's successor-designate.

Then Krancke explained the point of view of the Navy. Hitler listened in silence, and when Krancke had finished he started talking angrily.

Not about the transports, which were causing the trouble, nor about the long-standing feud between Göring and Raeder. Instead, he talked about the superiority of the British Navy 'which,' he said sarcastically, 'is able to sail through the Mediterranean without paying any attention to the Italian Navy and the Axis Air Forces'.

Krancke, taken aback by the sudden switch in the conversation and the violence of Hitler's voice, reported later to the Naval Staff: 'Numerous people were present at this discussion and there was no point in my protesting.'

But Hitler had by no means finished. 'Our own Navy,' he continued in the familiar, harsh voice, 'is but a copy of the British—and a poor one at that. The warships are not in operational readiness; they are lying idle in the fiords, utterly useless like so much old iron.'

Krancke reckoned it would be wiser for him to hold his tongue in case he provoked the Führer into any more of his vicious homilies; but when someone else reported that there was no British convoy traffic to Murmansk, he took a sheet of paper from his brief-case and said: 'I have just had this signal from the Operations Division of the Naval Staff.'

Typewritten on brick-red paper, and headed 'Secret! Officer only', it was timed 1345, and Krancke read it out:

U-boat reports by short signal a convoy 50 miles south of

134

Bear Island, course 070°, speed twelve knots. Convoy consists of six steamers. Weak escort. Vice-admiral Krancke inform Führer that C-in-C, Navy, approves in principle the operational use of Hipper, Lützow *and destroyers. Execution is in accordance with the decision of Group North dependent on the fact that according to the existing information the escort with the convoy is not in fact superior.*

Hitler was at once interested.

'Can the force get there in time and locate the convoy?'

'It is possible, my Führer,' replied Francke, and went on to give details of distances the ships would have to sail from Altenfiord, the speed they would steam at, and how far the convoy would have progressed along its track. He reported later: 'In this manner the Führer's previous statements were dealt with quickly.'

The chain of command for Operation Rainbow was from the Naval Staff (SKL) to its Operations Division (I/SKL), and then to Group North, commanded by Admiral Carls, with head-quarters at Kiel. From there it passed to the Flag Officer, Northern Waters, Admiral Klüber, with his headquarters in Narvik, and then to the Flag Officer, Cruisers (B. de K.), who was Admiral Kummetz, in the *Hipper*. Commanding the *Lützow* was Captain Stange.

The Operations Division and Group North had worked fast as soon as Herschleb's first signal, timed 1242, was received. In Berlin, the Naval Staff quickly warned Admiral Raeder so that he could get permission for the ships to sail.

While this was being done the Staff Officer, Operations at Group North, in Kiel, reported to Admiral Carls and the position of the convoy was plotted on the big chart in the operations-room. Its course as reported by Herschleb was drawn in; dividers were 'walked' along the course to determine where the convoy would be for the ensuing twenty-four hours. Judging from its present position and its destination it was unlikely to make any radical alteration of course.

The Operations Staff estimated it would take the *Hipper* and

Lützow five hours to get clear of Altenfiord, and another sixteen to get to the position the convoy would have reached by 0900 next morning. This would allow them to attack during the brief hours of half-light. . . .

Admiral Carls signalled to Admiral Klüber, hundreds of miles north of him at Altenfiord—he had gone there from Narvik—and B. de K., Admiral Kummetz: *B. de K. with six destroyers immediate notice for Operation Rainbow.*

Admiral Klüber had already received *U-354*'s signal, and guessing it would result in Operation Rainbow, had several minutes earlier signalled from the *Köln*, his headquarters ship across the fiord to Admiral Kummetz in the *Hipper*: Hipper *and six destroyers—three hours' notice.*

The arrival of this signal in the *Hipper* had the same effect as a brick in a hornet's nest: after it was taken to Admiral Kummetz he gave orders for the *Lützow* and the six destroyers lying at anchor nearby to be warned.

It was a picturesque but chilly scene: steeply sloping mountains like Kaaven, 3,130 feet high, Lassefjeld and Stove Hadde, now swathed in thick, smooth snow, surrounded the fiords; firs and pines, looking like toys dipped in icing sugar, littered the lower slopes up to the tree line. These mountains in their massive, Arctic majesty, and the broad, blue-grey waters of the fiords, combined to make the two capital ships look small and puny; the destroyers seemed but models, too small to be used by fighting men in the war at sea.

On board each ship there was scarcely-controlled excitement: going to sea was, for the men in the big ships, an unusual experience and one received with mixed feelings. Aboard British capital ships at this period going to sea was a monotonous and all too regular experience for the sailors to raise much enthusiasm either way. But among similar German ships it was different: they spent long weeks and months lying at anchor in the fiords, cut off from even a view of the open sea, with only a few small villages ashore, inhabited by sturdily independent and hostile people, many of them Lapps. The radio brought them the sickly-sweet strains of 'Lili Marlene' and news of the war. There were descriptions of the bravery of the men on the

Eastern Front, in the Afrika Korps and in the U-boats . . .
never news of themselves.

Long periods spent in ships at anchor produce a strange
psychological reaction among most men. They begin at first
to feel a reluctance to go to sea again—not the more obvious
eagerness. The sea and the enemy take on a more forbidding
appearance; an innate fear creeps in—not a particularly
definite fear, in fact rather more like a child's fear of the darkness, a distrust of the unseen and the unknown. Morale goes
down and even the more senior and experienced officers are
affected and powerless to do anything—even if they recognize
its causes. The only antidote is to put to sea; but Hitler's caution
usually prevented that.

Now, however, thanks to Admiral Klüber's signal, men were
at last bustling about preparing the ships for sea. Navigators
brought out folios of charts; engineers flashed up boilers or
started powerful banks of diesel engines; more signals went out
ordering tugs to be ready to help the *Hipper* and *Lützow* to
leave; minesweepers were sent out to sweep the exit from
Altenfiord; preparations were made to haul back the anti-
torpedo nets which enclosed the ships like underwater hen-runs.

Within a few minutes of *Hipper* receiving Admiral Klüber's
orders, Group North's arrived. They had been dispatched at
1245—five minutes after Herschleb's signal arrived from *U-354*.
By 1250 they had been passed on to the *Lützow* and the six
destroyers, in the abbreviated and rather more dramatic form
of: *Immediate notice.*

Ten minutes later Klüber followed with another signal to
Kummetz: Hipper, Lützow, *six destroyers immediately ready
for sea: report when you are ready to sail.*

The engineers were goaded into producing even greater
miracles, but ships' engines, whether the great boilers driving
turbines, or the more economical diesels, took time to warm
up. It was the engineers' perpetual grouse that after being left
idle for months on end, it was a sure bet that when they were
wanted, it would be in a tearing hurry.

While charts were unfolded and boilers flashed up, captains
prepared to receive their orders from Kummetz, and those men

137

who cared and had the time wrote a hasty last note home—
although every reference to the sailing of a ship would be
deleted by the censor ashore. But Kummetz was only warned
to be ready to embark on Operation Rainbow: it had not been
definitely settled yet that the convoy was to be attacked.

The decision theoretically rested with the Naval Staff and
Raeder; but the Admiral was wary enough by now to make sure
the Führer knew what was proposed, so that if he felt like it he
could exercise his powers as sea lord. That discreet signal,
therefore, was sent off to Krancke at the Führer's headquarters.

While Raeder and the Naval Staff mulled over all the aspects
of the proposed attack on JW 51B, it was comforting for them
to know the convoy was so close to Altenfiord that it was
unlikely the British could cut off their line of retreat; in addition, the convoy was being shadowed by *U-354*, and *U-626*
should also be on the scene to help within a very short
time.

On the other hand they could not avoid the fact that the
Führer was jittery about using the capital ships. Still, he had
received the discreet signal and, knowing what the Naval Staff
were proposing, could veto it. No veto came, however, and
Raeder decided to carry out the operation. He also hoped that
afterwards the *Lützow* could go on to carry out the commerce-
raiding plan. He signalled to Admiral Carls in Kiel:

*In view of the U-boat's short signal Naval Staff agrees in
principle to Operation Rainbow. In addition examine possibility
of operating* Lützow *in a separate operation* [i.e. Aurora].

Meanwhile Admiral Carls at Kiel had drafted out his orders
for Kummetz and they were signalled to him and to Klüber:

1. B. de K. with *Hipper*, *Lützow* and six destroyers to operate
against convoy JW 51B.[1] Operational command [will be exercised]
by Admiral Klüber.

2. Cover name 'Rainbow'. Sail as soon as possible. Report time.

3. Speed of JW 51B between seven and twelve knots. Position of
JW 51B at midnight 31st the area between 75° 30′ and 71° 30′ north,
36° and 43° east.

---

[1] PQ 20 in the German text: from now on, for clarity, the convoy will be
given as JW 51B in German references.

4. It is desirable to bring in [i.e. capture] single ships. There is to be no time wasted in rescuing enemy crews. It would be of value only to take a few captains and others prisoner with a view to interrogation. The rescue of enemy survivors by enemy forces is not desirable.[1]

5. The operation is limited [i.e. forbidden] south of 70° north.

6. Contact with the *Luftwaffe* should be maintained by Admiral Klüber.

At 1410 Kummetz signalled to Klüber: *Intend to pass through the net boom at Kaafiord at 1700. Request* [to be told] *own U-boat situation.*

At 1430 a boat brought Klüber and his staff weaving through the anti-torpedo nets which stretched in a square round the *Hipper*, the floats supporting them looking like closely-threaded beads on the water. He was piped aboard with the ceremonial due to an admiral, and Kummetz escorted him below to his cabin, where drinks were ready to be poured.

Klüber knew Captain Hans Hartmann, commanding the *Hipper*, and had met most of Kummetz's staff, and of course he knew Captain Stange, commanding the *Lützow*, who had come aboard earlier for the conference. Introductions were therefore brief and formal. He had brought the orders with him, and he outlined them to Kummetz, Hartmann and Stange. They said:

The task: to destroy JW 51B.

According to the existing report of *U-354* the convoy is not strongly escorted . . . it is suspected that the two British cruisers[2] and escorts which left Kola Inlet on the 27th December are with the convoy and it is expected that there are three to four enemy submarines at sea.

Procedure on meeting the enemy: avoid a superior force, otherwise destroy according to tactical situation.

U-354 and *U-626* are around the convoy.

The basis for the operation, Klüber told them, would be his own operation order, which he had just read, supplemented by the operation order of Group North and orders given by

---

[1] The implication in this well-turned phrase should not be missed. There would seem to be only one way to prevent this happening. . . .

[2] Force R, the *Sheffield* and *Jamaica*, and two destroyers.

Admiral Kummetz. After outlining the situation which, in his opinion, would face Kummetz and Stange, he added that a few hours of half-light would be needed to make full use of their guns. Torpedoes would be used only under certain circumstances—sure targets, for instance, and for sinking the merchant ships.

Both *Hipper* and *Lützow*, the Admiral emphasized, were warned particularly against the danger from the torpedoes of British destroyers because it would be difficult to see their tracks in the half-darkness.

Then Klüber handed over to Kummetz and sat back to hear how he was going to handle the tactical situation.

Kummetz said that the convoy would be steaming eastwards, and he proposed splitting his force into two parts—himself in *Hipper*, accompanied by the destroyers *Friedrich Eckholdt*, *Richard Beitzen* and *Z 29*, and the *Lützow* with the destroyers *Z 30*, *Z 31* and *Theodor Riedel*.

The whole force would sail together from Altenfiord, but during the night they would split up so that each group attacked the convoy from a different direction. The *Lützow* and her destroyers would be detached so that she would be in a position seventy-five miles due south of the *Hipper* at 0800. From then on the two heavy ships would turn and search eastwards along the convoy's wake, each with her three destroyers spread fifteen miles apart and fifteen miles ahead. The convoy should be found—they would have an accurate idea of its position from the shadowing U-boats—shortly after dawn. The *Hipper* would attack first from the north. This should draw off escorts, 'forcing the convoy to turn south and thus run, poorly defended, straight into *Lützow*', which would be approaching, with her destroyers, from that direction.[1] After the successful conclusion of Rainbow, he added, *Lützow* would detach her destroyers and go off alone to carry out Operation Aurora.

So much for the plans.

Our main interest in them in fact centres round one sentence in Admiral Klüber's orders—'*Procedure on meeting the enemy:*

[1] Admiral Kummetz was later criticized for splitting his forces and thus complicating timing and the identification of friend and foe, but the plan worked.

avoid a superior force, otherwise destroy according to tactical situation.'

This typifies the cautious attitude of the Naval Staff and Group North as a result of Hitler's fears for his big ships. In sea warfare, the old adage 'Nothing venture, nothing gain', is very true. Admittedly the loss of a pocket battleship as the price paid for the destruction of one small convoy bound for Russia would be a high one; but the mere sailing of a warship entailed some risk—the moving of a pocket battleship from Altenfiord to a base in Germany for a routine overhaul exposed her to the hazards of mines laid by the Royal Navy and RAF, torpedoes from patrolling Allied submarines, and air attacks.

No captain of a heavy warship engaged on such a foray as the proposed attack on JW 51B would unnecessarily risk losing his vessel; that would be understood, an innate part of his training for command, particularly in view of the type of warfare the German Navy was engaged in. Yet actually telling Kummetz and Stange with such emphasis that they were not to engage superior forces could have only one effect: to make them over-cautious.

The world already had an example of where over-caution could lead an admiral—less than two centuries earlier Admiral Byng had been charged that he 'did withdraw, or keep back, and did not do his utmost to take, seize and destroy the Ships of the French King, which it was his Duty to have engaged . . .' and he was shot. The rights and wrongs—and there were many —do not concern us here. But because of Hitler's fears two powerful ships were about to go into action with the knowledge that if they fell in with a more powerful British force and could not disengage (after all, the ability 'to avoid a superior force' does not always lie with the inferior one; indeed, often the fact that the other force is superior rules it out) they would have to account for their actions.

But, as will be seen later, the last—and most devastating— caution had not yet been enjoined on Kummetz and Stange: worse was yet to come.

141

12

Use Caution

'In war it is not permitted to make a mistake twice.'
—*Lamarchus*

THE conference aboard the *Hipper* finished at 1530 and Klüber left to go back to his headquarters at Narvik while Stange boarded his launch to return to the *Lützow*. There was plenty for him to do: apart from anything else he had to prepare the orders for the three destroyers which were to be part of his group and have them sent over to their senior officer, the Captain of *Z 31*.

For Captain Hartmann and the Admiral's staff officers in *Hipper*, too, there was plenty of work. Doctors brought in extra supplies of medical stores; gunnery officers and artificers checked over guns, ammunition and optical range-finders, while signals officers and ratings made last-minute checks on radar sets, making sure they were calibrated and that spare parts were available.

The minutes slipped by and soon it was 1645, a quarter of an hour before all the ships were due to sail. The anti-torpedo nets had been opened, captains were on their bridges, quartermasters were at the wheel, engineers waited for the first orders to come over telegraphs and telephones. The vessel guarding the entrance to the boom had been warned that the force was about to sail and the six destroyer captains waited.

The minutes slipped by—1650, and no sign of the tug which was to help the *Hipper* get under way. Five minutes passed and Kummetz started getting impatient. Another five minutes and it was 1700, the time when the *Hipper* should be passing the boom at the entrance to Kaafiord. Still the tug had not appeared out of the darkness.

Eventually, pursued by a series of rude signals, she arrived fifteen minutes late, and the *Hipper* was ready to get under way. Then a telephone on the bridge rang. It was the engine-room reporting that a flange on the starboard condenser pump had been damaged and would have to be repaired . . . it would take nearly half an hour.

Finally, shortly before 1745, the engine-room telegraphs were swung over, water boiled and bubbled under the great ship's stern, and she got under way.

Slowly, helped by the tug, the *Hipper* steamed down the long narrow sleeve of water which had been her home for so long. The *Lützow* joined and, followed by the destroyers, the force sailed through Altenfiord itself, where the water was 230 fathoms (nearly 1,400 feet) deep.

Almost immediately the force had to turn hard a' port into Stjernfiord, the narrow gap between the mainland and the island of Stjernoy. Here the water was not so placid: the swell from the Arctic Ocean rolled in between the mainland and the next island, Soro, and they had nearly thirty miles to steam before they were clear of land and threading their way past some reefs of rocks off-shore.

The weather was as good as could be expected. The wind was blowing south-west to west, Force 4 by the Beaufort Scale, which meant it was a moderate breeze of eleven to fifteen knots, and the sea was smooth with some swell. It was ideal for the men in the *Hipper* and the *Lützow* since their stomachs, which had become unused to being at sea, would not be strained too much.

As soon as the force was clear of the land Klüber sent a wireless message on the U-boat wavelength telling them Kummetz had sailed and that from noon next day they were 'to attack warships only when definitely identified as enemy'.

At 1840, an hour after the *Hipper* passed the boom, a coded signal was received on board from Klüber. It was quickly decoded and taken up to Kummetz on the bridge. He read, with mixed feelings:

Contrary to the operational order regarding contact against

143

the enemy [you are to] *use caution even against enemy of equal strength because it is undesirable for the cruisers to take any great risks.*

Thus the cumulative effect of the German Navy's losses made itself felt—not among the Naval Staff, who understood that ships *did* get sunk in war—but in the dark reaches of Hitler's mind.

Altogether they had not been heavy losses; they certainly did not dismay either Raeder or his Naval Staff. To Hitler, however, they were something his fevered imagination could conjure with. The *Bismark*, for instance, was a ship upon whose decks he had trodden; he had, standing on the searchlight platform aft, raised a gauntleted hand in salute after a brief speech to her crew drawn up before him. He had shaken hands with Lütjens, the gallant Admiral who had fought on until his ship sank under him.

Hitler's fears of a repetition, this dread of hearing that yet another of his proud warships had been sunk, had been so frequently repeated to Raeder that the Admiral had at the last moment felt he must send yet another warning to Carls at Group North, to make sure that no unnecessary risks were being taken. From Kiel, Carls had passed the buck with a cautionary signal to Klüber at Altenfiord.

Klüber, who had operational control over the ships, knew Kummetz would be careful, but he also knew where the caution originated. He decided to clear his own yardarms and sent the brief signal off to Kummetz. However, Kummetz did not know all this; he had simply received the unequivocal caution. It was hardly calculated to inspire him. 'An enemy of equal strength' could mean anything; there were no carefully worked out tables equating destroyers to cruisers. An enemy of equal strength to a heavy cruiser could, in a snowstorm and darkness, mean three radar-equipped destroyers. In daylight it might mean six; much would depend on the character and tactical skill of the senior officer and individual captains.

In other words 'an enemy of equal strength' could hardly be defined. Langsdorff fled from battle in the pocket battleship *Graf Spee*. Supposing Admiral Harwood had commanded her, and Langsdorff the three British cruisers? One feels that under those circumstances the *Graf Spee* would have stayed.

A gun, a torpedo, a range-finder, or a ship is merely the apparatus used by skilled men for fighting at sea. No one would suggest that any two fighter pilots would be evenly matched, since temperament, skill, training and natural aptitude often count more than miles per hour. So it is with a warship, though it is a fact all too often forgotten by historians. A destroyer of the same size, speed and armament of one nation is by no means the equal of a similar ship from another because machinery alone cannot take it into battle. The unknown quantities are the skill, character, courage and imagination of the captain, officers and ratings, which are indefinable.

The point is well illustrated in the battle, the preliminary moves of which have been described.

Later that evening, while Kummetz digested his terse warning signal, Hitler was having his usual evening situation conference. Krancke attended as usual and wrote later: 'I reported that the force had left port and would presumably locate the convoy in the early morning hours. The Führer emphasized that he wished to have all reports immediately since, as I well knew, he could not sleep a wink when ships were operating.

'I passed this message subsequently to the Operations Division of the Naval Staff, requesting that any information be telephoned immediately.'

Meanwhile Kummetz took his ships out to the west-north-west from Altenfiord before turning north-east to 'round the corner' of North Cape. In doing so he avoided the British submarines patrolling between the entrance and the Cape.

With *Hipper* leading, followed by the *Lützow*, and with the destroyers in a screen round them, they were soon making twenty-four knots, heading for the position where it was estimated that the convoy would be by dawn (or approximately half-light) next morning. Both the *Hipper* and *Z 31* had breakdowns but managed to repair them, although the force was delayed.

The last signal that day was sent by Klüber from Altenfiord addressed to Herschleb, who was still warily shadowing the convoy in the darkness with *U-354*. It said: *From midnight report position of the convoy at least every two hours. From 0200 transmit homing signals to B. de K.* [Kummetz.]

By 0100 next day, which was New Year's Eve, the German force had passed the latitude of North Cape, reputedly the northern-most point of the European continent[1] and described by Long-fellow as 'that huge and haggard shape . . . whose form is like a wedge'. Kummetz was now steering north-east towards the convoy's track.

There was no sleep for the Admiral that night and with his navigating officer he was busy poring over a large-scale chart of the Barents Sea. A line drawn from left to right across the middle of the chart represented the convoy's course; a diagonal line from the bottom left-hand edge indicated his own course, and where it crossed the horizontal line should be the point of interception. However, he could not be too sure how far along the horizontal line the convoy would be. It might have altered speed since *U–354* last reported, so he signalled to his force that at 0230 they were to start the reconnaissance sweep he had ordered before they left Altenfiord.

From that time the two groups of ships ploughed along in the darkness at eighteen knots, on slightly diverging courses, for just short of five hours, so that at 0800 they were seventy-five miles apart (see chart on page 110). Kummetz had chosen his position well, for he noted in his War Diary:

'0718 Bearing 060 two silhouettes.'

'0725 signalled to *Eckholdt*: *Bearing 092 several silhouettes. Investigate. Range about 170 hectometres*' [roughly nine nauti-cal miles].

Thus the stage was set for the Battle of the Barents Sea on this New Year's Eve.

---

[1] Actually Nordkyn, nearby, is slightly farther north

13

Action Stations

'I returned, and saw under the sun, that the race is not to
the swift, nor the battle to the strong . . . but time and
chance happeneth to them all.'—*Ecclesiastes*

EARLY on New Year's Eve, a few hours before the opening
rounds of the Battle of the Barents Sea, convoy JW 51B
was on an easterly course, driven well south of its planned
route by the heavy gale two days earlier, and also well behind its
time schedule. Two merchant ships, the trawler *Vizalma* and
the minesweeper *Bramble*, were still missing from the convoy.

Unknown to Sherbrooke, *Bramble* was about fifteen miles
north-east of the convoy and probably steaming a similar course;
while *Vizalma* and *Chester Valley* were both forty miles to the
north, steering east and making eleven knots, hoping to overtake the convoy but in ignorance of the fact it was south of
them.

The battleship *Anson*, cruiser *Cumberland* and three destroyers
had been south of the convoy until two days earlier, when they
had turned back. They had carried out their orders—to watch
for German capital ships coming up from the south—but their
role was not yet completed.

Burnett's Force R, the cruisers *Sheffield* and *Jamaica*, had left
Kola Inlet four days earlier and steamed westwards, run into the
heavy gale, then swept back eastwards and again turned west
towards the convoy.

Burnett felt that New Year's Eve would be a critical day and
intended to cover the convoy by steaming ten miles north of its
planned route and about fifty miles astern of it since Admiral
Tovey had laid down that the cruisers were not to approach
nearer—unless the enemy were located.

Although the Germans must have guessed the approximate route, they would be unlikely to know just how far along it the convoy actually was. They would have to steam along the track, east or westward, until they found the merchantmen. Force R, in that case, would best be able to intercept them from either ahead or astern. In view of the position of Altenfiord—which the convoy would have passed on New Year's Eve—he felt that astern was obviously the best choice since it was from that direction the Germans were most likely to approach.

The Admiral therefore planned that at 0845 on New Year's Eve his force would be steaming north-westwards at seventeen knots across the convoy's wake before turning into position behind it.

'My reasons for being in this position at dawn were twofold,' he wrote later, 'during the short hours when there was visibility I should have the advantage of light over any enemy that might appear,[1] and I might better avoid air reconnaissance which would lead on to the convoy.'

Unfortunately Burnett's knowledge of the convoy's assumed position on New Year's Eve was based on a signal from Admiral Tovey sent at noon four days earlier. It said: *I estimate JW 51B passes longitude of Bear Island* [at] *1600 on 29th.*

That estimate was based on the positions signalled by the two aircraft which flew over the convoy on Boxing Day, before the convoy had run into the gale. But, as mentioned earlier, the gale had blown the ships well south and put them behind their schedule. So when Burnett—who had no means of knowing this —thought he was crossing the convoy's wake fifty miles astern and turning eastwards to follow, he in fact crossed *ahead* of it and was steaming more than thirty miles *north* of its actual (as opposed to planned) track, and was incidentally quite near the *Vizalma* and her merchantman.

No one could be blamed; in fact one can be thankful that in the circumstances it was no worse. The navigator of the *Sheffield*, Eric Back, had not had an astronomical sight since leaving Kola Inlet four days earlier and was navigating by dead reckon-

---

[1] i.e. The enemy would be to the south, silhouetted against the lighter southern sky, while Force R would be in the darker northern sector.

ing. Because the gale had caused surface drift which would only be guessed, he was none too happy over his estimated position, although it eventually turned out to be remarkably accurate.

The same problem was worrying Peter Wyatt in *Onslow*. None of the ships had bubble sextants of the type used in aircraft and which had an artificial horizon. To get a sight with an ordinary sextant it was necessary to be able to see the horizon at the same time as a star. The combination was rare. Wyatt had managed to get a poor sight the evening before, but could not rely on it.

Thus as the German force approached from the south-west before dawn on New Year's Eve the convoy was closest to them and Force R was thirty miles beyond; *Vizalma* and the *Chester Valley* were even farther north. The *Bramble*, alone, was ahead of the convoy. In addition, convoy RA 51, homeward bound, had sailed from Kola Inlet the day before and was steering north, preparing to come round to the west towards Bear Island and the Greenland Sea (see chart on page 110).

Fortunately all the British ships had experienced a quiet night. For Sherbrooke in the *Onslow* it was now the seventh day at sea since leaving Iceland and, like the rest of the men in the escorts and the merchantmen, he was feeling very weary. The violence of the gale had worn everyone out, and with the crews of all the escorts doing alternately four hours on duty and four hours off it was difficult to catch up with sleep. Neither Sherbrooke nor his navigator, Wyatt, stood at watch; but they had to be on the bridge at all hours. In addition Sherbrooke knew from *Obdurate*'s sighting report the previous evening that the convoy had been spotted by a U-boat.

Then, in the early hours of New Year's Eve, came three signals from the Senior British Naval Office, North Russia. The radio direction-finding stations had detected a German destroyer off North Cape, a U-boat well ahead of the convoy and another U-boat to the south. Each signal contained the phrase 'reliable fix' but Sherbrooke considered they did not imply that German operations against the convoy had necessarily begun yet.

Shortly before that a shaded light flickered across from the *Orwell*, over the port side of the convoy, saying she was investigating 'Suspicious hydrophone effect'. A few minutes later she signalled 'No result'. It might have been Herschleb with *U-354* or possibly *U-626*. It could have been a shoal of fish, or a layer of particularly cold water, sufficiently dense to send back an echo.

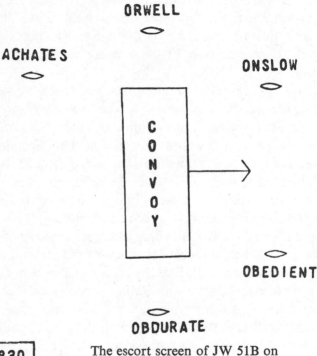

The escort screen of JW 51B on
31st December, 1942.

On board the *Onslow* early on New Year's Eve—as well as most of the other ships in the escort and probably the merchantmen—there was, as Peter Wyatt wrote later, 'an unspoken feeling that if the few reports we'd had meant the enemy was after us, then this would be the day. Or perhaps if they did not come today, then they wouldn't come at all. By the evening we would have the Russian submarine patrol line between us and the enemy, which should at least give us some warning of an attack.'

At 0740, which was virtually first light, when the darkness

lifted slightly to the south and one could just begin to make out the shape of the ship and become aware that the blackness was giving way to an indeterminate greyness, the *Onslow's* First Lieutenant was on the bridge. He was Lt Lewis King, a New Zealander, a man of small stature, humble of his capabilities but very much liked by everyone. The crew would do anything for him—a cause for perpetual astonishment so far as King was concerned. He bore the nickname of all First Lieutenants, 'Number One'.

With him was Peter Wyatt, his sextant handy, and looking vainly for stars. He was, in his own words, 'out for anything I could get'.

The look-out on each side of the bridge, the men at the guns, the quartermaster at the wheel, the men in the engine-room and the dozens of others on duty all over the ship, knew that the watch would change in twenty minutes and they'd be able to get below for breakfast and some sleep. It was a comforting thought, but it always seemed to make those last few minutes of the watch interminable.

Sherbrooke was also on the bridge and, as usual, saying little and apparently unaware of the idle chatter going on round him. Then, just before the watch changed, he said quietly to Lewis King: 'Number One, I have a feeling something is going to happen today, and I want you to see that all the hands are breakfasted by 0900 and changed into clean underwear.'

It may well have been one of the first times in the war that that famous question and answer of every seamanship examination—preparation for battle—had actually been carried out; and although both King and Wyatt knew that this day could be the critical one, the fact that Captain (D) had voiced his opinion quickened their pulses.

King gave the necessary orders and then filled in the deck log before handing over the watch. Deck logs—in effect brief daily diaries—were often needed only for courts martial or for helping to write an action report, but they had to be written up and signed at the end of each watch.

So King filled in the blanks: HMS *Onslow Thurs*day *31st* of *December 1942.*

From . . . . . . to . . . . . . and *at sea.*

Five on sick list.

Against the time 0800 he wrote a series of facts which represented all that the Admiralty were likely to be interested in in HMS *Onslow* at that particular time. Her two propellers were turning 111 revolutions each minute; the mean course being steered was 090° (due east); the wind was from the north-west —on the port quarter—and blowing Force 2 on the Beaufort scale, a convenient way of saying it had a velocity of four to six knots—it would be called a light breeze by a landsman. The sea was smooth with a long low swell; the barometer stood at 1004 millibars; the sea temperature was 41° Fahrenheit, while the air temperature was only 25° Fahrenheit. This topsy-turvy state of affairs was due to the effect of the Gulf Stream pushing warm ocean currents towards the British Isles and father north into the Barents Sea. Apart from giving Britain a more moderate climate it also keeps the waters open round Northern Norway and gives Russia one port which is ice-free all the year round—Murmansk, JW 51B's destination.

The air was so cold because there was no bountiful underlying Gulf Stream to warm it. This morning it was blowing from the north-west, chilled in its passage over the solid ice of the Arctic itself.

The watches changed in all the ships. In the merchantmen weary and cold second officers turned over to sleepy and, for the moment at least, warm third officers, and climbed down to the saloon for breakfast. Aft, on the poop, DEMS gunners who, for the last four hours, had huddled down behind lockers and gun shields, seeking what little shelter they could find, handed over to men who had spent nearly four hours in hammocks and bunks. The change of the watch was the one time when everyone was comparatively satisfied with his lot; those going off watch had warmth, food and sleep to look forward to; those coming on had, in reasonable weather, food inside them and the warmth that goes with it.

In the *Onslow* Sherbrooke's words to Lewis King were being translated into actions; and the change, slight as it was, from the usual routine soon produced the inevitable buzz of gossip

ACTION STATIONS

and speculation. Peter Wyatt went below to awaken Tom Marchant, the Torpedo Officer and second in command, who had kept the middle watch (midnight to 0400) and tell him of Sherbrooke's remark. Hastily, though sleep was at a premium, Marchant got up and went to the wardroom for a quick breakfast.

Three days earlier, on the 28th, the corvette *Hyderabad* had picked up a signal from the SBNO, North Russia, saying that Russian aircraft might be meeting the convoy. Unfortunately when it was decoded the signal appeared to refer to destroyers. Thus when the starboard look-out on the *Hyderabad*'s bridge reported at 0820 that there were two destroyers bearing 180° (due south), on the convoy's starboard beam, it was assumed they were Russian and Sherbrooke in the *Onslow* was not warned.

A few minutes later the starboard look-out in the *Obdurate*, which was zigzagging to the south of the convoy, reported: 'Two destroyers bearing 210°.'

Sclater, *Obdurate*'s captain, knew there was a chance that Russian destroyers might come out to meet the convoy, and ordered the report to be passed to Captain Sherbrooke. At 0830 a shaded signal lamp flickered, and the message was sent to the *Onslow*, out of sight on the other side of the convoy, via *Obedient*, which was ahead. This all took time—so much so that, had he known, Sclater would have sent it by wireless.

On the *Onslow*'s bridge the Yeoman spelled out the Morse letters. The time was now 0845 and the message said:

Bearing 210 degrees two destroyers.

Both Sherbrooke and Peter Wyatt immediately grabbed binoculars and went to the starboard after side of the bridge. They could see no sign of anything. The visibility was bad—it was darker than 'lighting-up time' on a dull, overcast winter's day in England.

Sherbrooke's face was impassive: no one on the bridge, from the look-outs to Wyatt, could guess what was crossing his mind. In fact he was thinking that they could be Russian—their patrols were highly unreliable and they appeared at any time in

153

unexpected positions—but was far from sure. He said, in his usual even voice: 'Tell *Obdurate* to investigate.'

So the signal, *Your 0830, investigate,* was passed to her via the *Obedient,* and soon they saw her turn away to starboard and steer for the rear of the convoy. The buzz soon went round the ship, adding its quota to the feeling of expectancy created by Sherbrooke's earlier warning.

In the *Obedient* Lt Hudson, who was the officer of the watch, had called his captain as soon as *Obdurate*'s signal started coming across. The general feeling on board was that the destroyers were Russian and someone expressed this view to Kinloch as he came to the bridge. He promptly replied: 'Not on your life! Sound off Action Stations.'

The minutes passed and the starboard look-out in the *Onslow,* a young Scot recently put up for a commission, reported a tanker at the rear of the convoy was dropping astern and show-ing 'Not under control' lights. They seemed to be brighter than was good for the convoy, but she was too far away for anything to be done about it.

In the meantime Sclater had increased speed and taken the *Obdurate* round to the stern of the convoy. He found that there were three destroyers and they were steering north in line ahead. The light was bad and everyone on the bridge tried to identify them, but even with powerful night glasses it was impossible. At 0915 they turned westwards, away from *Obdurate*, and then turned north-westwards again.

Sclater ordered them to be challenged by light. They did not reply. (If they had been Russian that would not have been un-usual.) He was still undecided about their identity when small red glows rippled along the side of one of them: she had opened fire. The shells fell short and Sclater ordered the *Obdurate* to turn away and transmit an enemy report.

In the *Onslow* Sherbrooke was watching the tanker when suddenly several red flashes appeared on the horizon in line with and beyond it. There was no mistaking them.

'Sound off Action Stations.'

A hand quickly went to the Action Stations alarm gong on the forward side of the bridge—its owner made sure it was not the 'Check Fire' or 'Life buoy' buttons on each side of it—and the urgent short rings warning of enemy surface ships shrilled through the ship, startling the off-duty watch of the ship's company as if they had suddenly received an electric shock.

Tom Marchant was already on his way to the bridge. His action station in any case was there, ready to control *Onslow*'s torpedoes.

The *Onslow*'s four tubes were ready for firing. The torpedoes could be set to run for 9,000 yards at thirty-five knots or 12,000 yards at thirty knots. Marchant knew that if they were to be used at all it would most likely be against an enemy cruiser which would probably have unrestricted manœuvrability, and the *Onslow*'s only chance of hitting her would be to fire all the torpedoes set at their fastest speed. In the escort orders he had said they were to be set at 9,000 yards. As a result the Gunner

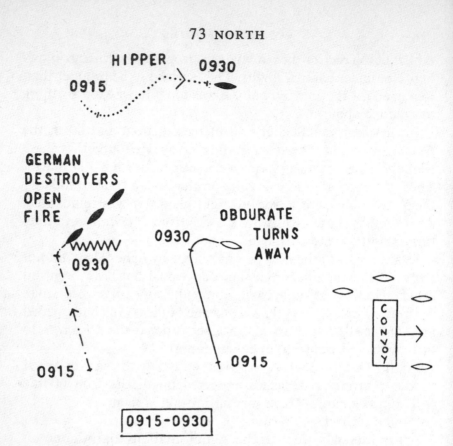

HIPPER 0930
0915

GERMAN
DESTROYERS
OPEN
FIRE

OBDURATE
TURNS
AWAY

0930

0930

0915

0915

CONVOY

0915-0930

(T) in all the destroyers had altered the speed settings to increase the amount of shale oil and air—the fuel for the torpedoes' engines—which would be supplied if they were fired.

The torpedoes had to be set to run at a certain depth, and the orders had said the optimum depth setting would be twelve feet. Some therefore had the compression of the spring on the hydrostatic valve altered to make them run at sixteen feet, others at twelve feet and some at eight. A depth of twelve feet was estimated to be just below the armour belt of a German cruiser.

All that remained to be done before firing the torpedoes was to set the torpedo sights on each side of the bridge. Each sight was a box containing a computor with eight triggers underneath (only four were in use). Knobs on the box would be turned to allow for the destroyer's own course and speed, others would set the enemy's estimated course and speed, and the torpedo's speed.

156

The computor solved the 'director triangle' and imparted to the sight the amount of 'aim off' to the right or left. The torpedo tubes were trained, when ordered, to the engaged side and locked at 90° to the centre line of the ship. When ready to fire the ship would turn away from the enemy target, the captain making sure she came round at a certain speed so that as the sight bar swung on to the target the torpedoes were fired, one at a time, and they would then have the correct angular spread between them.

Wilson, the Gunnery Officer, had been in the wardroom when the urgent summons of Action Stations sounded. He ran forward, climbed to the bridge and then up the ladder to the Director and into his seat. From there he could conduct the orchestra that was the *Onslow*'s main armament.

The Director was a large open nest above and behind the bridge, where men sitting in it had a clear and uninterrupted view of the horizon. The range-finder poked out on each side of the Director and the whole structure could train round in any direction (see picture 8).

Wilson sat in the back of the Director to the left, with the Rate officer on his right. In front sat the Range-taker, working the range-finder, and in front of him on each side of the Director sight were the Director Layer and Director Trainer.

These four men under Wilson were the eyes of the gunnery armament and aimed and fired the guns by remote control. The men at the guns had to keep them loaded, trained and elevated according to the readings transmitted to them at each position.

This method where only one man—the Director Layer—presses the trigger and fires the whole broadside at once represented one of the advances in modern naval gunnery, the result of lessons learnt from more than three centuries of fighting at sea. It is interesting enough to be described in more detail.

Director firing, as it is called, overcomes the many disadvantages of laying (the vertical movement of the gun—in degrees of elevation) and training (horizontal movement) each gun separately from the gun itself. It is difficult to point out a target to a gunlayer at each gun—being low down he cannot see as well

157

as the men perched in the Director; spray can cloud gunlayer's telescopes; each gunlayer has his own individual error—it might almost be called idiosyncrasy—and although small, the effect on a broadside means the shells would spatter about all over the place, instead of falling in an evenly spaced line across the target.

To avoid all this one sight, the Director Sight, is used, so that any error will affect all the guns alike and correction is easier.

The destroyers each had four guns, but the *Onslow* was the only one with 4·7-inch, the other 'O' class having First World War vintage 4-inch guns since the larger ones were not available when they were built. All the guns were hand-worked, and beneath each pair (two forward and two aft) were the magazines and shell-rooms.

When an enemy was sighted the whole Director trained round on to it, and the movement was transmitted to the guns, which followed, and to the Transmitting Stations (TS), the gunnery nerve-centre of the ship.

If the guns were pointed at a moving enemy and fired, the shells would miss because the guns had not been 'aimed off'. They must therefore be aimed off so that the shells landed where the enemy would be at the end of the shells' flight—not where he was when the shells left the barrels several seconds before. This aim off was calculated by a mechanical brain, known as the Admiralty Fire Control Clock, situated in the TS.

The basic problem was how to aim shells from a ship moving in one direction at say twenty-five knots so that they hit the target moving at twenty-five knots in another direction. To give the answer, the range was constantly fed into the Clock by the range-finder and radar; the enemy's course and speed came from the Rate Officer in the Director; the destroyer's own course and speed arrived automatically. There were other corrections to be made. Dip had to be allowed for (because the Director was mounted higher than the guns); and every time the guns fired the barrels were slightly worn by the shells and hot gases, entailing a correction for muzzle velocity. If all the guns were aimed at the same angle they would shoot in parallel lines and the shells would fall the same distance apart as the guns were spaced in the ship. To overcome this a correction was applied

158

to make them all converge on the point at which the Director was aimed.

To stop a shell turning over and over as it went through the air it was given a right-handed spin by the rifling in the barrel, and this spin made it wander to the right in the air. This amount of drift depended on the range and had to be added in. Then there was the wind blowing across the line of fire, and as it could affect the shells it had to be considered. As the shells rose high into the atmosphere the barometric pressure also had to be considered.

When all these factors were fed into the Clock it provided two answers—first the corrected range of the enemy, in degrees of elevation for the guns; secondly the deflection. Both were transmitted electrically to each gun so that when they were applied the guns were 'aimed off' correctly.

In the Director and TS were the 'gun-ready' lamps. Each represented a gun and as soon as the gun was loaded and ready to fire the lamps glowed. When all the lamps were lit an operator in the TS pressed the fire gong which sounded in the Director and at the guns. The Director Layer, who had been keeping the Director aimed at the enemy, then pressed his trigger.

As Wilson and his crew were settling down in the Director, men all over the ship had rushed to their own Action Stations, dragging on steel helmets and anti-flash gear.

In the Sick Bay Surgeon Lt Holland, the ship's doctor, prepared for any casualties and sent out medical parties to the first-aid posts. The forward one was in the supply-room on the starboard after end of No. 3 seamen's mess-deck, and was manned by a supply petty officer and the canteen manager. It was near the ship's company galley, bathrooms, engine-rooms, and the supply parties on the forward mess-decks handling ammunition up to A and B guns; it would deal with any casualties below decks forward.

The after first-aid post was in the officers' bathroom (see diagram on page 190), manned by a chief petty officer steward and a PO Cook, and was on the port side of the after accommodation covering X and Y guns, the Oerlikons, the searchlight platform in the waist of the ship and the after supply parties.

Casualties would first be dealt with at either of these two posts, Holland had planned; they would be moved to the Sick Bay, which was in the bridge structure directly under the chart house, when there was a lull in the action. It covered A and B turrets forward, the bridge, flag deck, radar and Asdic huts, and if there were a number of casualties extra accommodation was available in the Chief Petty Officers' and Engine Room Artificers' messes.

The Sick Bay was a tiny cabin, well scrubbed and full of the keen, searching odour of antiseptic, containing two bunks, one above the other. Five men were a crowd in the cabin. It was adequate for dealing with the usual illnesses and injuries of a destroyer at sea; it was far from adequate for dealing with the wounded in a stiff action.

Down in the engine-room Cdr Samways had given orders that connected up the second boiler and the ship would, in a short time, be able to make full speed. Bird, the anti-submarine officer, had been in the wardroom when Action Stations sounded and quickly made his way to the Plot, under the bridge, where he would work with Henderson, the Secretary, keeping the plot up to date; he also prepared to make enemy reports to the Admiralty and to Admiral Burnett in the *Sheffield*.

The other destroyers were also preparing for action. In the *Orwell*, for instance, Lt Tribe, the engineer, had been on deck talking to the Chief Stoker, trying to get as much fuel oil as possible out of two nearly empty fuel tanks aft. There might have been enough for another half-hour before having to change over; on the other hand they might lose suction. Their conversation was interrupted by the gun flashes astern.

'Change over,' ordered Tribe, 'and connect up No. 2 boiler.'

The *Orwell*'s captain, Nigel Austen, was less fortunate. He had a few minutes earlier left the bridge for the first time for several hours and gone to the toilet. Because of the amount of protective clothing everyone wore, this was a lengthy process. Action Stations was sounded off and in a few moments Austen came to the bridge complaining loudly that he had at last been caught with his pants down.

14

Hipper Attacks

'Every Commander is to take care that his guns are not
fired till he is sure he can reach the enemy upon a point-
blank . . .'—*Fighting Instructions, 1787*

IN the *Onslow*, as men scrambled to their Action Stations,
the soul-tearing clatter of the alarm rattlers still echoing in
their ears, Sherbrooke acted immediately on sighting the
gun flashes.

'Make to destroyers by light *Gun flashes bearing 270.*'

All he knew now was that somewhere astern of the convoy
were enemy warships. From the size of the gun flashes and the
range they were probably destroyers, and judging from their
original position and where the gun flashes showed them to
be now, they were obviously working their way round the stern
of the convoy.

'When in doubt, steer for the sound of the guns.' It was a
very old but fundamental principle of British fighting policy;
and it applied now as well as ever it did in the past, as did
another one—'It is *position* that matters, not speed.' Sherbrooke ordered, 'Port 25, Pilot. Twenty knots.'

There was still no word from *Obdurate*. Part III of his own
orders to all the escort commanders said:

'*Surface attack:* In the event of surface attack the sighting
vessel, on establishing belligerent identity, will make an enemy
report on the convoy R/T [radio telephone] wave and if a
destroyer on Fleet Wave, full power. . . .' Presumably she was
this moment transmitting her enemy report; these things took
time. And gunfire was a good enough enemy report to be working on for the present.

The next move had already been worked out by Sherbrooke

as long ago as 21st December, during that evening in his cuddy when he had paced up and down talking to his staff.

The time was 0933 and Sherbrooke ordered: 'Make to destroyers: *Join me.*'[1]

Obdurate was still at the rear of the convoy, several miles away, transmitting her enemy report. *Obedient* was on the far side of the screen and would have to join round the rear of the convoy, since it would be dangerous to steam through the columns of merchantmen. Only *Orwell* could join immediately. To her Sherbrooke signalled: *Join me. Course 270°.*

Already the *Onslow* was increasing speed to twenty knots and turning to port to head for the rear of the convoy (see chart on page 170). Bird ordered the Asdic dome, sticking out of the hull like a large blister, to be housed before it was damaged. It was no use at high speed anyway.

As the ship's bows started to swing there was a shout up the voicepipe from the wireless office:

'Office—bridge, office—bridge.'

Someone answered quickly and the voice called: 'Signal from *Obdurate*: *Three destroyers bearing 310. My position 73° 36' north 29° 00' east.*'

The whole ship began to throb as the propellers, increasing their speed, thrust her sharp bow into the swell and sliced spray up over the fo'c'sle.

Wilson in the Director, earphones clamped to his head, mouthpiece of the telephone slung round his neck, spoke into the microphone:

'Director—TS: testing communications.'

'TS—Director: communications well.'

A few seconds later the TS reported: 'All positions closed up, lined up and cleared away.'

Rapidly Wilson took the whole team—from the men in the Director to those in the TS working under the Gunner's Mate —through the check routine, and finally the TS reported: 'All positions, receivers checked.'

Now the *Onslow*'s four guns were ready to load: shells and

[1] i.e. The Fleet destroyers, *Obedient*, *Obdurate*, and *Orwell* which with *Onslow* formed the 'offensive' escort. The *Achates* and other escorts were to stay with the convoy.

162

charges had been brought up from the magazines and shell-rooms, and round each gun the seven-man team waited, swathed in anti-flash clothing, for orders to come through the telephone.

On the bridge Sherbrooke waited as the *Onslow* continued turning on to her new course of 270°. He was standing beside the compass and as usual he was quiet, expressionless, very much keeping within his own thoughts. He answered reports mostly by a nod of the head.

Next to him at the compass was the burly figure of Wyatt, clad in battle dress and an old cap, looking even more piratical with his thick black beard. He was watching the *Onslow* come round on to the bearing of the enemy destroyers, keeping an eye on the *Orwell* as she swung into position astern, and he was secretly worried about the accuracy of the *Onslow*'s position on the Plot, since he had not been able to get any decent sights recently.

Sherbrooke turned to Wyatt. 'I think they will be making up to the northwards, Pilot. Come round to north-west.'

Wyatt went over to the voicepipe and called down to the wheelhouse. Within a few seconds the *Onslow* steadied on 315°, which would put her in a better position to intercept the enemy destroyers.

On the port wing of the bridge, standing beside his torpedo sight, was Marchant: tall, his slim figure draped in a duffle coat, but looking as flamboyant as ever, and thankful that Peter Wyatt had given him the tip which allowed him to get his breakfast in time. Maybe he was going to get a chance of using his torpedoes at long last—though only destroyers were reported at the moment, and they'd be an impossible target. Pity those after tubes had been taken away—only four tubes left and *Onslow* the Flotilla Leader . . .

There was Foster, still apparently languid, but in fact very alert; near him the Chief Yeoman, looking just like a Chief Yeoman and busy with his message-pad, converting Sherbrooke's orders into the relevant code numbers in the signal book before giving them to the signalman to pass by lamp, or shouting them down the voicepipe to the wireless office. And

Williams, the Assistant Secretary, was standing at the back of the bridge, microphone in hand, waiting in case the close-range armament would be needed, in which case he would control its fire. Later the fact he had been on this convoy was to help him get his Czech wife out of Communist-controlled Czecho-Slovakia.[1]

And the bridge messenger, very young, possibly frightened, waiting for his first spell of action and at the moment bewildered by the fast-moving events, but only too ready to dash off at a second's bidding.

The look-outs, both experienced ratings, were lugubrious in their reports, as look-outs sometimes tend to be. A wealth of patience showed in voices which gave the impression that they would not be surprised at anything, and even if they were, they could quite adequately disguise the fact.

Suddenly Marchant saw a black shape emerging from a snow squall. 'What's that?' he called, pointing over the starboard bow. 'It's bigger than a destroyer!' The ship was almost bows on and Sherbrooke saw it instantly.

'Alter course straight for it, Pilot.'

Wyatt had just been going to call down the voicepipe to tell Bird to send off an enemy report on the basis of *Obdurate*'s signal, but this ship ahead, as he wrote later, was 'a large smoking monster, obviously a big ship and it could only be hostile'.

He called down the voicepipe: 'Starboard 10.'

He swung round the pelorus and took a quick bearing off the compass as Sherbrooke, in the same even voice, said: 'Make an enemy report, Pilot.'

A few steps to the starboard side of the bridge and into a voicepipe: 'Bridge—Plot: make an enemy report on Fleet wave, full power: *One unknown bearing 325, range eight miles, course 140* . . . Add our position and get it off quick!' The time was 0939.

[1] Williams on a ski-ing holiday in Prague after the war, met Sylva Langora, a well-known actress at the State Theatre. They wished to marry but the Czech Communist Government refused. Williams, desperate and having exhausted most lines of reasoning, finally said it was a poor way to treat a man who helped take arms to Russia during the war. It carried the day: Sylva Langora was allowed to marry and leave the country.

The action officer of the watch, Sub-lt Vaux, had already called up to Wilson in the Director:

'Bridge—Director: enemy in sight bearing 325°.'

Wilson had the Director trained ahead, looking for the destroyers. He had to move it round only a few degrees to starboard and there in his binoculars was the ship. She was nearly bows on, she was large, and she was moving fast. And she was a cruiser. That was all Wilson could make out—and that, even from his high vantage-point, was as much as could be seen from the bridge.

He spoke into the microphone linking him with the others in both the Director and TS: 'Enemy in sight bearing green oh-five . . .'

The Rate Officer beside him reported: 'Inclination 170 right. . . . Speed ten knots.'

The Director Trainer cranked the training hand-wheel and turned the Director a fraction until the crosswires in his binoculars were aimed at the cruiser's foremast; the Layer turned the elevating hand-wheel until his crosswires were on the base of the foremast.

The Range-taker focused the range-finder until the two images of the cruiser he saw in his eyepiece coincided, stamped on the 'cut' pedal, and the range was automatically transmitted to the TS below and fed into the ubiquitous Clock.

And the gunnery radar also had the range: the operator hunched over the set below could see the echo on the cathode ray tube in front of him. He turned a handle and moved a sighting wire along until it met the echo, pressed a pedal and automatically the range went off to the TS where the Gunner's Mate would decide, if they were different, whether to use the radar or range-finder range.

These things were happening simultaneously, but Wilson, eyes glued to his binoculars, was far from happy about the big ship ahead. Could it be one of Force R? The *Sheffield* or the *Jamaica*? Were they just going to open fire on a friendly ship? Was it all a ghastly mistake? He called the bridge.

But even in the last few moments the three destroyers originally seen by *Obdurate* came into sight, to the left of the big ship and obviously joining up with her. Once again the order went down the voicepipe: 'Send off another enemy report: *Three unknown* [warships] *bearing 325.*'

And the *Onslow's* operator transmitted, first to Scapa for the Admiralty, and then Murmansk for the SBNO, North Russia and Force R, *My* [previous signal time]: *Three unknown bearing 325.*

By now the big ship was moving across the *Onslow's* bows. There was no doubt now about her size. And a third signal went out from *Onslow*:

One cruiser bearing 340.

Wilson, now assured that the ship was indeed enemy, carried on with his stream of orders:

'All guns broadsides.'

This order to the TS was then relayed to the four guns: 'All guns load, load, load!'

At each of the guns ratings sprang into action: Projectile Supply, number five in the team, slammed a dull-yellow, 50-lb shell on to the loading tray; Cartridge Supply, number six, followed with the brass charge; the Tray Worker thrust them home, and the breech closed. The Layers and Trainers matched the pointers on their receivers, thus applying the deflection and elevation from the TS.

'Gun-ready' lamps flickered on in the TS and the Director. First B gun, then Y. But the A and X lamps did not glow. Wilson waited a few moments, impatient at the delay: already the order had come up from the bridge: 'Open fire when you're in range.'

'What's the delay in A and X?'

'Difficulty in loading,' reported the TS. Neither gun could get the breech to close, yet nothing seemed wrong with the mechanism.

The range was still far too great even for the *Onslow's* 4.7-inch although it was rapidly closing. *Orwell*, eight cables astern and following every move the *Onslow* made, was even worse off with her 4-inch, each of which bore the date stamp '1918'.

Meanwhile in the *Achates* Johns had sounded off Action

Stations immediately the original gun flashes were sighted and had altered course and increased speed to carry out his part, already laid down in Sherbrooke's escort orders. He and the two corvettes *Hyderabad* and *Rhododendron* and the trawler *Northern Gem* (as well as the *Bramble* and *Vizalma*, had they been present) were 'to proceed to place themselves in the best position to make smoke between the convoy and the enemy'.

The best position was to the north-west. This was to windward—what wind there was came from the north-west and would help spread the smoke in the convoy's direction. The merchantmen would soon be heading south-east, so the wind would carry it along with the ships. It was a position which would also keep the four ships between the enemy and the convoy, so they would not have to lay smoke on such a long front.

As soon as the *Achates* was in position Johns ordered the 'Make Smoke' button—it was on the starboard side of the bridge with the legend 'MAKE SMOKE——— STOP . . .' inscribed on a brass plate beside it—to be pressed. In the engine-room a loud gong sounded and the engineers opened the fuel injection valves so that more oil than could burn efficiently was fed into the furnaces; then, like a badly-trimmed paraffin lamp, black smoke poured from the funnel and trailed in a rolling and swirling black plume low over the water astern of her. The *Achates* was to the south-east of the *Hipper*, starkly outlined against the lighter part of the sky. She made a perfect target.

Meanwhile the enemy cruiser and the British destroyers, *Onslow* and *Orwell*—the *Obedient* and *Obdurate* were still catching up with them—were approaching each other at a mean speed of sixty miles an hour.

Sherbrooke watched the enemy through his binoculars. It was impossible to divine his feelings at this moment, the time for which twenty-nine years of naval training had prepared him. Every action was a crisis in the career of a senior officer. If he was successful, then he had merely done his duty; if he failed, whether owing to a long-thought-out plan miscarrying, or because he made the wrong decision when he had only a

167

split second in which to decide, then the Admiralty would quite rightly lose their trust in him. At a convenient time he would be relieved of his command and worse might follow. Their Lordships—the Lords Commissioners of the Admiralty, in all their dignity and wisdom—might 'express their displeasure', or it might end up with a court martial. At the moment the fate of a whole convoy and its escorts, together worth millions of pounds in cash, but of inestimable value in terms of badly-needed help for a hard-pressed ally, rested on him. If anyone could save it, then it was himself. If anyone could make a mistake which would result in its loss, then that man was himself. 'In war it is not permitted to make a mistake twice. . . .'

However, Sherbrooke was thinking of none of these things; his personal future and safety were not considered. He was trying to place himself in the enemy captain's position and divine what he would do in the circumstances.

Visibility was bad now in the half-light with intermittent snow squalls. It meant the enemy would not stand off at extreme range and shell the convoy at leisure. If he wanted to do any real damage, reasoned Sherbrooke, he would have to get in close. The captain of a big cruiser in low visibility would be very scared of torpedo attack; he would not be able to see torpedoes launched and would have to steam at high speed to keep enough freedom of manœuvre to dodge them.

It was as Sherbrooke had visualized it when he first received his orders to take JW 51B to Russia (except that he was short of two destroyers). His task was to drive the enemy away from the merchantmen, not to draw his fire: simply use the *threat* of those yellow-nosed torpedoes, already set for depth and speed, now resting in their tubes. And it was *in the tubes* that they were his most potent weapon. Once they were fired—however tempting the target—the enemy would no longer be scared of them; they would no longer be the main threat. The *Onslow*'s 4·7-inch, and the others' 4-inch, would hardly dent a German cruiser's armour, although good for morale. Nothing induces bravery so much as the thunder of one's own guns; likewise shells exploding aboard the enemy, even if they did not do a great deal of damage, might spread alarm and despondency among the Germans. The *Graf Spee* had not received much damage despite many hits by the 6-inch and 8-inch shells of the cruisers *Ajax*, *Achilles* and *Exeter*, yet she had fled (although the *Bismarck* fought well against truly terrible odds).

Tom Marchant, the second in command, was too busy estimating the enemy's courses and speed, facts he needed for his torpedo sight, to think of much else for the moment; but Peter Wyatt had more time. 'I think my thoughts were entirely fascinated with the situation—at last to *see* an enemy ship,' he wrote later.

The eyes of everyone on the bridge watched the enemy. What's her speed? Who is she? When will she open fire—and at whom?

Suddenly the darkly-menacing silhouette started broadening.

'She's turning to port!'

'She's scared of torpedoes!'

'What's her course now?'

Then, as the ship turned to port, four red spurts rippled down her side. The time was 0941.

'She's opened fire!'

'Four turrets—two for'ard and two aft.'

'Either *Hipper* class or the *Tirpitz*.'

'She's not big enough for a battleship; must be *Hipper*!'

'Eight 8-inch and twelve 4·1s, and she can make thirty-two knots.'

'But who's she firing at?'

Eight shells erupted in an almost straight line very close to the *Achates*: for a moment it seemed she was hit.

Sherbrooke knew he was getting rather far to the north and west of the convoy and decided to come round to starboard—on to a course of 025°—to make sure the cruiser did not get any closer.

'What's the *Hipper*'s range from the convoy, Pilot?'

'Six miles, opening, sir.'

More of the *Hipper*'s salvos fell round the *Achates*: one seemed to straddle her but she kept on steaming, faithfully laying the life-giving smoke-screen. Then the *Hipper* switched

169

her fire towards the convoy. Salvos exploded near the tanker
Empire Emerald, which still had not caught up with the convoy.

'Who the devil IS *Hipper* firing at?'

'Looks as if she's aiming at the tanker and ranging on us!'

She must be firing by radar—an interesting point, thought
Wyatt. The Germans *were* using radar then: their research
must be running parallel with ours.

'Enemy report from *Obdurate,* sir: *One destroyer bearing
180°.*'

That would be to the south of the convoy: well, there was
nothing Sherbrooke could do about it, and anyway the *Achates*
and the rest of them should be able to deal with her if necessary.
He had his hands full—still, Force R should be along soon.
Burnett would have picked up his enemy report.

'How far away are our cruisers, Pilot?'

'Between thirty and one hundred and thirty miles,' replied
Wyatt, quite aware this was a far from satisfactory answer;

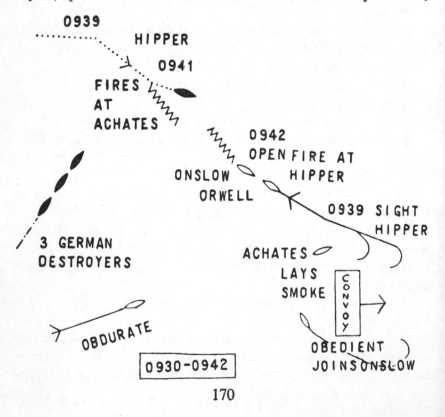

but it was the simple truth since he had been unable to get a sight. 'One to four hours away.'

One to four hours: and five minutes of the *Hipper*'s attention could sink all the 17th Destroyer Flotilla without a trace.

Despite the cold—*Onslow*'s forward speed induced a thirty-knot wind blowing round the Director—Wilson was tingling with excitement. The Director Layer and Trainer had their crosswires aimed on the enemy and reported 'Target'.

Down in the TS the Clock was working out answers and passing them to the guns in the form of elevation and deflection.

'Deflection set,' the TS reported to Wilson.

'Spread line.'

The Deflection Operator in the TS applied the deflection correction which made sure the shells fell in a zigzag, not in a straight line, giving at least one of them a greater chance of hitting.

The *Onslow*'s guns were now aimed to hit the *Hipper* with all the accuracy that British scientists could devise. It was a minute since the *Hipper* had opened fire at the *Achates*—a minute in which she had fired three more broadsides, a minute in which she and the *Onslow* had approached nearly a mile closer. Now she was in range. A quick look at the gun-ready lamps—A and X still not lit. The time was 0942.

'Shoot!' said Wilson into his mouthpiece.

'Fire!' said the range operator in the TS.

A man beside him sounded the fire gong. The Director Layer hunched over the sight, had his crosswires sighted on the base of the *Hipper*'s foremast. He pressed the trigger.

An electric current flowed at an immeasurably fast speed to an electric needle in the breech block of each gun, flowed into a thin iridio-platinum wire running through the primer in the base of the cordite charge, and fused it. The heat exploded the primer and ignited the cordite.

In a fraction of a second the cordite burned, producing a vast mass of gas which thrust the shell up the barrel, the rifling of which gave it a spin, and the shell left the gun at something like 2,750 feet per second—about 2,000 miles an hour.

The two guns—for only B and Y were firing—recoiled and

ran forward again to the firing position. Both breeches opened, the empty brass cartridge-cases were ejected, each was reloaded, and the two gun-ready lamps glowed again. In the meantime Wilson had spotted the fall of the salvo, passed corrections down to the TS and the guns were altered slightly.

The time was 0943. 'Shoot!' said Wilson again and again.

Then the *Hipper*'s silhouette became blurred and all but hidden in the darkness of a snow squall and Wilson had to fire relying only on radar ranges.

Down below in the radar office the Range Follower at the gunnery radar set watched the little blip on the trace of the cathode-ray tube. The trace jumped about a bit as the guns fired, but soon settled down. It was hard to concentrate with the guns firing and the excitement of knowing that at last the *Onslow* was engaging the enemy; but great concentration was needed to keep the sighting wire on the blip which represented the *Hipper* and also to call out the ranges so that they would be heard through a loud-speaker on the bridge.

As he listened, Sherbrooke was only too well aware that Wilson was shooting at the extreme range; and although the *Hipper* could be seen, perhaps the destroyer's camouflage was better than they thought, and the Germans may not have spotted them yet.

'Let's get a little closer, Pilot.'

Wyatt watched the compass and called a new course down the voicepipe to the wheelhouse. At the back of his mind he was working out the relative positions of the convoy, the *Hipper* and *Onslow*.

'Can't close in more than ten degrees from her course, sir, otherwise we'll lose bearing on the convoy too much.'

'Just keep her slowly closing, Pilot, and keep our "A" arcs[1] open, too.'

Just then Wyatt glanced astern to look at the convoy. 'My God, *Achates* has been hit: looks like an ammunition locker gone up on the fo'c'sle.'

But the little destroyer was still laying her smoke-screen, apparently unperturbed by the damage.

[1] The arcs of the horizon over which all the guns could fire.

Meanwhile, B and Y guns in the *Onslow* barked out every few seconds. The throat-catching smoke from the cordite charges drifted back over the bridge. The time was 0949.

From the *Onslow*'s bridge and Director men saw the *Hipper*'s silhouette slowly changing.

'She's altering away!'

'She's steering due south. . . . No, she's going on round to port.'

'Follow her round,' said Sherbrooke. 'Send an amplifying report.'

Wyatt yelled down the voicepipe to the Pilot: 'Make an amplifying report: *My so and so: enemy retiring.*'

In the Director the Rate Officer called out the *Hipper*'s new course, Wilson sent down his spotting corrections and the guns trained round a few degrees more and went on firing.

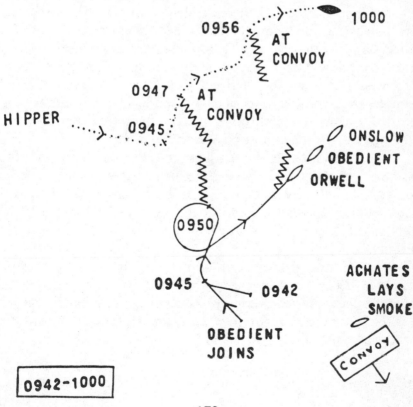

0942-1000

173

'She's making smoke.'

In fact the *Hipper* had steadied on due north, but by that time the destroyers were so far round on their turn that they completed the full circle and came back on their original course.

The *Orwell*, steaming almost in *Onslow*'s wake, was firing fast, and *Obedient*, with the *Obdurate*, was coming up on the quarter. Her position would be directly astern of *Onslow* and ahead of *Orwell*, and Austen signalled to her by light: *Am leaving room for you ahead of me.*

In the *Onslow* a shout came up the voicepipe from the Wireless Office, and the Yeoman reported to Sherbrooke: 'Captain, sir, from *Sheffield: Am approaching you on a course of 170°.*'

So Force R *was* north of them. No distance given and it could be up to one hundred and thirty miles away. . . . Still, what's *Hipper* up to now? Sherbrooke was far from happy. On the face of it he had successfully driven her off—the cruiser was steering north, away from the precious merchantmen. But was she really scared off? Perhaps she was just trying to get them to follow, playing the lame duck to lure Sherbrooke away from the convoy—yes, and let the three destroyers sighted earlier, or another group of ships, wade into the almost unprotected convoy. Sherbrooke quickly made up his mind.

'Make to *Obedient* and *Obdurate: Join the convoy.*'

There was no need to explain to Kinloch, who was the senior,[1] or Sclater, exactly what he meant: they would know he thought the convoy was threatened by other enemy ships and was sending them back to cover it. It was at this point that he felt the absence of *Oribi, Bulldog, Bramble* and *Vizalma* most keenly.

Obedient turned away out of the line, her bow wave and angle of heel caused by putting the helm over, giving her the classic appearance of a destroyer at high speed. Kinloch steered for the convoy, now eight miles away and signalled to *Obdurate*, who was quite close now, *Join me.*

[1] A signal telling Lt Cdr Kinloch that he had been promoted Commander in the half-yearly list of promotions, dated 31st December, came through during the battle.

Kinloch decided to steer across the stern of the convoy, laying smoke as he went, and then cover the merchantmen from the south-east—the direction in which their emergency turn away from the *Hipper* had taken them—since that was the most likely direction from which a second group would attack.

By now it was 1000 and Wilson ceased firing because the *Hipper* was eight miles away, hidden by snow squalls. He reported to the bridge that at the speeds they were steaming—especially when going to windward—spray was coming over the fo'c'sle, icing up the guns and freezing on eyepieces of binoculars in the Director. Sherbrooke reduced to twenty-five knots.

In the brief lull the guns' crews threw empty cartridge-cases over the side, out of the way; in the Director the Layer and Trainer wiped the frozen spray from the binoculars. Everyone waited for the *Hipper* to make the next move.

The convoy was by now steering to the south-east, away from the *Hipper*. The first that Captain Melhuish knew of possible danger was when PO Telegraphist Stephens appeared with a garbled wireless signal he had intercepted. It seemed to indicate unidentified warships behind the convoy.

Then at 0930 they saw the flashes astern as *Obdurate* came under fire from the destroyers. Immediately Captain Melhuish and his Yeoman, Matthews, clambered up the ladder to the 'monkey island' above the bridge. As he got to the top of the slippery iron ladder Melhuish slipped, his spectacles fell, and before he could recover his balance he had trodden on them. From now on he had to depend on Matthews' description of the scene.

Coloured lights had previously been rigged in case they were needed to signal emergency turns to the rest of the convoy. Now the time had come to use them. Matthews yelled down to another signalman who was waiting beside the switches in the wheelhouse, and a sequence of green and red lights came on— the preparatory signal for a 45° emergency turn to starboard. Melhuish waited until he was sure all the merchantmen had seen them, then ordered them to be switched off—the signal to execute the turn.

175

Turning the convoy even in the best of conditions was no joke since all the merchantmen were of different size and design. Each needed a different number of engine revolutions and different amounts of rudder to turn with; and none of the captains, although skilled seamen, was trained in performing evolutions in company with other ships. Fortunately the columns were short and there was the added stimulus that this, of all turns, was a very necessary one. Everyone, whether he came from Kent or Kentucky, London or New York, did his utmost to get round without dropping out of line or falling astern.

15

Onslow is Hit

'War should be long in preparing in order that you may
conquer the more quickly.'—*Publilius Syrus*.

KUMMETZ, standing on the admiral's bridge of the *Hipper*
eight miles away, was in fact very worried and uncertain
about the way the action was developing. To begin
with it had gone to plan; now confusion was creeping in all
round him.

As mentioned earlier, Kummetz had his force steaming
along with the six destroyers spread out in front each fifteen
miles apart. The *Hipper*, fifteen miles astern of the northern-
most destroyer, was seventy-five miles from the *Lützow*, which
was fifteen miles astern of the southernmost.

He was still steaming north-east, getting into position to
turn eastward and comb the convoy's track when, at 0715, he
crossed its wake without realizing it. Three minutes later two
silhouettes were sighted and the *Eckholdt* was dispatched to
investigate.

The look-out's report of the silhouettes had increased the
tension considerably in the *Hipper*. Kummetz waited anxiously
for the brief signal from *Eckholdt* which—he hoped—would
tell him what opposition he was up against. Waiting . . .
waiting . . . these were always the worst moments of all. An
attack on a convoy—on paper an easy task; but in the forefront of his mind were the words '. . . use caution even against
enemy of equal strength because it is undesirable for the cruisers
to take any great risks'.

Nine minutes later Kummetz could himself occasionally see
the silhouettes as they steamed through patches of bad visibility, but they were no more than black blobs on a blurred
grey and black backcloth.

'Probably our own destroyers are in wrong position,' he noted. 'I have *Hipper* turned towards silhouettes in order to diminish our silhouette and also to get clarification that it is really the convoy before I give the alarm.'

He gave an order to *Hipper*'s captain, Hartmann, and at 0742 the cruiser came round to a course of 100°—almost due east and, coincidentally, within a few degrees of the course the unsuspecting convoy was steering. He reduced speed to ten knots to overtake the ships only slowly and give himself plenty of time to see what was going on.

Five minutes later a larger silhouette was sighted fine on the starboard bow and *Hipper* came round to 110°. Then excited look-outs reported more silhouettes until, at 0753, a total of nine could be made out. 'This can only be the convoy,' declared Kummetz.

However it was still too dark to attack and a minute later the *Hipper* turned right round and steered away from the convoy on an opposite course.

'The sighting of the convoy gets rid of all the tension,' noted Kummetz. 'For me it was a question of attacking it by day because I maintain that to operate with cruisers against destroyers by night would demand the utmost effort by the cruisers. It is still not too late! I am convinced that I would not easily obtain a similar chance to attack with my forces. Everything depends on making full use of this opportunity.

'Only speed of action can achieve the solution of the problem of the danger of torpedo attacks which have to be considered in the light of my directive [from Admiral Klüber] not to take any serious risk.

'All I have to do now is to detail a destroyer to maintain contact; otherwise everything else can be formed up ready to attack at first light as instructed. With all the good luck I have had so far as sighting the convoy is concerned, it is a pity that I had not sighted it an hour earlier because *Lützow* is now positioned about seventy-five miles to the south. She cannot be in position for the first attack at first light.'

At 0800, while the merchantmen were unaware that they were being followed and Sherbrooke ordered everyone in

Onslow to be breakfasted by 0900, the *Hipper* signalled *Eckholdt* that she was to shadow the convoy. This was followed two minutes after by a wireless message to the whole force: *Hipper attacks from the north at first light.*

To get back into the attacking position at first light, Kummetz again turned the *Hipper* and headed eastwards after the convoy, increasing speed to twenty knots.

'I decide, in order to make use of the coming twilight hours which are essential for this operation,' he wrote, 'to attack with *Hipper* at dawn even if the destroyers are not in company. *Eckholdt* must for the time being remain as convoy shadower.' He added that there could be no question of having the destroyers join up with the *Hipper* and *Lützow* while it was still dark 'because of danger of getting mixed up'.

While Kummetz was making these lengthy decisions—about 0830—the *Obdurate* had sighted the *Eckholdt* and her consorts shadowing astern of the convoy, warned Captain Sherbrooke, and had been ordered to investigate them.

As Sclater turned back to do this, Kummetz decided, in view of the approaching dawn, to sort out his six destroyers and signalled at 0907: Beitzen *group* [*Eckholdt, Z 29*, and *Beitzen*] *to* Hipper *and* Z 31 *group* [*Z 31, Theodore Riedel* and *Z 30*] *to* Lützow.

The cruiser's operators were still transmitting the signal when look-outs reported silhouettes in sight again, following it up with the news that there were at least five ships.

Five minutes later, at 0915, Kummetz, who had taken the *Hipper* in a good deal nearer, did not like what he saw. He noted: 'Visibility very poor. Everything seems hazy. Cannot make out whether I am dealing with friend or foe. A total of ten ships now in sight, some of which look like destroyers. It cannot be said for certain whether our own shadowing destroyers are not among them. It is therefore essential to exchange recognition signals.'

The *Hipper*'s captain pointed out the nearest destroyer and ordered it to be challenged. But there was no reply to the winking signal lamp. In the meantime the *Eckholdt* had signalled: Eckholdt, Z 29 *and* Beitzen *have formed up round convoy.*

179

This was followed very shortly afterwards by a signal from Captain Stange, many miles away to the south in the *Lützow*, saying that he was approaching on a north-easterly course at twenty-six knots.

Just then the flashes of gunfire were sighted in the direction of the silhouettes—'evidently coming from our own destroyers,' said Kummetz. It was in fact the *Eckholdt, Z 29* and *Beitzen* firing at *Obdurate*.

The *Hipper* was now approaching the convoy from the north-west with her radar giving a very confused picture—echoes were coming back from several ships. Her eight 8-inch guns were loaded with high-explosive shells—they would cause more damage against the thin steel plating of merchantmen and destroyers than armour piercing: even a near miss would spray the ship with splinters.

Hartmann, the *Hipper*'s captain, and his gunnery officer watched carefully through binoculars. Way over on their starboard bow, just visible in the half-light, were the silhouettes of the merchantmen, hulls loaded down to their marks with arms for Russia. But up to windward of them, between the *Hipper* and the convoy itself, a British destroyer was beginning to lay a smoke-screen. She was steaming fast across the convoy. The smoke pouring from her funnel hung low on the water, an ever-lengthening and impenetrable black curtain behind which the convoy would very soon be safe—since the radar was getting such a confused series of echoes—and through which the *Hipper* would not dare steam for fear she found the watchful destroyers lurking on the far side, ready to carry out a torpedo attack.

Obviously this ship must be prevented from completing her task. Hartmann asked Admiral Kummetz for permission to open fire and received it. He turned the *Hipper* to port to bring all four 8-inch turrets to bear and gave his orders. A few moments later, at 0942, the *Hipper*'s guns thundered out and eight shells fell very close to the destroyer (which was in fact the *Achates*). More broadsides followed and within a few seconds the spotting officer reported a straddle and a possible hit.

Suddenly look-outs spotted another British destroyer steaming in fast on the starboard bow. Both Hartmann and Kummetz immediately realized she was in a good position to make a torpedo attack. The destroyer was in fact the *Onslow*, followed closely by the *Orwell* which the Germans had not sighted, and she opened fire. A few moments later she altered course slightly to port to keep between the *Hipper* and the convoy.

But as Sherbrooke had guessed, the Germans were very scared of a possible torpedo attack and misconstrued the reason for his turn. The *Hipper*'s log records:

'0944: A destroyer approached from the south-east and then put her helm hard over. She had fired torpedoes.'

Hartmann promptly ordered the *Hipper* to come hard-a-port and swung away to the northwards, turning his stern to the *Onslow* and *Orwell* and presenting a smaller target to the torpedoes he thought had been fired. By doing this he was forced to steer away from the convoy—just as Sherbrooke had planned. To complete the illusion of a torpedo attack, someone in *Hipper* reported seeing one approaching.

Thus fear and imagination helped Sherbrooke's boldness. *Hipper*'s first attack on the convoy had been beaten off by two destroyers using only the threat of their torpedoes. A bee dies once it has used its sting; and the *Onslow* and *Orwell* were in a similar position. Once their sting, the torpedoes waiting ready in their tubes, was used and missed, then the *Hipper* would have nothing to fear from them and they would surely die under the weight of her guns.

As she turned away the *Hipper* opened fire with her after turrets, but the shells fell between the *Onslow* and the convoy. She was probably firing by radar. Just before he altered away Kummetz wirelessed to the rest of the force: *I am in action with convoy in* [position given]. *Course 090°, speed ten knots.*

Although he had been temporarily driven off, he was full of admiration for the way Sherbrooke's destroyers were handled. He wrote:

'The [British] destroyers conducted themselves very skilfully. They placed themselves in such a position between *Hipper* and the convoy that it was impossible to get near the ships. They also made very effective use of a smoke-screen with

181

which they tried to hide the merchant ships. They tried to dodge *Hipper*'s fire by taking avoiding action and using smoke. Their relative position forced *Hipper* to run the risk of a torpedo attack while trying to use her guns on the ships.'

Kummetz realized he had been outmanœuvred by Sherbrooke in his first attack on the convoy and prepared for the second. He turned the *Hipper* eastwards at 0957 on to a course parallel to the *Onslow* and *Orwell* and opened fire with all four turrets. However, both destroyers fired back vigorously and three minutes later the *Hipper* altered away to the obscurity of the north-east.

All the time Kummetz was being driven farther away from the convoy, and although this meant that because of the bad light and the shortcomings of the radar it was out of effective reach of his guns, it would perhaps give the *Lützow* a better chance when she attacked from the south. Then he saw the enemy had followed round boldly—almost impertinently—on his starboard quarter, carefully keeping between him and the merchantmen.

Four minutes later, at 1004, he decided to make his third sally and this time the *Hipper* came round to the south-east to a course converging on the *Onslow* and *Orwell*. For four minutes she steamed along, her 8-inch guns blazing away. But although the two British destroyers weaved to dodge the shells, they still stubbornly steered in an easterly direction, effectively cutting Kummetz off from the convoy.

Once again, at 1008, he took the *Hipper* away to the north-east and ceased firing, as if to regain his breath. Then at 1013 he decided to make his fourth attack and turned the *Hipper* to the south-east to bring all her eight 8-inch guns and as many of the 4·1-inch anti-aircraft guns as possible to bear on the two destroyers and overwhelm them. At the same time he signalled to his force: Hipper *to north of convoy and there are four enemy destroyers between us and the convoy.*

This was an ambiguous signal because the *Onslow* and *Orwell* were the only two ships then fighting him off. The *Obedient* and *Obdurate* were steaming down towards the convoy, and the *Achates*, already badly hit, was still faithfully laying smoke.

182

Kummetz's own three destroyers now formed up astern of the *Hipper*, which was increasing speed and firing fast at the *Onslow* and *Orwell*. They in turn were steaming along just forward of her beam. It was an unequal contest and, since the *Hipper*'s gunners would soon get the *Onslow*'s range, it could surely have only one outcome.

The *Hipper*'s eight 8-inch guns fired a broadside weighing more than 2,000 lb, and the six 4·1-inch anti-aircraft guns added another 200 lb. In reply the *Onslow*'s two guns (two were still frozen up) fired a 96-lb reply and the *Orwell*'s four 4-inch a 124-lb broadside. A total of more than 2,200 lb versus 220 lb. Thus the *Hipper* had the advantage of being able to fire nearly a ton more of high explosives and in addition she knew the guns of the *Onslow* and *Orwell* could do her little harm.

On the *Onslow*'s bridge every man was busy and absorbed with his particular job: Marchant, for instance, was maintaining a flow of up-to-date torpedo control information in case the torpedoes should be fired. He wrote later: 'After the initial preparation for action was completed, my thoughts switched almost momentarily to the tubes' crews who were "closed up" down there abaft the funnel on the upper deck, watching the dim, huge shape of the enemy and quietly waiting for the order to "Train port" (or starboard, as the case might be). They were glancing now and then with looks of the utmost confidence towards the Gunner (T), Frankie Tibbs, a bulwark and versatile member who was in general charge, and the Chief Torpedo Gunner's Mate, an equally efficient and reliable Chief Petty Officer who quietly inspired confidence by his example, loyalty and zeal.

'Instantly my mind flashed back, as it has so often since, to a day when, as a boy under training in HMS Ganges, I was completely captured by a picture in the recreation-room depicting a scene, presumably from the First World War, of a line of battleships steaming in line ahead in rough seas and intermittent moonlight. In the foreground was the waist of one of the screening destroyers with her torpedo tubes trained in readiness, and in the shadows were the tense, taut and muffled figures of the tubes' crews, poised for the danger which was for ever lurking under such conditions. Beneath the picture were the words "When thou passeth through the waters I shall be with thee." All this passed through my mind in a few seconds, but I felt that their comparative physical inactivity, and the strain of remaining poised and watching, was part of a great purpose the result of which we might that day see.'

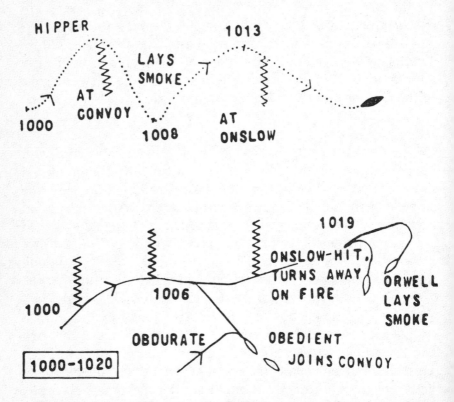

Wyatt was watching the *Onslow*'s course and keeping a wary eye on the *Hipper*, giving helm orders as necessary; and Sherbrooke was planning the action like a good chess-player, trying to keep as many moves ahead of the *Hipper*—and any of her consorts—as possible.

A and X guns were still frozen up—the crews were trying to close the breeches by the highly unorthodox method of banging them with shells. B and Y guns had ice forming on the outside of the barrels as spray came aboard, despite the fact they had each fired more than sixty rounds and would normally have been quite hot.

Wilson had been following the dark shape of the *Hipper* with the Director. As she turned towards them for the third time at 1004 he immediately opened fire, backed up a few moments later by the *Orwell*, which was still keeping station 1,000 yards astern of the *Onslow*. Again the ominous red glows rippled along the *Hipper*'s side as her 8-inch guns fired.

Sherbrooke spoke to Wyatt: 'Come round on to a more parallel course, Pilot.'

Wyatt bent over the voicepipe to the wheelhouse. 'Starboard 15—steer oh-eight-oh.'

For four minutes shells exploded in neat and deadly lines of eight round the two ships. Then once more the silhouette shortened and the *Hipper*'s guns ceased firing.

'She's altering away!'

'Steadying on about 045°.'

'What's she up to now?'

Then slowly the silhouette began to lengthen. The time was 1011.

'She's coming round again.'

'Steering about 080°.'

'There—she's opened fire again!'

'Radar reports he can see the salvos leaving *Hipper*.'

And so he could: tiny blips were detaching themselves from the large blip that was the cruiser and speeding along the trace towards the *Onslow*.

'Salvo coming . . . coming towards . . . steady . . . going right . . . going right . . .'

The eight shells fell in a closely-spaced geometrically precise straight line one hundred and fifty yards ahead of the *Onslow*, right across her course, and erupted in high, smoke-tinged waterspouts.

'Salvo coming . . . coming towards . . . going right . . . going right.'

Eight more shells burst one hundred and fifty yards ahead: the *Hipper*'s gunners had overestimated the *Onslow*'s speed.

'By jingo, they're small spreads!'

The *Hipper*'s gunners were not 'spreading the line': instead all her guns were being aimed so that the shells fell in a straight line, not a zigzag.

'Salvo coming . . . coming towards . . .'

'Shall I try and dodge them again, sir?'

The *Hipper*'s gunners now knew they had the range and had only to correct for line. They were firing rapid broadsides.

Every few seconds the *Onslow*'s two guns fired back and the smoke and specks of burning cordite from A gun blew aft over the bridge. But no one had time to notice it because the destroyer was now in great danger: the whole of a heavy cruiser's broadsides were being aimed accurately at her. Marchant was on the port side of the bridge with Sherbrooke a few feet away to his right; Wyatt was beside the compass, between and slightly behind; Williams was at the back of the bridge on the port side with a look-out by him; another look-out, the young Scot, and the yeoman were on the starboard side.

Four salvos—more than four tons of explosives—up to now. Wyatt spoke once again into the voicepipe to the wheelhouse, ordering another sudden alteration of course in a desperate attempt to fox the *Hipper*'s gunners.

'Salvo coming . . . coming towards . . . going left . . .'

Heavy thumps shook the ship and splinters hummed across the quarter-deck. The first of the eight shells in the fifth salvo burst close along the port side, and a jagged piece of the casing cut through the thin plating of the hull into the engine-room. The other seven shells went over the ship and burst in the sea beyond.

'Alter towards!'

'Port 20—steer oh-seven-oh.'

'Salvo coming . . . coming towards . . . going right . . .'

A succession of thuds shook the ship once more: splinters whined over the bridge and spray showered up; again the first shell of the salvo exploded within a few feet of the port side, between A and B guns, making a dent six inches deep and splitting the riveted plating. The other seven shells went over to explode in the sea on the starboard side.

'Alter towards!'

'Engine-room report damage. . . .''

'Port 10—steer oh-six-oh.'

'Salvo coming . . . coming towards . . . coming towards . . .'

The radar operator had a fraction of a second before he died in which to realize that the shells would fall almost on top of him.

There was a heavy detonation behind the bridge: a shell, the fifth in the salvo, had come in from ten degrees abaft the beam and over the 25-ft motor-boat to burst on the edge of the funnel, ripping it open down a riveted seam from top to bottom. Blast down the funnel itself blew open some of the boiler side casing doors and lifted the safety valve so that high-pressure steam shrieked out, streaming upwards in an ever-widening plume.

Splinters slashed the funnel so that it looked like a pepper dredge; hundreds more, blasted into razor-sharp slivers, were flung forward into the two radar offices only a few feet away, killing an operator. Others cut all radio aerials, went through the Director and sliced into the back of the bridge, killing the young Scot in the starboard look-out position. A splinter, ricocheting down off one of the gunnery radar aerials protruding forward from the top of the Director, hit Sherbrooke in the face.

But on the bridge, although every man knew the ship had been hit somewhere aft and was nearly deafened by the insensate shriek of escaping steam, and almost unnerved by the screams of a mortally wounded seaman, the immediate job was to dodge any more hits. Wyatt concentrated on the compass.

'Port ten—steer . . .'

A few moments later Marchant heard—almost sensed—a grunt from someone standing to his right. He glanced round to see Sherbrooke's face a mass of blood. Wyatt, realizing there had been a bad hit aft, was looking momentarily over his left shoulder and saw Wilson standing up in the Director, shouting something. When he looked forward again he saw blood all over his battledress and for a moment thought he had been hit himself. Then he saw Sherbrooke.

Before any of them could do anything to help their captain more thuds, mingled with the crash of their own guns, made the ship shudder and a double flash forward showed that two of the *Hipper*'s 8-inch shells had burst somewhere on the foredeck. Almost immediately flames billowed up in front of the bridge. Cordite charges started to blaze, adding their searing heat to the holocaust.

Sherbrooke ('It was difficult to understand how he saw or spoke at all,' Wyatt wrote later) realized the next hit might be fatal for the *Onslow*. In any case he would have to turn away immediately and slow down to reduce the bellows effect of the wind on the flames.

'Come hard to starboard, Pilot, make smoke and come down to fifteen knots.'

Marchant pressed the 'Make Smoke' button and Wyatt yelled into the voicepipe 'Starboard 20, revolutions for fifteen knots!'

The *Onslow* heeled over as she turned away, empty brass cartridge-cases rattling and rolling into the scuppers. The foredeck in front of the bridge was a swirling mass of angry flames making an unearthly red glow in the Arctic darkness and giving a crimson tinge to the black smoke and white steam spewing up from the funnel. In the light of the flames dead and dying men could be seen scattered round A and B guns forward.

From astern Austen, in the *Orwell*, had seen the salvos falling near the *Onslow*; then the flash of a hit on the funnel was followed by the two hits forward and the whole ship dissolved into a cloud of smoke and steam which streamed aft from a pulsating nucleus of fire. He thought she was going to blow up and immediately came round to port to keep clear.

A few moments later he saw her alter away to starboard. Immediately the *Hipper*'s gunners switched target and her 8-inch salvos starting falling with deadly monotony round the *Orwell*. Austen ordered her to make smoke to help screen the *Onslow*.

At the same time he had only a few seconds in which to decide the next move. With the *Onslow* out of action he was now the *Hipper*'s main target and the only ship effectively placed to fight her off from the convoy.

Should he try to make a solo torpedo attack on her—an attack probably doomed to fail because of the *Hipper*'s tremendous gun power, and which would almost certainly mean the destruction of his ship? Or would it be better to turn away and cover the stricken *Onslow*? That would leave the *Hipper* open to come down on to the convoy. . . .

It was an awful decision to have to make, and could mean the sentence of death for his whole crew.

Then, as he watched, he saw the *Hipper*'s dim silhouette changing and at the same time the shells stopped falling round: the Germans themselves had saved him making the decision, for the *Hipper* was turning away, retiring to the east into the dark anonymity of a convenient snow squall. Thankfully Austen turned the *Orwell* back to cover the burning ship.

On the bridge of the *Onslow* Sherbrooke was still in command, insisting that he was able to remain there.

'Most of A and B guns' crews killed, I'm afraid, sir.'

'*Hipper*'s shifted fire to *Orwell*.'

'Get a report from the engine-room on this damage.'

'You need help, sir, I've sent for the SBA.'

'No, no, I can see,' said Sherbrooke. 'Where is *Obedient*?'

'About five miles to the south, sir. *Orwell* is joining us.'

'Yes, he'll be no good on his own.'

Reports started coming through to the bridge from various parts of the ship.

One of the last two hits had been on the ship's side almost at deck-level between A and B guns, tearing a hole measuring six feet by five feet. Blast and splinters killed nearly every one of A gun's crew. Almost all of the forward Fire and Repair Party were also killed, and splinters had cut all electric leads, pierced every steam pipe and ventilation trunk in the compartment, and a particularly large one dented the barrel of A gun. A bad fire flared up immediately. (See diagram on next page.)

The second shell hit the edge of B gun deck a few feet away and just in front of the bridge. The explosion ripped out the steel plating as if it was cardboard and splinters riddled the gun-shield ten feet away, killing most of the crew and jamming the gun itself. Blast killed the men in the ammunition supply party

189

round B gun support who were only a few feet away from the explosion. Another big fire, above and aft of the first one, started raging in the CPOs' mess directly under the bridge. Cordite charges, which the ammunition supply party had been handing up from the magazine below B gun, immediately started blazing, generating intense heat and spreading the fire still farther.

Meanwhile, amid the deafening noise of steam escaping from the safety valve, and the smoke and heat blowing back from the fires a few feet away from them, Wyatt and Marchant tried to persuade Sherbrooke to go below for treatment. But he refused and stayed in command, despite his terrible wound.

Marchant sent Lewis King, the First Lieutenant, forward to find out exactly what damage there was—particularly if the hull was holed—and a messenger was ordered to fetch the doctor.

Holland was in the tiny Sick Bay two decks below the bridge, attending to casualties who had just been brought in. He had

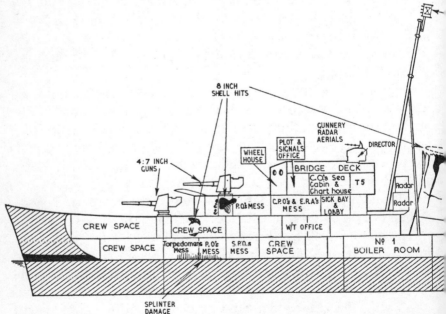

190

a first-aid bag slung over his shoulder and a hypodermic syringe, which fitted into a small metal case, like an old-fashioned fountain-pen clip, attached to his jacket.

The messenger was excited and out of breath: 'You're wanted on the bridge, sir.'

'I remember being horrified to think that anyone needed me there,' Holland wrote later. 'I was not sure who required me, only that I should go.'

Leaving Hanley, the young Sick Berth attendant, in charge he climbed up to the bridge, conscious as he went of the increasing din and the acrid stench of cordite, burning paint-work and smoke.

He found Sherbrooke, blood streaming from his face, standing against the binnacle. By the flickering light of the flames it took only a few seconds to see that a splinter had smashed his left cheek-bone, nose and the left side of the fore-head and that his left eye was hanging down his cheek.

'I am afraid you'll have to come below, sir.'

'Can't you patch me up here?'

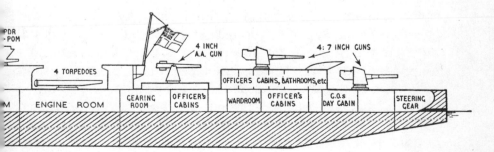

'No, sir, I am afraid you'll have to go to your cabin.'

After hearing that the leak in the engine-room was not serious and had been plugged, Sherbrooke finally agreed, after much urging, to go below. He called Marchant over.

'Torps, you can take over here while I go below and get patched up. Tell *Obedient* what's happened and order him to take over temporary command. Do what you can with the fires, and as we aren't much use now it would be a good idea to fall back on the convoy and home the cruisers. Keep me informed.'

Holland helped his almost blinded Captain down the ladder to his sea cabin on the deck below the bridge. It was very small —simply a bunk, desk and a wash-basin. The electric light would not work because the supply had been severed, and someone produced a hurricane lamp.

Sherbrooke was eased into his bunk—he could hardly see at all. His Leading Steward, Fraser, held the dim lamp while Holland dressed the wounds, having to pack the one over the bridge of the nose to control the hæmorrhage. Finally, without a word of complaint from Sherbrooke, the task was completed with a morphia injection.

'Watch out for hæmorrhage and let me know if there is any change in the Captain's condition,' Holland told Fraser, and then left to deal with other casualties.

'When I came out of the Captain's cabin the ship seemed to have taken on a terrific list,' Holland wrote later. 'Everywhere there was thick smoke and the smell of burning paintwork, and I remember struggling uphill from the cabin to the ladder in the centre of the ship.

'I must say I felt terrified; I don't really know what I was terrified of—a sort of vague feeling of impending dissolution. For the only time in my life my knees were knocking and I suppose it was that one does not expect the Captain to get hit. He was a tower of strength and in some way one felt he would be left standing when everyone else had caught a packet. Whatever it was, I had a feeling that if I had half a chance I would have taken to my heels. But there was not much scope for that, and I seem to remember having left my "Mae West" in the Sick Bay for a rating who was supposed to be in bed with tonsillitis (he had, however, turned to and was a great help to us in moving the wounded aft. He never reported sick again— a sort of shock treatment seemed to have cured him!).'

16

The Last Signal

'The winds and the waves are always on the side of the ablest navigators.'—*Edward Gibbon*

THE *Onslow*'s condition was now critical. Reports of serious fires forward were coming into the Damage Control Centre. The worst resulted from the hit between A and B guns, and the crew space was well ablaze. Pieces of burning debris tumbled into the magazine below—where the cordite charges were stowed—and Leading Seaman Richard Uren, who was in charge, immediately ordered it to be flooded in case it caught fire and exploded.

As soon as the valves had been opened to let water fill the magazine he organized his men and started tackling the fires. The smoke was almost blinding. Uren grabbed a hose and, finding a particularly serious blaze, frequently scrambled almost into the flames themselves to get at the seat of it.

On deck, where the two hits forward had wiped out almost all of the crews of A and B guns, the only man left on his feet at B gun was Able Seaman Thomas Cunningham. Dazed and shocked by the explosion, but undismayed at finding the rest of his crew lying dead or badly hurt, he started dragging the wounded from the flames leaping up and down a few feet away and threatening to spread. As soon as they were safe he went back to the fire and helped fling cordite charges and shells— which were already hot from the flames and in danger of exploding—over the side into the sea. One of the men he helped drag away was the captain of the gun, Able Seaman Leonard Hooper, who had received a fatal head wound. Hooper's subsequent 'fight for life for seven days and nights astounded his medical officers', according to the citation for his posthumous

194

mention in dispatches. (Uren and Cunningham were each awarded the DSM.)

Lewis King, the First Lieutenant, arrived down on the fore-deck to find nearly the whole of the forward part of the ship on fire. Dead men were lying around the guns; more were scattered in the POs' mess and the crew space below it. With the Fire and Repair Party wiped out he had to find more ratings to start tackling the fires. A quick inspection showed the fire in the POs' mess beneath B gun had spread to the wooden lining, fitted as insulation against Arctic conditions, and to the hammocks and was blazing fiercely. The heat was so great that it could be felt in the wheelhouse and Plot—the cabin where the automatic position-plotting machine was kept—just beneath the bridge.

Hoses were hauled out—they had been stowed away in warm places to prevent them freezing up solid—and rigged. All hatches and doors leading forward were closed in a fruit-less attempt to suffocate the flames. The hoses were dragged through shell holes into compartments lit only spasmodically by the flames and which were full of thick, choking smoke.

When Lt Kevin Walton, the Senior Engineer, arrived to help fight the fires he found they could not tackle a particularly bad one. It could apparently be reached only by going through the burning mess-decks. Walton, however, quickly found that it was possible to get at it by climbing down through the shell hole. Dense smoke was pouring out and it was almost impossible to breathe.

Although he could not see whether the deck several feet below the hole had been shot away, he quickly tied a handker-chief over his face, lashed a rope round his chest, gave the free end to a rating to hold, and lowered himself down into the smoke. He then had two hoses led down after him and for twenty minutes sprayed the flames before being relieved. (For this and other work, described later, he was awarded the DSC.)

While King and Walton led the parties fighting the fires forward, Marchant and Wyatt on the bridge were busily handling the ship. Marchant could not find out the extent of the damage and was unable to see the few feet down from the bridge because of the flames and smoke. He sent Williams forward to find out what he could and report back as fast as possible.

Down in the engine-room, where the hit on the funnel had sent a shower of debris tumbling down into No. 1 Boiler-room and blown open the boiler casing, Engine-room Artificer Roy Howarth and Stoker PO Arthur Heaman worked fast to clear the boiler uptakes, close the casing and continue steaming the boiler. (Both were later awarded the DSM for their courage and leadership.)

Leading Telegraphist Donald Grant started repairing the damaged wireless aerials while PO Telegraphist Frank Lovett rectified the A.C. supply, putting all the wireless receivers back in action once again. Then, after a lot of patient work—despite the fact that the fire in the CPOs' and ERAs' mess below was making the Wireless Office almost unbearably hot and filling it with smoke—he managed to repair a very intricate fault in the main transmitter.

Up in the Director, Wilson had been so concentrating on his job of controlling the guns that he had not realized the funnel, a few feet away, had been hit, even though splinters had cut through the canvas weather screen behind him.

Then one of the gunnery radar operators had reported, without any excitement in his voice:

'Shan't be able to pass any more ranges, sir.'

'Why not?'

'Set's blown up, sir.'

'Sure you can't get *anything* out of it?'

'No, sir, there's a bit of a mess down here.'

The second hit a few moments later had put all the gunnery fire control circuits out of action—Wilson was trying to shout this information down to the bridge when Wyatt turned to look aft, as described earlier.

Realizing he could do nothing in the Director, Wilson then climbed down and immediately went aft through the smoke to X and Y guns—helping a wounded man to the After First Aid Post on the way—to get them into local control. He found Y gun all right but X gun was still having trouble.

196

The Ordnance Artificer was working on it, trying to get the breech to close. Earlier when the crew had first been unable to close the breech they assumed there was ice on the shell—it had been in the ready-use racks on deck. They had taken a new shell from below, rammed it home, followed it with the charge and again tried to close the breech. But still it stuck. They had then sent for the Ordnance Artificer and started stripping the breech, thinking it had a fault. The ice in the groove behind the extractors, which was causing all the trouble, could not be seen.

After arranging to give fire orders to the guns by telephone from the bridge—the only available method left—Wilson went to the TS to find Tibbs and arrange for him to pull out the electric leads forward, thus eliminating the short circuits which were causing additional small fires.

But the most harrowing task of all fell to Holland, the surgeon, and Hanley, the Sick Berth attendant. More than forty of the *Onslow*'s crew had been killed or wounded within two minutes.

Because of the noise of the ship's own guns firing neither men had realized the ship had been hit until three casualties were brought into the Sick Bay. Two were put into the only bunks, while the third stayed on a stretcher. Haemorrhage was controlled, dressings applied and morphia injected. While they were doing that, several more wounded men were brought along because the Forward First Aid Post in the supply-room on the seamen's mess-deck had been wrecked. When the Sick Bay was full casualties should have been put in the CPOs' and ERAs' messes just forward of it, but the lighting there had failed, and they had to be put down on the deck outside the Sick Bay.

Hanley had worked on those cases when Holland was called to the bridge to attend to Captain Sherbrooke. It was a difficult task because, apart from anything else, of the amount of clothing the men were wearing. A wound in the shin meant that a seaboot, two thick stockings and a sock, trousers and knitted underpants had first to be cut away.

While attending these men, Hanley discovered that the CPOs'

and ERAs' messes nearby had caught fire: flames were licking up and setting the wooden insulation and hammocks ablaze. Smoke started to pour back into the Sick Bay. He warned the new Fire Party and carried on. More wounded were being carried and dragged in all the time and put down on the deck.

To get at the flames the fire-fighting teams had to drag hoses through the Sick Bay flat,[1] across the wounded, many of whom were unavoidably soaked with water. Holland wrote later: 'When I got back to the Sick Bay flat things were in an awful tangle: hose-pipes, wounded men, blood and smoke—one had difficulty in making out what was going on. The place was untenable and I had to get the wounded away.'

He found that the after part of the ship was not damaged and decided to evacuate the men to the After First Aid Post, in the officers' bathroom. He ordered every rating with no special job to help carry the wounded aft.

Many of the men wore so much clothing that the special stretchers, which should have wrapped round them, could not be secured because the straps were not long enough to allow for the extra bulk. But somehow they were carried aft, along slippery decks which were by now sloping as the ship listed. While this was going on an urgent message arrived from the After First Aid Post asking for the doctor or SBA at once. Hanley immediately hurried aft and found many more wounded had been taken there from various parts of the ship, in addition to those being evacuated from the Sick Bay. Several of them were in a very serious condition; at least two were already dead.

He arranged for the more serious cases to be put in bunks in various cabins round the wardroom. When there were no more bunks the wounded men were wrapped up in blankets and put on the deck. The less serious cases—those who could be lowered down the companion-way—were taken to the wardroom.

Holland arrived and he and Hanley worked as fast as possible, trying to sort out the worst cases from the mass of

---

[1] A flat is a non-continuous deck. In this case it was in effect a lobby from which doors led off to the Sick Bay, CPOs' Mess and other compartments.

wounded men so that they could be dealt with first. In the bitter cold fingers were so numb that it was often almost impossible to rip the watertight packing from field dressings. For the time being it could only be first aid: serious surgery was out of the question. With forty casualties to deal with—many of them likely to die, or actually dying—it was a case of quickly cutting away clothing, a brief examination, dressings put on and secured into place, a tourniquet applied if necessary, and morphia injected to ease the pain.

As soon as possible Holland went back to the Sick Bay to salvage dressings and instruments. The paint on the bulkhead was already bubbling with the heat of the fires, overcoming the usual smell of antiseptic. Spare blankets were collected, and hot water bottles were given to the worst cases to ease shock. Later they would get warm, sweet tea if they could safely drink it. But all too often Holland or Hanley had to order a body to be taken away. Some of the men were so badly wounded that even under morphia they tried, in their agony, to sit up and rip off their dressings, and in between treating other cases the first-aid men had to keep a watch on them.

Not all the wounded could be brought into the First Aid Post. One rating in the TS had his left leg broken, and had fallen down between the high-angle control table and a bulkhead. He was jammed there because of the heavy list of the ship. Other men in the TS crew had already patched him up, and Holland applied further dressings, put the leg in splints, gave him morphia and made sure he was made as comfortable as possible, covered with duffle and sheepskin coats. (The man had to remain in the same position until the *Onslow* slowed down to enter harbour twenty-four hours later.)

While Holland attended to the casualties,[1] Wilson tried to get the two remaining guns into action again, King and Walton and all available ratings fought the fires forward, Foster worked at the communications and Samways looked after repairs. Marchant, with Wyatt's help, still had to fight the ship.

Summing up the situation at this stage he later wrote:

'Both the forward guns had been put out of action by hits

[1] He was subsequently awarded the DSC and Hanley the DSM.

and the after guns by failure of power and the formation of ice
in the breech blocks. The remaining hands available forward
were employed in fighting the fires, along with those who could
be spared from aft. We had also sustained various splinter
holes in the engine-room and boiler-room, and at one stage
the appearance of things produced a very alarming picture.
We were, of course, making thick smoke, and the safety valves
had lifted, the smoke and steam giving a beautiful study in
black and white. The ship was gradually taking up a list to
port due to the near miss; the bridge was almost uninhabitable
because of the choking smoke from the fires forward; the noise
rendered speech practically impossible; and then came a phone
call from the engine-room to say that there was a fire in one of
the boiler-rooms and that water was making its way into the
engine-room. Most of the electrics, including that for the
W/T and Asdics, had been wrecked and the only wireless available, with jury aerials since all others had been shot away, was
the Fleet Wave.'

As soon as the jury aerials were rigged, Marchant signalled:
Have been hit forward.

He ordered Moorman, the Yeoman, to signal by light to
Obedient—whose captain, Kinloch, was now next in succession
by seniority to Sherbrooke—*Have been hit forward and in the
engine-room.*

As soon as Sherbrooke had been helped below a further
signal was flashed to Kinloch: *Captain (D) wounded. Take over
for time being.*

It was also essential that Admiral Burnett, commanding the
two cruisers which were steaming to their aid, should be informed what had happened. Amidst the smoke, wreckage from
damaged transmitters and the din of the steam escaping from
the safety valve, an operator tapped out in Morse the signal:
*Have been hit forward and in the engine-room. Am retiring on
convoy making smoke-screen.*

Then, while Kinloch ordered the *Obdurate* and *Orwell* to
join him, two more signals from *Onslow* gave him all the rest
of the information he needed to know to fill in the picture:
Forward magazine flooded. Fire in forward boiler-room and *Am*

proceeding to southward of convoy to home R.A.D. [Admiral Burnett].

Just about this time the minesweeper *Bramble* transmitted a brief signal, *One cruiser bearing 300°*, but only the *Hyderabad* picked it up. Apparently she assumed the signal—the last ever received from the *Bramble*—had been picked up by other ships of the escort, for she did not pass it on to Kinloch, who was unaware of it until several days later.

17

Lützow Joins In

AFTER dealing the *Onslow* a crushing blow without realizing it Admiral Kummetz ordered the *Hipper* to increase to thirty-one knots—full speed—and steer to the east-north-east, with his three destroyers in company. The convoy was now more than twelve miles away to the south-south-west steaming, he hoped, into the guns of the *Lützow* and the three destroyers.

Suddenly, at 1036, a destroyer or corvette—the look-outs could not be certain which in the darkness and snow squalls—was sighted on the port side, steering away from the *Hipper*.

'I directed the *Hipper* to engage this ship, which was at first taken to be a corvette or a destroyer and later confirmed as a destroyer,' wrote Kummetz, 'because it would have meant a very unpleasant link on the lee side of the firing in an engagement with the convoy. After finishing off the destroyer I intended to resume the action with the convoy. The destroyer was probably an escort stationed on the flank of the convoy.'

In fact, the 'destroyer' was the 875-ton minesweeper *Bramble*, commanded by Cdr H. T. Rust, and manned by seven officers and 113 ratings. She had one 4-inch gun firing a 31-lb shell against the *Hipper*'s eight 8-inch and twelve 4.1-inch. Immediately the *Hipper* was sighted, Rust must have sent off an enemy report—received only by the *Hyderabad*—knowing nothing could save him.

But the *Hipper*'s guns did not sink her, even though they were firing for six minutes, and at 1046 Kummetz ordered the *Friedrich Eckholdt* by radio-telephone: *Sink the destroyer in position 1500. Destroyer was first fired on by* Hipper.

Kummetz then swung the *Hipper* round to get nearer the convoy again. He wrote: 'Proceeding south with the *Hipper* group in order to get close to the convoy I was aware that with the decreasing visibility I was taking a risk. But I was hoping, after maintaining a heavy fire on the destroyers, to find one or more gaps in the defence through which I could attack the merchant ships.

'To make a destroyer attack was out of the question owing to possible confusion with the enemy. As the action developed I should no longer have been able to assemble our own destroyers round *Hipper* before darkness, and would thus have left her without destroyer protection at a critical period. On top of this, an attack by only two destroyers (*Eckholdt* had not yet rejoined) would have been futile.'

As the *Hipper* steamed at thirty-one knots to overtake the convoy the merchantmen made another emergency turn and had a very narrow escape from destruction.

Some time earlier, almost twenty minutes after the *Onslow* had been hit and at the same time as Kinloch had taken temporary command of the escort and was steaming astern of the convoy, the *Rhododendron*, stationed on the port quarter of the convoy, signalled that she had sighted smoke bearing 197° at a range of seven miles. But Kinloch wrote afterwards, 'As this was about two miles ahead of the leading ships of the convoy and nothing had been received from them the report was considered false.'

Ten minutes later the *Rhododendron* again signalled that she had sighted an 'unknown man o' war' bearing 165°, only two miles away and steering north-east.

If this report was accurate, Kinloch reasoned, the enemy warship would be steering right across the bows of the convoy, only a few thousand yards off, from west to east, yet she had not opened fire. He wrote: 'As the convoy was approximately on this bearing, *Rhododendron*'s report could not be accepted.'

But the *Hyderabad*, stationed on the starboard side of the convoy, had in fact sighted two destroyers crossing ahead from west to east, and then a large vessel, and had made no report.

The large vessel was the pocket battleship *Lützow*.

More than an hour earlier Captain Stange had brought her up from the south as ordered and, at 0922, sighted silhouettes

203

(just before the German destroyers originally opened fire on *Obdurate*). The flashes of the destroyers' guns were bearing almost due north and, a few minutes later, more gun flashes were seen. An entry in the *Lützow*'s log asked, '*Hipper* in action with convoy?'

At 0951, after several more silhouettes had been sighted, Stange received Kummetz's signal saying the *Hipper* was in action with the convoy. For the next fifty minutes he steamed slowly north-east to intercept the convoy. At 1035 the *Lützow*'s smoke was spotted by the alert *Rhododendron*.

After sighting an unidentified vessel to port, the *Lützow* then turned 20° to starboard on to a course of 060°, east-north-east, and the log noted: 'Snow squalls on the port bow—poor visibility—brief twilight—sky heavily overcast.'

Stange was now steering across the bows of the convoy. 'Several targets sighted through snow squalls,' it was noted in the log. The nearest was reported to be three miles off and the farthest seven. 'No identification possible.'

Two minutes later gun flashes were seen on the *Lützow*'s port quarter. (It is impossible to say where they were from because neither the *Hipper* nor the British ships report firing at that time.) *Lützow*'s log continues, against the time 1050: 'Impossible at first to ascertain whether dealing with friend or foe by reason of the poor light and the smoke and mist on the horizon.

'To avoid observation from *Lützow* being obscured by the snow squalls and smoke drifting south, I decided to proceed at low speed in the vicinity of the convoy, clear of the snow squalls, in order to take advantage of opportunities for attack as visibility improved.'

But Stange had missed a golden opportunity. He had three destroyers with him, each armed with eight torpedoes. Two of them had five 5-inch guns, and the other four 5-inch. The *Lützow* herself had six 11-inch, eight 5·9-inch, six 4·1-inch guns and also eight torpedo tubes. Yet he had let all his force pass within two or three miles of the merchant ships, the prize for which Operation Rainbow had been planned, without opening fire or launching one of its thirty-two torpedoes.

As he passed across their bows there was no British escort vessel whatsoever nearby: the *Hyderabad* was on the starboard side of the convoy, the *Rhododendron* on the port quarter beyond it, the *Obedient, Obdurate,* and *Orwell* astern and, therefore also beyond the merchantmen, the *Achates* on the starboard quarter laying smoke, and the *Onslow* still astern as she steamed towards the head of the convoy.

However, the orders from Kummetz—which Stange knew had come from the Naval Staff in Berlin—were to be cautious. He had done that. As a result he had failed to destroy the ships of the convoy which, at that time, were keeping perfect station and were—apart from *Rhododendron*—completely unaware of the *Lützow*'s presence.

Ironically, Kummetz's plan had worked perfectly: the *Hipper* had drawn off the escorts to the north of the convoy; the convoy had turned south and run, unprotected, into the *Lützow* . . . only the *Lützow* had not fired a shot.

Stange, having passed across the convoy's path, then turned away south-east on a parallel course ahead of it, and at 1115 signalled to the *Hipper*: *Position* [given] *course 120°, speed twelve knots, enemy lost to sight on south-easterly course in snow squalls*—Lützow.

Almost immediately, Stange altered course to the eastward 'to avoid the bad weather and keep clear of the smoke of the convoy'. This put the merchantmen on the *Lützow*'s port quarter, where visibility was very poor, but they could still see the silhouettes of the ships. Suddenly they saw the flashes of guns and almost at once sighted a big ship to the north, which was also firing. Stange wrote: 'Exchange of recognition signals proved it to be one of our own ships, apparently in action with enemy ships, likewise indicated by gun flashes on the port quarter. The first impression is that the firing is aimed at *Lützow*. However, as there is no evidence of fall of shot, it becomes evident after exchange of recognition signals that it is the enemy with whom *Hipper* is now engaged.

'Seeing no possibility of approaching the convoy from the east, owing to the persistent lack of visibility, I decided to turn west, to bring under my fire the enemy engaged with *Hipper* to the north and, at the same time, to maintain contact with *Hipper* before the onset of darkness.'

At 1126 the *Lützow* circled and headed north-east, towards the *Hipper*, and was followed by the three destroyers, *Theodor Reidel*, *Z 30* and *Z 31*. The convoy was on the port side 'in snow and smoke'.

Ten minutes later silhouettes were sighted on the port bow and identified as destroyers. Speed was increased to twenty-four knots. 'The intended engagement of these vessels is abandoned due to gathering darkness and extremely poor light,' Stange noted.

The *Hipper*, coming south-westwards at thirty-one knots towards the convoy, claimed to have sighted two destroyers on her port side at 1106 and opened fire on them. In fact there were no British destroyers anywhere near that position, but the target might have been the *Bramble* which, after being attacked earlier, had perhaps limped away to the eastward.

At this time Kinloch was leading the *Obdurate* and *Orwell* and gradually overhauling the convoy, passing down its port side. With the *Onslow* and *Achates* damaged, they were now the only destroyers which could defend the convoy against the pocket battleship, heavy cruiser and six destroyers attacking it.

At 1055 the *Obdurate* sighted an enemy warship to the eastward, approaching the convoy. The Commodore had just made an emergency turn. This enemy vessel was in fact the *Lützow*, now waiting hopefully for the weather to clear. At 1100 the snow squalls cleared up for a short while and the *Obedient* sighted her and two destroyers five miles away to the eastward, steering south.

Kinloch led the three destroyers round towards her, making smoke to hide the merchantmen, and then came round on a parallel course, steaming between the enemy and the convoy.

Then at 1106 the enemy opened fire—but not at them. From the British destroyers this ship appeared to be the same one they had just seen—the *Lützow*—but in fact it was the *Hipper*, which was approaching at thirty-one knots, steering south. Her bearing was almost the same as the *Lützow's*. The *Hipper* was firing at what, as mentioned earlier, was possibly the *Bramble*.

At 1115 Kinloch signalled by wireless to Johns in the *Achates*, still faithfully laying smoke to the westward, *Join me. Prolong the line to port*, but he replied: *Holed forward. Maximum speed fifteen knots*.

Kinloch then ordered him to join the *Onslow* at the head of the convoy and take her under his command.

As seen from *Onslow* earlier, the *Achates* had been badly damaged right at the start of the action when, beginning to screen the convoy with smoke, she had become the *Hipper's* first target.

The cruiser's first salvo missed but her gunners quickly corrected so that the second and third straddled, and although Johns was weaving to dodge them, the first shell of the fourth salvo burst in the sea close along the port side, just forward of the bridge, while the rest went over.

The near miss flung up hundreds of splinters. They ripped through the *Achates'* thin steel plating into the shell-room and magazine, killing and wounding some of the supply party handing up ammunition and letting water flood in; more smashed the search radar set, wounded two of the port Oerlikon guns' crew, a signalman and look-out on the bridge. Others riddled the Stokers' Mess, cutting down most of the Fire and Repair Party, and more flooding started. Loftus Peyton-Jones, the young First Lieutenant, and Peter Wright, the Engineer, immediately formed more repair parties and set to work. At the same time wounded men were carried away to the Sick Bay and First Aid Post to be treated by MacFarlane, the ship's doctor and the Sick Berth attendant, assisted by Drummond, the canteen manager, Allan Jones, an officer's steward, and Able Seaman Platt, who was in charge of the Forward First Aid post.

The repair parties tried to close the magazine and shell-room hatches and plug the holes in the stokers' mess-deck, but both the strongbacks—levers used for shutting the hatches—had been lost in the explosion. By the time those from the after magazine and shell-room had been brought forward so much water had poured in that the whole mess-deck had to be abandoned.

The steam ejector was connected up to pump out the magazine and shell-room, but it was then found that the steam line had been shattered. Ratings then manhandled the portable electric pump forward and started it working. After twenty minutes it was obvious to Peyton-Jones and Wright that the pump was making no progress against the inrush, so the mess-deck was closed down altogether and hatches and bulkheads shored up with baulks of timber to ease the strain on them.

The electric pump was then carried farther aft to start pumping out the ERAs' and Stoker POs' messes, which were slowly beginning to flood through the splinter holes in the ship's side, but the pump broke down and twenty minutes passed before it was working again.

With many tons of water swilling about below deck the *Achates* slowly trimmed down by the head; but Johns continued steaming his ship across the stern of the convoy, laying the smoke-screen, while his officers and men did all they could to save the ship.

Then, at 1115, came Kinloch's signal. Johns found it impossible to steam at more than fifteen knots because of the amount of water entering through the splinter holes, and when Kinloch then ordered him to join the *Onslow* at the head of the convoy he hauled out clear of his own smoke-screen to move up.

Immediately the *Achates* was spotted by the *Hipper*, which was now coming down from the north-east to attack the convoy again (see chart on page 225). Once more the German gunners got the range immediately and salvos started spurting with deadly accuracy round the destroyer. Johns at once increased speed and started zigzagging to try to dodge them.

Peyton-Jones had been at work directing repairs forward when he heard the *Hipper* was in sight once more and immediately went to the TS, which was on the upper deck below and abaft the bridge. Suddenly there was a tremendous crash and the ship shuddered from what was obviously a direct hit.

He dashed out of the TS, looked forward and aft along the upper deck and saw the hit had not been there, and started for the bridge.

'At the foot of the first ladder,' he wrote later, 'I was met by a white-faced youngster sent by the Yeoman to fetch me. On arriving in the wheelhouse it became obvious that the hit had been on the bridge above. The deckhead was bulging downwards and a somewhat dazed coxswain, Daniel Hall, was ruefully regarding the wreckage around him.

'The usual way up to the bridge was barred, so stepping out on to the port Oerlikon platform I clambered up the remains of the outside ladder. The familiar scene was unrecognizable—just a blackened shambles of twisted metal with the remains of a few identifiable objects sticking grotesquely out of the wreckage.'

Among this fantastic jumble of what had been the compass platform before one of the *Hipper*'s 8-inch shells burst right on it, were lying the mercifully unidentifiable remains of those who had been standing there as the *Achates* tried, unsuccessfully, to dodge the salvos—the Captain, Lt Cdr Johns; the No. 2, Lt Eric Marland; the young Navigator, Sub-lt Kenneth Highfield; the signalmen, look-outs and A/S operators. And over it all was the acrid stench of high-explosive fumes.

'Farther aft,' wrote Peyton-Jones, 'the damage was less severe although still effectively flattened as if by some giant hammer smashing down from above. Here men were lying, not all of them dead. I leant over Fred Barrett, the young Sub-lieutenant who had been directing the gun armament, but he had been too badly wounded to tell me anything.'

Quickly Peyton-Jones climbed over the wreckage and the bodies, coughing from the fumes, and saw the Yeoman, Albert Taylor, leaning against the ripped and twisted after-screen. By some miracle he had escaped with only wounds, while almost everyone round him had been killed.

Taylor straightened up as he saw Peyton-Jones and slowly —maddeningly so to start with, but becoming more coherent as the initial shock cleared from his mind and his full senses returned—reported what he knew.

Peyton-Jones, at the age of twenty-four, was now in sole command and could not have faced a more desperate situation. The *Hipper*'s shells were still bursting round the ship, and she was steaming at twenty-eight knots out of control, turning in a tight circle and heeling 20° to port. Flames were licking up from just in front of the bridge and every instrument —including the compass—had been smashed.

He scrambled forward across what was now only a crater of scorched and tortured metal to get the *Achates* under control again. A hole torn in the deck by the shell led to the wheel-house and served as a voicepipe. He shouted an order down to the coxswain, Hall, and a few seconds later heard Hall's reassuring voice saying the wheel was now amidships. Hall was the only man left alive in the wheelhouse; the bodies of the telegraphmen were left lying beside their shattered instruments.

Then Peyton-Jones, with Taylor's help, tried to sort out the tactical situation while still dodging the *Hipper*'s shells.

'I knew only what little I had gleaned from my occasional visits to the bridge to report on the progress of affairs between decks,' he wrote, 'and the present situation was somewhat obscure. Certainly the convoy was still there with its close corvette and trawler escort.

'From the Yeoman's report on the exchange of signals with the *Obedient* it was apparent that she had now taken over as Senior Officer in place of the presumably damaged *Onslow*, which had been sent to the disengaged side of the convoy. It was equally apparent that we were in no state to take anyone under our orders, and until we had our own situation under control it seemed best to stay where we were and make the only effective contribution to the defence of the convoy of which we were capable—laying smoke.

'Orders were accordingly passed by word of mouth to the engine-room to recommence making smoke and as the black clouds started rolling out of the funnel the ship was conned on a broad weave across the stern of the convoy.'

But the *Hipper* had not yet finished: another salvo straddled the *Achates* and a direct hit burst in the seamen's bathroom on the port side. This put the TS out of action, killing most of its crew. It fractured the after-bulkhead of the now-flooded stokers' mess-deck, and hurled splinters through the ship's side abreast of the ERAs' and stoker POs' messes, flooding them, the torpedomen's mess-decks and the Low Power room. Lighting and power to the forward part of the ship were cut off.

Then a second salvo straddled, one shell bursting close along the port side and smashing large holes in the hull abreast of No. 2 Boiler-room. Water quickly spurted in and it had to be abandoned. Splinters also holed No. 1 Boiler-room, but the steam ejector managed to keep down the flooding.

The ship's immediate future gave little cause for hope: forty men had been killed and many more wounded. The ship had a 15° list to port and it was increasing; she was down by the head with more water pouring in every moment.

While Peyton-Jones, with the help of Hall and Taylor, was getting the ship under control again, the ominous fire on B gun deck, where cordite charges had been set ablaze by the shell exploding on the front of the bridge, seemed to be spreading. A group of ratings started tackling it, helped by spray flying over the foredeck, and managed to put it out. Sub-lt Davidson, whose cheerful face had appeared apparently from nowhere, then collected men together to replace the B gun's crew, most of whom had been killed, so that they could fire back at the *Hipper*. But the gun mounting had jammed. At the same time a messenger was sent back aft to tell Y gun to open fire, but he was killed on the way—probably by splinters from a near miss —and they never received the order.

Mercifully the *Hipper* finally stopped firing and Peyton-Jones was able to send word to the engine-room to reduce speed to twelve knots and ease the strain on the damaged hull.

Steering became more difficult as the ship slowly increased her list to port and trimmed even more down by the head. A compass was brought up from one of the boats and wedged in the wrecked forward bulkhead of the wheelhouse. The bearings it gave were obviously inaccurate but better than nothing at all.

While this was being done Peter Wright, the engineer, appeared on the shattered bridge to report. The news was hardly cheering to a man who had been in command for only a few minutes: in addition to the flooding of No. 2 Boiler-room, more of the lower-deck compartments were filling up. In addition

211

MacFarlane, the doctor, must have been killed : he could not be found anywhere.

The task of tending the wounded now fell on men like Able Seaman Platt, who had already been knocked down once by blast from a shell and soaked by seas sweeping over the fo'c'sle, Drummond, and Allan Jones. They were joined by Supply PO James Cole, who had been working on the Plot until the bridge was hit. Although badly shaken, he immediately started giving his wounded shipmates first aid.

All over the ship men were, merely by carrying out their duties, performing acts of gallantry. It was yet to cost many of them their lives. There was, for instance, Stoker PO Robert Bell, who was in charge of No. 2 Boiler-room. When the near miss brought water flooding in, he rallied his men, maintained steam pressure in the boiler as long as he could, and tried to plug the holes. All the lights went out, but Bell struggled on in the icy water—which rapidly rose up to his waist—until ordered to abandon the compartment.

Able Seaman McIver first dragged wounded shipmates out of a rapidly-flooding compartment and then made several journeys along the upper deck despite the rain of splinters from near misses. Then, after the bridge and wheelhouse were hit, he went up and later relieved the wounded Hall at the wheel.

PO Telegraphist William Bartrip, who was in charge of the W/T department, struggled without lights to repair his damaged transmitter and receivers. At the same time Telegraphist Eric Dickenson—who fortunately was to survive—started to rig jury aerials to replace those shot away. He was knocked down by blast from one of *Hipper*'s shells before he finally managed to finish the job.

As the work of trying to keep the *Achates* afloat went on with desperate urgency on the shattered decks below, Peyton-Jones patiently conned the ship round, shouting his helm orders through the hole in the deck, on to a course parallel with the convoy.

.   .   .   .   .

The *Hipper*, after leaving the *Achates*, then turned to starboard, as if to steer across the stern of the convoy, and opened fire on the *Obedient*. Kinloch promptly ordered the destroyers to turn in succession to starboard to a parallel course. At 1122 the *Hipper* was steering 305° and at a range of just over four miles the *Obedient*, *Obdurate* and *Orwell* opened fire.

Meanwhile Captain Melhuish, the Commodore, standing on the monkey island of the *Empire Archer* with his Yeoman, Matthews, was warned that the *Hipper* was on the port quarter and he ordered an emergency turn from south-east to south, thus putting the enemy astern.

Once again Matthews yelled down to Madley, the Leading Seaman in the wheelhouse standing by the switches. On came the green and red lights for a 45° turn to starboard. At another yell from Matthews he switched them out, and the merchantmen began to make their fifth emergency turn in good order.

The *Hipper* had been firing at the three destroyers—concentrating on *Obedient*—for six minutes when suddenly the *Obedient* was straddled and splinters from the shells cut away her wireless aerials. Until the jury aerials were rigged an exasperated Kinloch could communicate with the other destroyers only by light, so he decided to turn over command of the escort temporarily to Sclater, in the *Obdurate*. The signal *Take charge of destroyers* was made at 1139.

When the *Hipper* finally drew away to the westward at thirty-one knots the three British destroyers turned and put down a smoke-screen to help cover the convoy.

In fact Kummetz had turned away because he had become worried about the possibility of the three destroyers making a torpedo attack. As he did so he signalled to the *Lützow*: *In action with escorting force. No cruiser with the convoy.* The signal was timed 1136.

Within a few moments twenty-four shells suddenly exploded round the *Hipper*. Force R had arrived.[1]

---

[1] Kummetz's signal, timed 1136, was obviously sent before Force R opened fire. *Hipper*'s log says they opened fire at 1139, while *Sheffield* and *Jamaica* gave the time as 1130.

18

Shoot . . . Shoot . . . Shoot!

A{\scriptsize T} 0830 that morning, when the *Obdurate* had sighted the destroyers astern of the convoy, Admiral Burnett with Force R was steaming north-west across what he thought was the convoy's wake. A quarter of an hour later, when *Obdurate* had been ordered to investigate the destroyers, Admiral Burnett thought he was ten miles north of the convoy's track and about thirty miles astern of it, a good position, as explained earlier, from which he could intercept any enemy warships approaching the convoy to attack it from astern. Unfortunately, as we have already seen, his plan was upset by the convoy being well south of its proper track and behind schedule, so Admiral Burnett was about thirty miles due north of it.

It was still dark to the north but lighter to the south. The temperature was 16° below freezing and, except for the guns and radar, the two cruisers *Sheffield* and *Jamaica* were well iced up.

Both Admiral Burnett and Captain Clarke, who commanded the *Sheffield*, were on the bridge. The Admiral was a stocky man, always cheerful, with a ready and hearty laugh. The ratings liked him and regarded him as lucky—in contrast to his predecessor, Rear-admiral S. S. Bonham Carter, who had been flying his flag in the cruiser *Edinburgh* with convoy PQ 15 when she was torpedoed and sunk, and had transferred to the *Trinidad*. Within a fortnight she too was sunk. This unfortunate coincidence was too much for the sailors, who from then on referred respectfully to their life-jackets as their 'Bonhams'.

Because Admiral Burnett was quiet and calm on the bridge, never interfering or fussing, he was also popular with the officers. With a natural and almost boyish approach to physical

214

training and games, particularly golf and tennis, he liked a glass of wine, and was good company. Having flown his flag in the cruiser *Scylla* when with sixteen destroyers—the 'fighting destroyer escort'—he covered PQ 18, he was no stranger to Arctic conditions.

Captain Clarke was a different type of man: slim, thin-faced, with a great store of nervous energy. He was confident and proud of his ship's company. By this stage of the war roughly 60 per cent of the officers and ratings in the ship were 'Hostilities Only'. These men who only a short time before had been civilians had blended with the ship's company with astonishing rapidity, and there was no discernible effect—even in the judgment of the sternest of senior officers—upon the day-to-day fighting efficiency of the ship.

'I believe this can be attributed mainly to the existing atmosphere in warships which were so frequently involved in alarms and excursions,' Captain Clarke wrote later. 'The influence of those who had been in the ship for a longer period and were more "salted" gave confidence to the newcomers.'

The *Sheffield* had been in a wide range of operations since the beginning of the war: apart from a few short periods in dockyard hands she had been actively at sea since September 1939. She had been engaged in the Norwegian operations, taken a notable part in the *Bismarck* chase, helped fight convoys through to Malta, been shot at from every direction during the North Africa landings, and was now getting to know the Arctic quite well. All these things married up to produce a tough and resilient ship's company. Even though a large proportion of the men had not experienced all those operations, they unconsciously absorbed the atmosphere from those who had.

The effect was to produce a confident, efficient, philosophical and cheerfully grumbling crew. The same went for the *Jamaica*, now following close astern of the *Sheffield*. It is worth noting that it was just this sort of experience and confidence that the officers and men of the German Navy, from admirals to junior ratings, lacked so completely.

.   .   .   .   .

At 0858, Able Seaman George Parkinson and Ordinary Seaman John Moore, the *Sheffield*'s surface radar operators, picked up an echo seven-and-a-half miles away to the north-west. Immediately this was passed to the *Jamaica* and both ships went to Action Stations.

On the bridge with Admiral Burnett and Captain Clarke was the *Sheffield*'s Navigator, Lt Cdr Eric Back, who would actually handle the ship in action, while up in the Director Control Tower (DCT) Lt Cdr Orford Cameron ordered the thickly-greased millboard discs covering the muzzles of the guns to be removed.

Down below in magazines and shell-rooms supply parties loaded the cordite hoists to the guns with flashless charges and the shell hoists with CPBC[1] fused so that the left and right guns in each turret would fire shells set to delay and the central guns non-delay. The centre guns of B and X turrets would also fire night tracer so that they could easily be seen in flight. (In the *Jamaica* eight of the twelve guns were to fire night tracer to distinguish her fall of shot from the *Sheffield*'s.)

Each shell weighed 112 lb and the charges, cordite in silk bags, 30 lb. The Gunnery Control was similar to that in the destroyers except that it had many refinements, and in the TS the more complicated Admiralty Fire Control Table was used instead of the Admiralty Fire Control Clock.

In the *Jamaica*, Captain Jocelyn Storey already had his orders and knew what to do in a surface action: he would keep the *Jamaica* conforming with the *Sheffield*'s movements and following about five cables (half a mile) astern. On the bridge with him was his navigator, Lt Cdr Hugh Moore, who would be watching the compass and the outline of the *Sheffield*, making sure the ship kept her station. In the DCT Lt Cdr John Scotland went through the routines for preparing his twelve 6-inch guns for action.

Look-out bearings were passed in both ships, and each DCT swung round on to it, followed by the guns.

[1] Common Pointed Ballistic Capped: the then latest 6-inch armour piercing shell. The 'Ballistic Cap' was a light steel nose fitted on the shell to streamline it and so increase the range for a given charge.

Meanwhile more radar reports were coming in. There were in fact two echoes, one large and one small, steering eastwards. The immediate reaction was that the size of the echoes ruled out the possibility of them being U-boats, and since it was thought the convoy would be a good deal farther ahead of the echoes, they must be either stragglers (perhaps a merchant ship and an escort) or, more ominously, enemy surface ships.

Further information arrived on the bridge: the echoes were steering 090° and were apparently making twenty-five knots—a great deal faster than a merchantman.

'As this contact appeared to have possibilities,' Admiral Burnett wrote, 'I at first hauled away to the south-east and then closed in order to track and establish touch.'

At 0904, as the cruisers turned away in answer to the Admiral's orders, a blurred object was seen on the bearing. The Directors and guns of both ships trained on to it, and it was held by ordering spotting corrections and adjusting the 'enemy speed' settings in the TS.

But very soon it became clear that the two ships held by

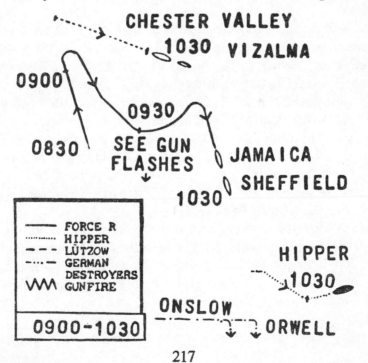

the radar were doing only ten knots, not twenty-five. Burnett decided to carry on steaming south-eastwards and continue to track them by radar.

For half an hour nothing happened: the strange ships continued steaming eastwards without any alteration of course and speed. The ranges and bearings were plotted on the chart and their tracks drawn in, but it did not provide any clue as to their identity; only that they were following what should have been the convoy's track.

Then, at 0932, the reflection from gun flashes was sighted in the sky to the southward. Burnett wrote later that he thought it was high-angle fire, 'probably at Russian aircraft'. He continued: 'As I was not satisfied with the innocence of the original radar contact I continued to track it.' He altered course northeastwards to close on a converging course.

In fact, although he was not to know it, the ships to the north which he was tracking were the *Chester Valley*, still being shepherded by the little trawler *Vizalma*. The shooting to the south was from the three German destroyers firing at the *Obdurate*.

The Admiral was in a perplexing situation. He did not know the actual position of the convoy, whose safety was his primary objective, and which he supposed was to the east. Past experience had taught him that stragglers were to be expected after heavy gales; and the brief gunfire seen to the south could have come from one or more detached escorts.

Fourteen minutes later, at 0946, the reflection from obviously heavy gunfire was seen in the southern sky. This was the *Hipper* opening fire on the *Achates*.[1] Almost at the same time Captain Sherbrooke's enemy report of three destroyers was received and relayed to the *Sheffield*'s bridge.

The Admiral, however, was still far from happy about the actual position of the convoy, and although he suspected by now that it might be well south of its estimated position, he held on for some minutes, still steering north-east. Then at 0955—after reading the enemy report and while the *Onslow*

---

[1] The time is from Admiral Burnett's report: the *Onslow* and *Obedient* gave it as 0941, and the *Hipper* as 0944.

and *Orwell* were making their feint torpedo attacks on the *Hipper*—'I hauled round to 170°, increased speed to twenty-five knots and steamed towards the sight of the guns. It was by this time presumed that the original contacts were stragglers from the convoy, the convoy itself apparently being much to the southward of its route.'

If one wanted to pass judgment on Admiral Burnett's decisions one can argue that the *Sheffield* and *Jamaica* could have intervened in the action earlier had Admiral Burnett at once applied the fundamental principles of British fighting policy 'When in doubt steer for the sound of the guns', and 'The unfailing support given in battle by one British unit to another'.

On the other hand, one can perhaps argue more strongly that the 'safe and timely arrival' of the convoy was his main task, and the convoy was still not located.

Captain Clarke later wrote: 'From the apparent distance away of the gunfire, and the convoy's position as signalled, it seemed we had forty or fifty miles to go. The best part of an hour and a half—time in which the enemy were free to do more or less what they pleased. Not a comforting thought. Again, who were the enemy? All the chances were that the units at Altenfiord had come to sea in full strength. As far as we knew that might mean the pocket battleship *Lützow*, the heavy cruiser *Hipper*, the 6-inch cruiser *Nürnberg*, and as much as a flotilla of destroyers; not to mention tactical co-operation from previously disposed U-boats.

'To hold the ring on our side were by then only five destroyers, two corvettes and one trawler with the convoy, and ultimately to drive off the enemy there were just the *Sheffield* and the *Jamaica*—two 6-inch cruisers.

'As we drove south it seemed to me a strange unnatural calm settled down upon us all. I had, over the ship's broadcasting system, described to the ship's company the situation as it appeared to us on the bridge, and there was little or nothing to do in the material sense.

'Communications were checked and re-checked; gun mountings were trained from side to side to ensure there was no interference from the considerable ice which still lay over the exposed parts of the ship. Chief Yeoman of Signals Fuller remembered to hoist our silk Battle Ensign (a gift from the city of Sheffield); the doctors laid out the tools of their trade; and away in every corner of the ship, many isolated and alone under firmly-clipped hatches, men watched their dials and instruments—and waited.

'What goes on in the minds of those inevitably committed to battle and, moreover, battle against superior strength? Each one who has experienced this will in detail probably answer differently, but perhaps each will admit one thing. He is afraid: not of the enemy, but of fear itself.

'For myself there was first that familiar sinking feeling in the pit of the stomach, followed by a kind of icy detachment in which my thoughts rushed on me: now was the real moment when I must forget nothing I had ever learnt. One personal lapse, one professional mistake, one omission, one error of judgment and I would fail the others. All this became the more emphatic when I glanced around me.

'There was the Admiral, looking just the same as usual. He'd been under fire before, too. It didn't worry him. We all knew his reputation. It would not be he who made the mistakes. My officers, trustworthy and experienced; there wouldn't be failures there. The men, hardened and salted by training and sea time; each would, I felt certain, be a credit to the ship. And on the port quarter, her bow wave foaming dimly in the darkness, the *Jamaica*—in perfect station. "Remember your next astern." I trusted I wouldn't forget that one. Her captain and I had joined the Naval College together thirty-two years ago. We knew each other well. That helped, too.

'The next half-hour seemed to pass very quickly. At intervals there were more gun flashes ahead, getting nearer all the time. No one seemed to notice the intense cold. Early in the turn south the Admiral had wirelessed our approach course, partly as an encouragement to the lonely convoy escort, and partly to help identification should we contact our friends first. There would be only a few hours of dim twilight, and telling friend from foe at any time in the confusion of the circumstances we were likely to meet would not be simple.

'Our object was clear—the safe arrival of the maximum number of ships of the convoy now under attack and, if at all possible, the continued undetected advance of the homeward-bound convoy (RA 51, which had sailed from Murmansk the day before) now to the eastward of the battle area. This would be achieved if the enemy could be sunk or driven to abandon their operation, preferably the former.

'It must, however, be admitted our forces were woefully inadequate for the purpose. To redress the adverse balance we *might* achieve surprise; fortuitously such light as there would be in the early stages would be behind the enemy and not us; we had trained in end-on firing which would allow us to present a minimum target to the enemy's superior weight of fire. Finally there was no reason why the enemy should know we were unsupported.'

Both cruisers were now doing thirty-one knots—almost their maximum speed under ideal conditions. Fuel oil was being consumed at a fantastic rate—each ship was burning thirty tons an hour, turning water into the super-heated steam needed by the turbines to develop 75,000 h.p. The oil, after passing through heating tanks to reduce its viscosity so that it would be atomized easily, was being pumped through half-inch pipes to each of the eight furnaces, and then forced out through nine sprayers which whirled like the familiar devices for watering cricket pitches. Air was being sucked in by fans eight feet in diameter to mix with the oil in the correct proportion to make sure it burned without making smoke. This was turning water into steam at 700° Fahrenheit—three times the temperature of boiling water—before being fed into the turbines. The noise was almost as much as the human mind could stand; speech was impossible.

On the bridge of each ship it was bitterly cold: the forward speed created a strong wind so that for the men it was similar to standing up in an open car driving at thirty miles an hour on one of the coldest days of an English winter. From where Admiral Burnett and Captain Clarke stood on the forward side of the bridge, behind armour-plate glass wind-screens, the bows seemed very near. Fine spray was flying up from the sharp stem and blowing back over the deck, freezing and adding more to the ice already there.

Ceaselessly the operators at the surface radar set cranked their aerials this way and that, searching for echoes. At the same time in the Director Control Tower the Gunnery Officer and his crew scanned the horizon to the south with binoculars. This was probably the coldest Action Station in the ship as the wind howled in through the open sighting ports, frosting binoculars and freezing the men who had to sit over their instruments, unable to move to restore their circulation. The range-finder, sticking out on each side below, was out of action even before the battle, because spray had frozen solid on the windows. Everything would have to depend on the accuracy of the radar ranges when the time came to open fire, and one could only hope the enemy was having similar difficulties.

By 1020 Admiral Burnett could make out what seemed, from the gun flashes, to be two separate actions being fought out several miles to the south of him. One was almost dead ahead, the other on port bow. The horizon was certainly lighter in that direction, but only comparatively so. He could see smoke lying low over the sea, like menacing banks of black fog, hiding both friend and foe. Behind it—and probably in it, too— Sherbrooke and his destroyer team were fighting for the life of the convoy. Had the enemy got among the merchantmen yet? With the tiny escort, it would not be Sherbrooke's fault if they had.

Now, Burnett knew, everything depended on him. But he could not go steaming at full speed into the midst of the smoke without positively identifying the targets; he might intervene from one direction while the main threat came from the other. And, just as admirals and captains of earlier centuries had to try to keep the weather gage so, in the darkness, he had to keep the light gage, attacking from the darker sector an enemy silhouetted against the lighter southern sky. In that way he might be able to make up for the comparative weakness of his own cruisers by surprising the enemy, perhaps delivering a knock-out blow before they had time to recover. The great thing was to avoid steaming into the fray like a bewildered and angry bull dashing through the gate into the arena, not knowing where the picadors and matador were waiting for him.

At 1030 the invisible, probing radar waves from the *Sheffield* bounced back to the receiving aerials from a large ship ahead. The operator read the range off the scale on the cathode-ray tube and passed it to the bridge. It was ten miles away.

This was called 'Target A' in the *Sheffield*, and two minutes

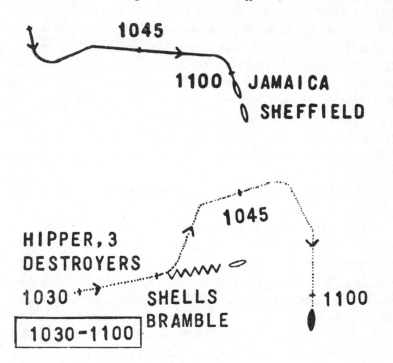

later the radar picked up another big ship more than fifteen miles away on the port bow. This was called 'Target B'.

The ranges and bearings were plotted as soon as they came in from the radar operators, and the Plot showed that Target A was steering fast to the east, across the *Sheffield*'s bow, while Target B was steaming to the north-east on a closing course. However, the radar could not yet pick up any other ships round these two, so Burnett had no idea where the convoy, Sherbrooke's destroyers or the enemy destroyers were.

But the *Sheffield* and *Jamaica* were approaching the enemy at a rate of a mile every two minutes, and if Burnett kept on the present southerly course the enemy would draw to the eastward and would not be silhouetted against the lighter sky if and when they came in sight. In addition the banks of smoke merging into the half-light, and the gun flashes flickering here and there combined to present a very confused picture, so Burnett ordered the two cruisers to turn to port on to a course parallel with Target A, thus retaining the light gage and keeping the range steady for the present. The time was 1035. (The *Hipper* was firing at the *Bramble* between 1036 and 1042.)

Target A was seen from the *Sheffield*'s bridge for a few moments and although they could not identify the ship she was larger than a destroyer and therefore enemy. (She was in fact the *Hipper*.) Radar showed her altering course to starboard at 1054, steering southward away from Force R, so Burnett turned to starboard to conform. Radar then reported that there were two smaller ships in company, and they were presumed to be German destroyers.

For nearly a quarter of an hour the British cruisers followed southwards. They saw Target A (*Hipper*) firing to the eastwards —the two tracer shells in the salvos could clearly be seen from the *Sheffield* and the high trajectory showed her target was some distance away. The enemy was not using flashless cordite and was firing fast—roughly seven salvos a minute. At 1112 Admiral Burnett altered course to 190°, directly towards Target A, the *Hipper*.

The over-all position at this time was that the *Sheffield* and *Jamaica* from the north were watching the *Hipper* steaming down towards the convoy, firing to the eastward at what she claimed were destroyers, but which were certainly not British. Target B picked up by the *Sheffield*'s radar was probably the *Lützow* which earlier had been beyond the convoy and steering across its bows, but was now steaming on its port side, waiting hopefully for the weather to clear. Kinloch with the *Obedient*, *Obdurate* and *Orwell*, was manœuvring between the *Lützow* and the merchantmen.

As Burnett turned directly towards the unsuspecting *Hipper* she shifted her fire to the *Achates*. She could now be seen from the *Sheffield* and *Jamaica*, a dark blur against the black smoke

224

lying across the horizon to the south, but she was end-on and still could not be identified.

When at 1128 the *Hipper* swung round to starboard and opened fire on the *Obedient* she placed herself broadside on to the British cruisers, who immediately identified her.

Now was the moment for Force R to strike, and Burnett acted promptly. He ordered the *Sheffield* to come round to starboard,

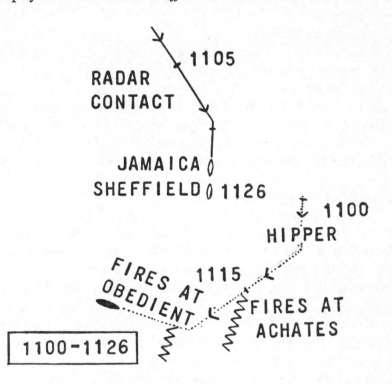

and the *Jamaica* followed her round. A few moments earlier Cameron, the *Sheffield*'s Gunnery Officer, had reported to Captain Clarke that he would be able to spot the fall of shot.

All the information being fed into the TS by the Director and the radar—range 16,900 yards (eight miles), enemy course 270°, speed thirty knots—was combined with details of *Sheffield*'s own course and speed; the Layer and Trainer at the Director sight had their crosswires sighted on the base of the enemy's foremast.

At the order 'Broadsides' from Cameron in the *Sheffield*

and Scotland in the *Jamaica*, shells and charges had been rammed home, breeches had been closed, followed by the interceptors. These latter completed the firing circuit and lit up the twelve gun-ready lamps in front of each of the gunnery officers.

On the *Sheffield*'s bridge Captain Clarke, watching the enemy and the range dial, spoke to Admiral Burnett: 'Permission to open fire, sir.'

Burnett nodded.

Clarke bent over the voicepipe to the DCT: 'Open fire!'

Cameron spoke into his microphone: 'Shoot!'

The fire gong sounded its 'ting ting' and the Director Layer, his left hand automatically spinning his elevating hand-wheel, squeezed the trigger with his right hand, and the electric circuits to the guns were completed. Twelve 112-lb shells from A, B, X and Y turrets sped towards the *Hipper* at 2,000 miles an hour—nearly three times the speed of sound. The time was thirty seconds after 1130.

A few moments later the *Jamaica* opened fire.

As the salvos thundered out each gun, weighing six-and-three-quarter tons, was flung back by the tremendous power of the cordite, stopped after exactly $30\frac{1}{2}$ inches by the recoil cylinder, and then thrust back into position by the run-out springs.

More shells and charges came up the hoists, the breech-workers flung open the breech and a blast of hot air automatically cleared the cordite chamber of any burning residue. A soaking wet rammer—better known as a 'woolly-'eaded bastard'—was thrust in to clean it, another shell was then rammed home, and a charge followed. The tube was changed; the breech and interceptor were closed.

One by one the gun-ready lamps flickered on again in the DCTs in front of Cameron and Scotland. The Director Trainers and Layers were still tracking the *Hipper*; the spotting officers were still waiting for the first shells to fall.

The gunnery radar operator suddenly reported in *Sheffield* that he could see on his set their own salvos going through the air.

'Shoot!' Cameron said once again. 'Shoot!' repeated Scotland. The time was exactly 1131.

They both watched their first salvos. The tracer shells described the familiar and seemingly leisurely arcs towards the *Hipper*. At last they were shooting at a really substantial target, and it seemed, as always, rather unreal.

The *Sheffield*'s first salvo was not seen to fall—it was probably

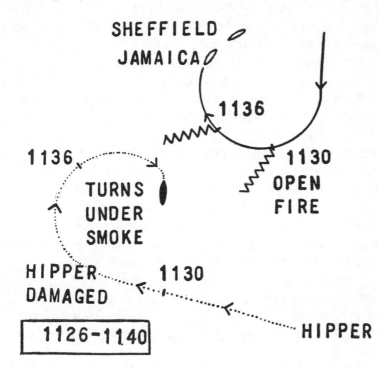

SHEFFIELD
JAMAICA
1136
1136
TURNS
UNDER
SMOKE
1130
OPEN
FIRE
HIPPER
DAMAGED
1130
1126-1140
HIPPER

over, hidden by the *Hipper*'s bulk. The second was also over; the third was to the right, the fourth hidden by the *Hipper*'s cordite smoke and the fifth accurate. At least one shell landed between the funnel and the mainmast, exploding six- to nine-millionths of a second after hitting. The dull red glow could be seen from the *Sheffield*'s bridge. *Jamaica*'s first three salvos missed, but at least one shell from each of her fourth, fifth and sixth hit the enemy. Both ships were firing at intervals of less than twenty seconds.

Burnett achieved complete surprise with his attack: the *Hipper*'s 8-inch turrets were all trained round to port, firing at the *Obedient*, and the *Sheffield* and *Jamaica* had fired more than four salvos before she could train them round.

The extent of the surprise aboard the *Hipper* is shown by these eloquent extracts from her log:

'Enemy approached at high speed. Six falls of shot lay close to the ship. Enemy could not be identified. He was taken for a destroyer. Observation conditions against the northern horizon are worse than those against the southern horizon. On top of this the Admiral's [Kummetz's] bridge was affected by blast and dazzle from our own guns.

'1133: *Hipper* was hit on the starboard side in Section VIII. No. 3 boiler gradually filled with oil and water and had to be shut off and abandoned. With it the starboard turbine stopped and maximum speed was decreased to twenty-three knots.

'1134: *Hipper* fired a single salvo from main armament at the enemy to starboard and then turned to starboard.

'1137: *Hipper* received two hits on the port side. Fire broke out in the aircraft hangar.'

As the *Hipper* started coming round to starboard towards Force R, the destroyers with her began to lay a smoke-screen.

Admiral Burnett immediately turned to starboard as well at a range of four miles, keeping step in a deadly minuet. It was difficult for him to know exactly what the *Hipper* intended to do now; but whatever it was, the range was quite close enough and by conforming to the *Hipper*'s movements he stood a better chance of keeping all his guns bearing and the enemy silhouetted.

To the Admiralty, Burnett signalled: *Am engaging enemy.*

With the range down to four miles the British cruisers' 6-inch guns were getting a chance of doing some damage to the *Hipper*, and they waited for her to straighten up. But instead she came on round towards them and then, in the half-light, ran into the smoke laid by her destroyers and disappeared from sight.

What was she doing behind the smoke—continuing a full circle to steam off in the direction she came? Or would she try to escape to the east, south or west? Indeed was she *trying* to escape?

Burnett decided she was going round in a complete circle and told Captain Clarke to bring the *Sheffield* round as well. But she had only completed three-quarters of the circle when a low dark object was seen on the port bow. It could only be a destroyer, but enemy or friendly?

If enemy, it was in a perfect position to fire torpedoes into the *Sheffield*.

Admiral Burnett immediately ordered the *Sheffield* to steer towards, to comb any possible torpedo tracks.

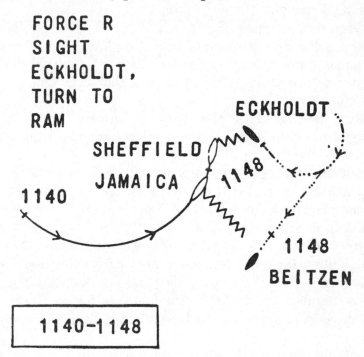

FORCE R
SIGHT
ECKHOLDT,
TURN TO
RAM

ECKHOLDT

SHEFFIELD

JAMAICA

1140

1148

1148

BEITZEN

1140-1148

By that time the gunnery officers of both *Sheffield* and *Jamaica* had caught sight of the *Hipper* again and fired nine salvos before they were warned of a destroyer right ahead.

As the *Sheffield*, doing more than thirty knots, followed by the *Jamaica*, steadied on a course heading directly for the destroyer everyone on the bridge strained his eyes to try to identify her.

'Think she's got two funnels. . . .'

'The *Onslow*s have only one.'

'Yes—two funnels!'

229

'Don't think she's one of ours,' declared the Yeoman. 'Funnels too far apart.'

'On and ready to fire!' reported Cameron from the DCT.

'Make the battle challenge,' ordered Captain Clarke.

A special pattern of coloured lights, which were changed daily, were switched on.

Everyone on the bridge waited for the pre-arranged reply.

From the bridge of the destroyer three white lights came on, forming a triangle. The wrong answer. . . .

'Open fire,' snapped Clarke.

'Shoot!' said Cameron into his microphone.

The six guns of the two forward turrets thundered out, the shells' trajectory being almost flat since the target was less than two miles away.

'Ram the blighter, Nobby', growled Burnett.

Captain Clarke brought the *Sheffield* round on to a converging course.

Suddenly, through their binoculars, they saw sparks as shells smashed into the enemy destroyer, followed a few millionths of a second later by the orange glow of detonation. Fires broke out.

A second salvo roared from the forward turret and burst short; Cameron ordered 'Up 400' and the third salvo was fired. Spurts of angry red flame showed several more shells exploding on the destroyer; the forward funnel burst into flames, another fire started on the quarter-deck.

'Put your helm over,' said Burnett. 'No need to buckle our bows now.'

Eighteen seconds later the fourth salvo—fired at a range of only just over a mile—smashed into the enemy, followed by the fifth and sixth. By the seventh the enemy, the *Friedrich Eckholdt*, was almost completely smothered in smoke and flame, and the *Sheffield* was turning to port to avoid ramming. Fixed sight procedure was used for the next three salvos. 'As we swept down on the target she was disintegrating before our eyes,' Captain Clarke wrote later.

The shattered *Eckholdt* was passing so close now that first the two twin 4-inch anti-aircraft guns opened up from the starboard side, followed by the rhythmic and rapid tom-tom beat of the multiple pom-poms. A and B turrets forward trained round and then finally ceased firing, brought up by safety stops so that blast should not damage their own ship. By this time the *Eckholdt* was down by the stern and almost completely on fire. Then X and Y turrets aft trained round forward as the enemy came into their arc, and, using radar ranges with the flames as the point of aim, fired five more salvos.

The 6-inch, 4-inch and pom-poms were all hitting the *Eckholdt* hard; she was so overwhelmed that she had no chance to use torpedoes or train her turrets. As the *Jamaica* steamed past her yellow and green pyrotechnics were soaring up into the sky from the nest of flames which were gradually being dowsed as the ship sank low in the water.

The *Jamaica* had been abused by various people in the *Sheffield* a few seconds earlier for shooting away from the *Eckholdt*, but as they passed the sinking ship they saw why: there had been a second destroyer (the *Richard Beitzen*) astern of the *Eckholt* and, seeing that the *Sheffield*'s opening salvos did so much damage to the leading ship, Scotland in the *Jamaica* had fired at the potentially more dangerous second one. She had, however, turned sharply to port under smoke and escaped into the murk to the south-west.

The *Sheffield*'s fire gives some indication of the damage which a cruiser, if she is handled in a determined manner, can do to a destroyer.

After turning to starboard towards the two British cruisers Kummetz in the *Hipper*—still under the impression he had been attacked by a destroyer—hid in the smoke-screen. When he emerged a few minutes later and was engaged by the *Sheffield* and *Jamaica* (before they tackled the *Eckholdt*) he thought this was another force. He wrote:

'A fresh opponent now appeared, of a type not easily distinguished, firing at *Hipper* from the north. She appeared from the way in which she fired to be a cruiser.

'I thus found myself between an enemy cruiser and the convoy's destroyers standing to the south.

231

'I had to extract myself from this unfavourable tactical position; in addition to which the survey of the situation as a whole had become more difficult owing to the waning light.[1]

'To attack to the.south, thus drawing away from the cruiser and nearer the convoy, was out of the question, given the uncertain condition of *Hipper*. Furthermore I could not release the destroyers to operate on their own, as they were standing by *Hipper*. I therefore decided to withdraw all ships from the scene of the action to the westward.'

This message was sent from the *Hipper* by radio-telephone at 1137, addressed to all ships in the force: *Break off action and retire to the west.*

At this time the German destroyer *Friedrich Eckholdt*, commanded by the Senior Officer, 5th Destroyer Flotilla and followed by the *Richard Beitzen*, was steaming north-west, after having been detached to sink the *Bramble*, looking for the *Hipper*.

Sighting the two ships ahead the *Eckholdt*'s captain spoke by radio-telephone to the *Hipper*:

'Cruiser and destroyer in sight bearing 300°. Is it you?'

The *Hipper* did not reply immediately and he asked another question, since seconds were vital:

'On what bearing are you in relation to the convoy?'

'Am north of the convoy,' replied *Hipper*.

Almost immediately the *Eckholdt*'s captain saw the ships ahead open fire on him. The *Hipper* has made a mistake, he must have thought, and yelled into his radio-telephone:

'You are firing at me!'

A fraction of a second later the captain of the *Richard Beitzen*, just astern, realized the *Eckholdt*'s mistake and exclaimed over the R/T: 'No! It is a British cruiser!'

But, as already described, the warning was too late. The *Eckholdt* was badly hit almost immediately—the price she had to pay for mistaking two British cruisers for the *Hipper* and a destroyer—while the *Beitzen* managed to escape.

The *Hipper* kept calling up the *Eckholdt*, but there was no reply.

[1] In addition to the waning light, areas of funnel smoke, patches of mist and snow flurries added to the difficulties for both sides.

Four minutes later, and twelve minutes after his original retirement signal, Admiral Kummetz again signalled to his force: *Break off engagement and retire to the westward.*

As *Lützow* signalled to him *I am closing you*, Kummetz described the situation in the log as follows: 'At this point *Eckholdt*'s condition was uncertain. W/T contact had failed and her accurate position was unknown. She was last seen at about 1115 from the Admiral's bridge while attempting to sink the British corvette or destroyer (the *Bramble*).

'Later a fire was seen in the direction in which she was last sighted. It is possible that by this time she was beyond all aid. I could no longer obtain a general picture of the scene. I could not clear up this situation, nor could I send in the destroyers to help the *Eckholdt* as I needed them to protect our own ships, and had to reckon with the risks they would run.'

Kummetz also commented: '*Hipper* has received a hit which might have far-reaching effects. The aircraft hangar is on fire. The fire is being got under control and one hit appears to have gone into the boiler-room which is evident from the thick black smoke which comes out of the funnel and air vents, obscuring all vision aft.'

With the *Hipper* steaming away to the westwards as fast as she was able in her damaged condition, Admiral Burnett, having disposed of the *Friedrich Eckholdt*, had also turned west to resume the battle. At 1200 (when the *Hipper*'s radar reported that only one radar beam could be detected astern, and its signal strength was decreasing) Burnett was about thirteen miles away on the *Hipper*'s starboard quarter. At 1202 he signalled to the Admiralty and Murmansk: *Enemy cruiser hit. Have lost touch. Enemy destroyer left sinking. . . .*

Seventeen minutes earlier, at 1145, Lt Herschleb, still on the scene in *U-354*, had sent a signal back to Admiral Klüber in Altenfiord which, after being forwarded to Hitler, was going to play its part in the destruction of Germany's surface fleet. It said: *According to our observation the battle has reached its climax. I see nothing but red.*

233

19

The *Lützow* Challenges

HEN the *Sheffield* and *Jamaica* made their surprise assault on the *Hipper* at 1130 she had, as mentioned earlier, just straddled the *Obedient*, shooting away her aerials, and David Kinloch had successfully driven her off.

As the three destroyers steamed south in the half-light to catch up with the convoy again it seemed possible to hope once more. *Hipper* had been last seen steering away to the westwards and then a few minutes later gun flashes showed she had run into some heavy opposition—obviously Force R. The convoy and escorts could apparently breathe a sigh of relief while the *Hipper* was tackled by something more of her own size.

Ahead of the convoy the *Onslow*, leaking badly, pumping and fighting fires, steamed on; the *Achates* was astern, still laying smoke and slowly sinking. On either quarter were the *Rhododendron* and *Northern Gem*, and the *Hyderabad* kept watch on the starboard beam.

In the *Onslow* Captain Sherbrooke was now under the effect of the morphia and apparently in no great pain. Beside his bunk, watching in the dim light of the hurricane lamp for signs of hæmorrhage, and passing on messages as they came down the voicepipe from the bridge, was his steward, Fraser, a young Scot from Lossiemouth. It was a harrowing time for him: apart from the fear that his captain might die—he certainly appeared to be terribly wounded, and there was no telling how deeply the piece of splinter was embedded between his eyes—there was the knowledge that the ship might yet sink, and the chance of surviving with such wounds in the icy water would be negligible.

However, few in either the convoy or the escorts had much time to relax and let the earlier tension escape: two minutes after they had seen Force R engage the *Hipper* they sighted more of the familiar red glows of gunfire over on the port quarter of the convoy, and a few seconds later the corresponding flashes as shells burst among the columns of merchant ships. The *Lützow*, hanging round to the eastwards, had now decided to rejoin the *Hipper*. In doing so she passed within nine miles of the convoy and opened fire.

Captain Mclhuish, the Commodore, again signalled an emergency turn to the convoy and together they came round from south to south-west, away from the *Lützow*. The shells

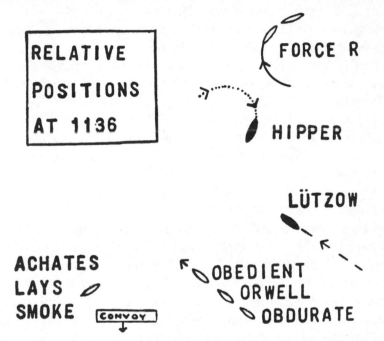

missed the merchantmen but before they were hidden by smoke they sustained the only damage inflicted by this vastly superior German force—the American ship *Calobre*, owned by the North Atlantic Transportation Company, and whose captain was the Vice-commodore of the convoy, was hit by a few splinters. No one was hurt.

Kinloch brought his three destroyers round to port, steering across the stern of the convoy, and laid more smoke to screen the merchantmen from the *Lützow* on their new course.

235

The *Lützow*'s log shows she first opened fire at the convoy with her six 11-inch guns, but almost at once a combination of the Director sight and range-finders icing-up and the muzzle-flash from A turret blinding the men in the forward Director forced them to stop.

The pocket battleship then opened up with her secondary armament (eight 5·9-inch), using ranges supplied by the radar. 'This,' the log noted gloomily, 'is not always accurate. No hits observed.'

It added: 'Two enemy destroyers (or corvettes?) in the convoy returned fire without success. Fall of their shot consistently short. One of our accompanying destroyers joined in the firing at first but then ceased fire.'

The British ships returning the fire were of course the three destroyers; and it is hardly surprising their 4-inch shells were falling short, since they were firing at extreme range.

Force R's attack on the *Friedrich Eckholdt* had not gone unobserved in the *Lützow*, and the log said: 'Towards noon a vessel was sighted to starboard, at a great distance, under heavy fire. After one hit extensive fires broke out. After a further period a mast-high pillar of flame was observed, whether a friend or foe was not then clear. . . .'

There was a somewhat ironical reference in the *Lützow*'s log to Admiral Kummetz's signal just before Force R took him by surprise. Against the time 1148 was written: 'Signal timed 1136 [received] from B. de K.: *In action with escorting force. No cruiser with the convoy.*' The log added, almost ruefully, 'From subsequent deliberation and the results of later observation, it transpires that there must have been cruisers with the convoy.'

The *Lützow* did not come any closer to the convoy; instead Captain Stange continued steering to the north-west and passed out of sight of the British destroyers. He intended to join the *Hipper*, then completing her circle after being attacked by the *Sheffield* and *Jamaica*.

However, the *Hipper*'s course, when she emerged from the smoke-screen, brought her across the stern of the convoy and when the *Obedient*, *Orwell* and *Obdurate* suddenly spotted her approaching from the darkness to the north, and only four miles away, they assumed it was the same ship they had just apparently beaten off, the *Lützow*, coming back to attack again.

Immediately Kinloch, Austen and Sclater altered course to port together without signals to fight off this new assault, and this put *Obdurate* at the head of the column. As they turned the *Hipper* altered away. Sclater, temporarily the Senior Officer, steadied on a similar course and the three destroyers opened fire. The *Hipper* replied almost immediately, aiming, as was her habit, at the leading ship. *Obdurate* was straddled and hit by splinters; but the bold tactics seemed to have worked once again, for the *Hipper* turned to the north-west, away from the convoy, and disappeared into the darkness.

As the merchantmen were now some distance off, the destroyers turned back towards them, staying to the north-west in case the *Hipper* should reappear on the scene. During this period they had received various signals from Admiral Burnett asking for information, and they had been relaying details of the enemy's course and speed, as well as the convoy position.

With the three destroyers coming back from this last attack by the *Hipper* just after noon, their share in the battle was over, although they did not know it. At 1223, nearly twenty minutes after they had turned away, they saw gunfire in the distance to the north and west. Sclater considered this to be Force R driving off the enemy, and signalled to Kinloch to this effect, saying he intended rejoining the convoy. Kinloch agreed.

At the same time Tom Marchant, in the *Onslow*, realizing that the convoy was now at least temporarily out of danger, signalled to the Commodore in the *Empire Archer*: *Action being fought out 010 degrees, 20 miles. Enemy cruiser hit. Enemy destroyer left sinking.*

The *Sheffield* and *Jamaica* now had various contacts on their radar screens to the south-west of them, steering the same course. One was obviously a large ship, and Admiral Burnett correctly estimated it was Target A, the *Hipper*, retiring to the westwards after her brush with the British destroyers.

Captain Clarke, describing this period later, wrote: 'Though both our cruisers turned to the westward immediately the local menace [the *Friedrich Eckholdt*] had been disposed of, the major enemy was already out of sight and it was not for another twenty minutes that we again located something large away ahead on the port bow, and at a range too great for effective fire. This one, at least, was apparently now set upon withdrawal but, on the basis of the general knowledge of the German forces in northern waters and what we had already seen, there were still other threats about.'

Neither he nor Admiral Burnett was left in doubt for long. Half an hour after the turn to the west—a period during which Eric Back, the *Sheffield*'s Navigator, managed to get three star sights with his sextant and thus fix the ship's position—lookouts sighted silhouettes on the port beam. The time was 1223.

They were almost certainly two destroyers steaming a parallel course. Were they friendly or enemy? If the latter they were in a fine position for a torpedo attack, and Burnett ordered the *Sheffield* to turn towards them. They were in fact escorting the *Lützow*.

A minute earlier the *Lützow* and her destroyers—which, as mentioned earlier, had been coming up from the south to join the *Hipper*, but had altered course to the westward in accordance with Kummetz's signal—had sighted the two cruisers and identified them as destroyers, probably German. A few moments later the officers on the *Lützow*'s bridge had doubts and ordered the *Lützow*'s recognition signal to be made.

At this point the *Lützow* herself had not been sighted from the *Sheffield*. She was directly in line with the two destroyers and when the *Lützow* signalled it was thought, in the near-darkness, to be from one of the destroyers.

The signalman in the *Lützow* flashed dot-dash-dot-dot three times.

In the *Sheffield* Fuller, the Yeoman, read it.

'Making LLL. Not our challenge.'

'Repeat it back,' ordered Captain Clarke.

This might fool the Germans for a few valuable moments while the two cruisers prepared to open fire.

By a mistake a further challenge was flashed from the *Lützow*

—the letter G, repeated three times. Captain Clarke, seeing the ruse seemed to be paying dividends, ordered it to be repeated back.

Clarke had, a few moments earlier, ordered Cameron, the Gunnery Officer, to open fire, giving the bearing of the enemy destroyers. However when the DCT, high above the bridge, came round on to this bearing, Cameron first saw a heavy ship. The Director Layer and Trainer quickly brought their crosswires on, radar ranges were passed to the TS, and the guns were loaded, trained and elevated. Cameron, for the 41st time in the action, ordered 'Shoot!' The time was 1229—six minutes after the silhouettes of the destroyers had first been sighted.

In the gathering darkness the flash of the guns firing blinded the men on the *Sheffield*'s bridge for a moment. 'To our dismay,' Captain Clarke wrote, 'the first salvo passed well over the enemy destroyers, clearly indicating that some grave error had apparently occurred.

'What actually happened, though, was simple enough. I, on the bridge, had given the bearing of the targets correctly, but without specifying in so many words that the targets were destroyers. The Director crew had obediently placed themselves on the bearing ordered only to observe through their high-powered telescopes something we had not seen on the bridge—a heavy enemy unit several thousand yards behind the destroyers, but precisely on the same bearing. Very naturally the Gunnery Control had assumed the larger target was the object of my instruction, and had fired accordingly.'

The *Sheffield*'s first salvo was very accurate, although it could not be seen from the ship. The *Lützow*'s log said: 'The enemy opened fire as orders were being given to our own guns. First salvo straddled. Subsequent salvos very accurate.'

The *Lützow* replied with her 11-inch and 5.9-inch guns a minute later at a range of just under eight miles.

The *Sheffield* and *Jamaica* had been steering for the *Lützow* for four minutes, and during that time the pocket battleship's salvos regularly fell a mile short. Suddenly more shells started falling round them. They were from the *Hipper* which, steaming away westwards at twenty-six knots, had earlier picked up the

Sheffield and *Jamaica* on her radar. Admiral Kummetz could see their attack on the *Lützow* and the pocket battleship's reply ('*Lützow* was very useful to me in keeping the shadowers off'), and he ordered the *Hipper* to join in, noting that 'the appearance of gun flashes gave the impression that they were cruisers'.

The *Hipper*'s gunnery was much more accurate than the *Lützow*'s, even though the range was far greater, and the *Sheffield* was quickly straddled.

At this point Burnett was facing a critical stage in the battle. An 8-inch cruiser, the *Hipper*, was firing at him from fine on the port bow while a pocket battleship, the *Lützow*, engaged him from broad on the port beam. And in the darkness ahead there were at least two, possibly five, destroyers carrying at least sixteen, possibly forty, torpedoes.

The destroyers, which could hardly be seen, were by far the greatest menace. Captain Clarke, referring first to the *Hipper*'s shells, wrote: 'I know I was aware that we were under fire once again, but I was not conscious particularly of the proximity of the shells. My mind was entirely concerned at the time by the destroyer threat. I remember noticing with some apprehension the columns of water which surrounded the *Jamaica*, and, curiously enough, I was afterwards told that those in the *Jamaica* were equally concerned about the ordeal we appeared to be undergoing. Neither evidently appreciated that what was happening to his consort was also happening to him.

'It is clear now that both ships were more than ordinarily fortunate in escaping damage at that stage and perhaps our misdirected fire, followed by the *Jamaica* also engaging the same target, did in fact spoil the accuracy of at least one of the enemy and contribute to our immunity from a concentration of 11-inch and 8-inch shell.'

Amid the crash and flash of the *Sheffield*'s guns—they were firing at intervals of between twenty and thirty seconds—the acrid smell of cordite smoke, the bitter cold and the fact that he had been on the open bridge for many hours, Admiral Burnett had to decide the next move; and he had only a few moments in which to do it.

The enemy destroyers might at that very moment be wheeling in the gathering darkness, preparing to attack; they might have already launched their torpedoes. Admiral Burnett gave the order to turn away, and the *Sheffield*, followed by the *Jamaica*, heeled over as she came round to starboard at high speed and steamed clear of the destroyer threat.

Coincidentally, Captain Stange turned the *Lützow* away at the same time, 'as the enemy's fire was accurate'. Ironically enough he had not yet correctly identified the *Sheffield* and *Jamaica* as cruisers, and the *Lützow*'s log adds 'I feared a torpedo attack by the destroyers. The light was now too poor to permit of a torpedo track being sighted in the darkness'.

Admiral Burnett wrote in his report: 'At 1224 I altered course to the westward to maintain touch and determine the enemy's intention to withdraw, reducing speed for a period to twenty-seven knots so that I would be in a better position to cut off the enemy should he decide to turn to the east and attack the convoy once again.

'I maintained touch with [*Hipper*] until 1300 and [*Lützow*] until 1345; in a further fifteen minutes it was established that all contacts were lost and I was confident that the enemy were definitely retiring.'

Admiral Burnett could have continued to shadow the *Hipper* and *Lützow*, making use of his limited radar and risking a co-ordinated attack in the darkness (for the Arctic twilight had now ended) by the German destroyers. This was, despite the poor show they had put up so far, a considerable danger; indeed, any British destroyer captain in the enemy's position would have regarded the opportunity as a gift.

However, shadowing the enemy once he was sure they *were* retiring back to their base, was pointless for Admiral Burnett. His three most important considerations were to remember that (*a*) his primary task was the protection of the convoy, and a fruitless chase after a fleeing enemy did not come under that heading; (*b*) a third of the enemy's supposed surface force, the *Nürnberg*, was not accounted for, and might even now be attacking, or preparing to attack, the convoy; (*c*) the convoy —which had not yet been sighted by Force R—was now more than forty miles astern while the homeward-bound convoy, RA 51, was also now coming into the picture.

The Admiral therefore took the cruisers in a sweep to the south until at 1609, with almost complete darkness, he reached the limit of the Russian submarine area. Then he swept to the northward, 'In case any German ships who were not satisfied that their objects had been achieved should have doubled back with the intention of attacking the convoy from the rear after dark.'

After talking over the radio-telephone to the *Lützow* and *Richard Beitzen,* the officers in the *Hipper* decided that the *Friedrich Eckholdt* was probably lost. Kummetz sent off a guarded signal on the U-boat wavelength at 1233 which said: *No contact with* Eckholdt. *Enemy is shadowing the formation. Detachment of* Lützow *impossible.*

The *Hipper*'s log says that at 1237 the enemy had turned away, and at 1250 Kummetz noted: 'The enemy ships which were maintaining contact on the port quarter are no longer visible. It is now quite clear to me that at least as far as that formation is concerned I have been confronted by at least one enemy cruiser, if not two.

'At this time I cannot decide to send a [wireless] message to Admiral Klüber since the shadowers have just been shaken off and because in view of the continuing obscure picture of the hit on the *Hipper*'s No. 3 Boiler it appears necessary to maintain wireless silence.

'Since he has not made any great endeavour to maintain contact and is obviously not endeavouring to regain contact, it can be accepted that he will bring no other operational group against us but will return to the convoy.'

At 1253 it was reported that the enemy radar transmissions astern could no longer be picked up, and two minutes later a signal was received on board the *Hipper.* Addressed to Admiral Kummetz, it was from Admiral Klüber who, from the rocky fastness of Narvik, said simply:

Return at high speed. Two enemy cruisers confirmed in Murmansk area. One of them Jamaica.

The irony of having received that signal exactly two minutes after the final radar contact had been lost astern with what he guessed was almost certainly those two ships can hardly have been lost on Kummetz. However, it was left to Captain Stange, following astern in the *Lützow*, to have some afterthoughts about the action. The log says:

'Enemy radar closes down after sweeping astern. The impression was now gained that the shadowing vessels have broken off the pursuit. As we withdrew from the scene of the action, the unsatisfactory feeling reigned that, in spite of the general position, which was apparently favourable at first, we had not succeeded in getting at the convoy or in scoring any successes at all.

'On the other hand there was a feeling of relief that, while a comprehensive survey of the position was not possible, we had managed to distinguish friend from foe in time and that we were not mistaken by our own forces. I was deeply concerned with this throughout.[1]

'It is astonishing *Lützow* was not hit in action with the cruisers, in spite of the salvos which constantly straddled or fell close. The sad fact remains that *Freidrich Eckholdt* was lost.'

By way of postscript the following summary of ammunition expended during the battle may be of interest:

Hipper: 375 rounds of 8-inch (eight guns)
         203 „ „ 4·1-inch (twelve guns)
  (Total 578)

Lützow: 86 „ „ 11-inch (six guns)
        76 „ „ 5·9-inch (eight guns)
  (Total 162)

Sheffield: 583 „ „ 6-inch (twelve guns)

Jamaica: detailed figures not available, but about the same as *Sheffield*.

---

[1] Stange was at this time apparently unaware that the *Friedrich Eckholdt* was lost because she mistook the *Sheffield* for the *Hipper*.

20

Achates Fights for Life

WHILE Force R finished the job of driving off the *Hipper* and *Lützow*—a task so successfully begun by Sherbrooke and continued by Kinloch—the convoy continued steaming south, led by the badly-damaged *Onslow*. At 1445, as soon as it was apparent that the Germans had quit for good, the convoy came back on the course for position G, the next to last point on the chart before the convoy split up, some ships going into Murmansk and others on to Archangel, farther to the east.

A little earlier, at 1328, a very large explosion, the glow from which lasted for two seconds, was sighted to the north-north-east from *Onslow*. It is difficult to account for this unless it was the *Friedrich Eckholdt* finally blowing up. The position where she was attacked was now on that bearing from the convoy, and if it was her, then the crew must have had a dreadful struggle since she was first hit at 1130. She was not actually seen to sink by either British or German forces.

In the *Onslow* by now Tom Marchant had a better idea of the damage the ship had suffered. Fourteen men were dead, three were dying and twenty-three more were wounded. The ship was leaking badly from a hole on the port side, was down by the bows and listing to port. This list put the hole under water and caused more flooding.

In addition tons of dead water from the fire-fighting hoses were collecting on the port side of the upper mess-decks and passages, and also in the Torpedomen's Mess on the lower deck, increasing the list even more. All available men were hard at work bailing with buckets and a hand-pump until the electric portable pump could be rigged. This was effective, but it weighed 400 lb and took some moving about.

Somehow the ship's bows had to be lifted as much as possible and the list to port reduced. If this could be done it might then be possible to give the ship a list to starboard to keep the hole on the port side out of the water.

It will be remembered that the forward magazine, on the port side, had been flooded. This was the main cause of the list, though of course enormous weights of water in the other flooded compartments also helped to keep the bows down. It was realized that if the forward shell-room (next to the magazine but on the starboard side) was flooded as well it would counter-balance the list and ease it considerably. This was done and the fresh-water tank and reserve feed tank on the port side were also pumped out.

Fortunately some of the large fuel oil tanks were empty, and it was decided to flood one right aft on the starboard side. This acted as the heavier man on a see-saw—the buoyant midship section of the ship acting as the pivot—and, combined with the other measures, raised the bows in the water as much as possible and also gave the ship a slight list to starboard.

The hole was now immersed only when the ship rolled to port. It could not be plugged, however, because it was hidden under lockers and the wooden Arctic sheathing. The portable pump managed to keep the water down to a depth of two feet for the time being, while the sea was calm. The danger from heavy seas—when the big hole in the superstructure under B gun would also let the water flood in—was considerable.

Marchant wrote later: 'A weather report was received about 1800 which indicated heavy weather would probably be encountered at the approaches to Murmansk. As the ship was virtually of no use to the convoy and in view of the fact that submarines would now constitute the greatest menace, against which we had no Asdics, it was considered that the safe arrival of the ship was the main objective.'

He went down to see Captain Sherbrooke—the first opportunity he had had of leaving the bridge since the action began. He described it later:

'Captain Sherbrooke had asked to be kept informed through-out of the shape of events, and my impression on going to see him at 1830 in his sea cabin midst the strong and pungent smell of cordite, burnt wood, rubber and paint, and in the dim light of a solitary oil lamp, took me instantly to the day I had seen the spot in the old wooden *Victory* where the surgeon "plied his trade".'

There were various alarms and excursions round the convoy in the afternoon when ships were sighted and radar contacts made. Kinloch, who had again taken over as Senior Officer from Sclater once the *Obedient*'s aerials were repaired, could not know for certain if all the German ships had been driven off, and was very conscious of the fact that the enemy might still be shadowing astern of the convoy.

When he went back on to the bridge after seeing Captain Sherbrooke at 1830, Marchant signalled to *Obedient*: *In view of large holes in fo'c'sle which will be dangerous if weather deteri-orates consider it advisable to proceed to Kola Inlet forthwith. Captain (D) concurs.*

Kinloch immediately agreed, and later signalled to Marchant to pass the convoy's position, course and speed to the Admiralty as soon as the *Onslow* was clear of the convoy.

Slowly the battered destroyers increased speed and drew away from the merchant ships and their escorts to start a race with the falling barometer. Bound for Kola, the *Onslow* could make twenty knots before the high bow wave and occasional roll brought the hole under water again.

Peter Wyatt worked out a course for Kola Inlet, many miles away to the south-east, while down below the surgeon, Holland, worked patiently with Hanley, the SBA, to nurse the wounded. Later, in the darkness and bitter cold, came the melancholy task of burying the dead.

Just after midnight the *Onslow* sent the following signal: Obedient *has taken over S.O. Escort JW 51B. Position course and speed of convoy at 2000/31st: 72° 42' north, 32° 30' east— 110°—8½ knots.* Onslow *damaged and proceeding independently to Kola. Estimate time of arrival 0700/1st January. Apparent situation on leaving convoy at 2000/31st as follows:* Achates *damaged. Whereabouts uncertain. Remainder of escort and 12 merchant ships undamaged.* Bramble *and two merchant ships not in company since 29th.*

Unfortunately the *Achates* had sunk many hours earlier, after a brave but unsuccessful fight to save her. At about noon, when it seemed likely that there would be no more attacks on the convoy, Peyton-Jones had ordered the men to be fallen out from Action Stations and marshalled into repair parties under the Engineer, Peter Wright. With every available man working desperately to plug the hundreds of splinter holes, shore up damaged bulkheads and help pump, there was little else Peyton-Jones could do but wait.

Taylor, the Yeoman, managed to salvage a small signal lamp from the wreckage, and was ordered to ask the *Hyderabad* if the smoke-screen they were laying was effective and of value. The corvette replied to the effect that it was 'most useful', so it was continued.

Time on the bridge between 1200 and 1300 passed slowly. Peyton-Jones wrote later: 'Peter Wright and Davidson looked up occasionally to make brief reports of progress, the former on the losing battle to control the flooding in the ship and the latter on the measures being taken to collect and care for casualties, of whom by now there were a considerable number. But on the bridge there was little to do but wait and think. . . . Meanwhile it was getting dark and cold.'

The situation, though serious, was not then considered to be critical; but slowly, almost imperceptibly, the list to port increased. From 15° it went to 17°, then 20°. All the time more splinter holes, as yet unplugged by the hard-working repair parties, were submerged. This brought more flooding and in turn further increased the list.

Finally Wright came to the bridge with the news that it was no longer possible to maintain steam in No. 1 Boiler—the only one left. Slowly the *Achates* wallowed to a stop. She was three miles on the starboard side of the convoy and the nearest ship was the trawler *Northern Gem*.

Peyton-Jones ordered the Yeoman to make a signal to her, and shortly after 1300 the battered signal lamp flashed: *Not under control. Please stand by me.*

He then ordered Davidson to prepare to have the ship taken in tow from aft, but when Davidson returned a few minutes later to say the ship was heeling so much that it would be difficult if not impossible to get any cable aft, Peyton-Jones told him not to bother but instead to prepare the boats and rafts for launching.

'I must admit I had grown so used to the list to port that I had not realized how bad it was,' he wrote later. But when eventually he went to the after end of the bridge and saw that the whaler, still hanging in its davits, was awash, 'it was brought home to me just how great the odds were against remaining afloat'.

After a final word with Peter Wright, Peyton-Jones ordered everyone on to the upper deck. Slowly but inexorably the ship continued to heel over. The sea crept across the sloping deck like the tide rising on a steep sandy beach. First the lower wire of the stanchions went under; then the water reached the base of the funnel and lapped round the base of Y gun mounting.

Davidson, helped by several of the crew, including PO Batchelor and Leading Seaman Wells, quickly went round cutting the lashings holding down the Carley floats and rafts —the latter simply thick nets threaded with cork floats.

While they were doing that, Peyton-Jones considered firing the torpedoes, set to 'Safe' and jettisoning the ready-use ammunition stowed on deck in lockers and round the guns; but he quickly saw that it could not help the ship now.

Down below the list seemed far worse and it was becoming difficult for the men to climb up and down the ladders and companion-ways. As soon as the order for everyone to get on to the upper deck was passed round men rushed down to get the wounded up from the Sick Bay and First Aid posts. Many could hardly help themselves and had to be dragged bodily up crazily-angled ladders; others could just walk with assistance. But many could not be moved, and Drummond, the

Canteen Manager, and Steward Allan Jones decided to stay below with them—although they knew the ship was in danger of capsizing and if that happened they would be trapped.

While the wounded were being evacuated, PO Telegraphist Bartripp quickly went round the bridge, wheelhouse and wireless office making sure all the confidential books (secret ciphers, orders and reference books) were locked in their safes—a precaution against them floating clear, should the ship sink, and being picked up by the enemy.

Down in the engine-room Stoker Joseph Colley struggled to help a wounded man climb slippery ladders to the upper deck and comparative safety.

The *Achates* was now a dying ship; with her splinter-riddled port side almost completely submerged the water was pouring in as if strained from a colander and slowly drowning her. She still heaved sluggishly as the swell passed under her, but her reaction was heavy, as if she knew she was doomed.

With most of the wounded now lying on the steep gradient of what was supposed to be the upper deck, Peyton-Jones clung to the side of the bridge and watched for the *Northern Gem*, but she appeared to be hanging back. (Skipper Lt Horace Aisthorpe, who was commanding her, later explained that the *Achates'* first signal had been so difficult to read—hardly surprising since it had been made with a salvaged box-lamp—that he thought it was being made by an enemy destroyer as some sort of *ruse de guerre*, and he feared a trap.)

Peyton-Jones then ordered Taylor to signal the *Northern Gem* once again. Taylor braced himself and trained the lamp. He had managed to get the first few letters off when the ship started to roll over, quite slowly but with a terrifying certainty, as if she could no longer hold out against the suffocating weight of the sea inside her.

Immediately several men started dropping Carley floats and rafts clear; others grabbed handholds to stop sliding down across the ship and into the sea, to be trapped by superstructure and rigging. But with a laboured sucking and gurgling, punctuated by dull metallic crashes as gear broke adrift, the *Achates* continued rolling until she was on her beam-ends, water flooding down her now horizontal funnel and surging through hatches and shell holes into the decks below. Drummond and Allan Jones were immediately trapped with the wounded shipmates they had refused to leave; and all were drowned.

On the bridge Peyton-Jones and Taylor scrambled up the deck as it slowly reared up and became vertical. They clambered out on to the side of the wheelhouse—which was now horizontal since the ship was lying on her side—and found the door gaping open at their feet like the entrance to a dank and murky subterranean cavern. They saw two men scrambling about inside trying to escape—one of them was Barrett, the badly-wounded Sub-lieutenant. Between them they dragged the two men clear.

Peyton-Jones just had time to unsling his binoculars from round his neck and hang them on a convenient projection when the ship capsized completely and the icy water surged over their heads.

For a few moments the ship paused, her rudder and propellers in the air, then she slid below the waves as if weary of waiting.

'In the turmoil of the next few minutes I lost touch with my late companions on the side of the bridge, but remember noting with satisfaction the number of Carley floats and rafts that had floated off and mentally congratulating Davidson on his work,' Peyton-Jones wrote.

'One empty Carley float was only some twenty-five yards off and to this I quickly swam and climbed on to it. My principal concern now was that the *Northern Gem* might not see us in the gathering darkness and so for several minutes I held aloft the special light with which these floats were provided, thanking Providence that it was functioning correctly.

'Calling to various heads bobbing in the water eventually congregated some fifteen or twenty men round the float, among them Hall, the coxswain, and Bartripp, the PO telegraphist, both as unruffled as ever. Some were supporting their wounded shipmates and these we manhandled on to the float. I told them *Northern Gem* was on the way to pick us up and we started singing "Roll Out the Barrel".'

250

(It was at this point that Bartripp reported that he had successfully locked away all the confidential books.)

The ship had rolled over and sunk so quickly that many men were probably taken down with her, among them the Engineer, Peter Wright, who was last seen encouraging his men as they were forced to leap for their lives, and McIver, rescued a few moments earlier from the wheelhouse.

Now great bubbles of air and fuel oil came to the surface, bringing with them the pathetic pieces of flotsam that were all that now remained of the *Achates*.

The bitterly cold water took men's breath away at the beginning and numbed their senses, but gradually they collected in small groups round floats, or clung to pieces of wreckage. Stoker PO Robert Bell, for instance, shouted encouragement to the men round him, trying to cheer them up with wisecracks. Nearby was Supply PO James Cole, who had been with wounded men on the upper deck when the ship capsized. He had managed to help heave some of them on to floats.

Farther away Able Seaman Charles Brightmore, who had been severely wounded at his Action Station in the Director when the bridge was hit, did what he could to keep the other men cheerful. The chief boatswain's mate, PO Frank Batchelor, had stayed with the ship until the last moment, making sure the Carley floats and rafts drifted clear. Now he swam round, waiting.

The redoubtable Stoker Colley quickly collected survivors round him and started off community singing. The temperature of the sea at that time was about 33° Fahrenheit.

Aisthorpe was now very close with the *Northern Gem*. A few minutes earlier, when he had first received the signal from the *Achates*, he had used some very strong language, as the prospect of towing a wildly-yawing destroyer all the way to port was not a pleasant one. He told his First Lieutenant to get the towing-wire ready and added that he should try and get at least two 15-fathom lengths of chain shackled on to the outer end.

Men began hauling the thick intractable wire—as always it became possessed of a devil which twisted it into kinks and caught bights on the slightest projection—out of the *Northern Gem*'s hold.

251

But as Aisthorpe watched the destroyer he could see she was getting lower in the water; and then he saw her begin to roll over. He ordered the towing-wire to be stowed away again and took the trawler close in, stopping within 250 feet of her as his crew grabbed heaving lines and prepared rescue nets.

'Men could be seen scrambling on her side as she slowly turned over,' Aisthorpe wrote. 'Someone from the *Achates* started singing "Roll Out the Barrel", and within a few seconds it was taken up by quite a number of the crew. As we waited there we watched her turn keel up, and then the men started jumping off and making their way as best they could towards us.'

Dozens of tiny red lights, fitted to the men's life-jackets, came on while here and there were the brighter white lights attached to the Carley floats. In the gathering darkness they looked like grotesque fairy lights reflected in the water.

But the *Northern Gem*'s bulwarks were high, the swell threw the rafts about, and many of the half-frozen men could do little to save themselves. Thick rescue nets were hung down the sides, but within a short time few had the strength to climb up. The trawler's crew, however, did not hesitate. Several of them scrambled down on to the Carley floats and helped haul the survivors aboard; others climbed down the nets until they were in the water, lashed themselves on, then secured ropes round the men so that they could be hauled on deck. More of the crew clung precariously over the trawler's side, helping the numbed men the last few feet that was all the difference between life or death.

All the time the swell sucked and dragged at the floats and rafts, trying to dislodge them as both survivors and the trawler-men struggled to keep each one alongside until the last man was dragged to safety. As soon as one rescuer was too frozen to continue another took his place; many who would not otherwise have been rescued were saved by the speed at which the trawler-men worked, risking their own lives in their determination that no one should be lost.

Aisthorpe saw a man lying in the bottom of a Carley float and called down, 'Come on son, jump for it.' But the man just looked up blankly. Steward James Fleming promptly climbed down into the float to tie a line round him so that he could be hauled aboard. When this was done the man slid down on to the deck, not attempting to go below. 'I spoke to him,' Aisthorpe wrote later, 'and said "Come on son, you can't lie there, it's too bloody cold", but he just looked at me. He tried to speak but couldn't. I got one of the crew and between us we got him down below for treatment. We didn't know at the time that he was the young Sub-lieutenant who had been badly wounded on the *Achates*' bridge.'

Peyton-Jones's raft had been some distance away from the *Northern Gem* and they paddled over towards her. A man on the trawler's deck flung a line and he made it fast to the float. As it drew alongside, however, everyone crowded to one side and it capsized.

'Willing hands stretched down to haul us out of the water,' Peyton-Jones wrote, 'but what with the swell and the height of the trawler's bulwarks it was no easy matter and we had to wait with what patience we could muster. Many had not the strength to hold the ropes that were thrown them, and the crew of the *Northern Gem* climbed out on to the rubbing strake to heave them inboard. Even so it seemed to take a long time and while waiting I climbed back on to the Carley float and took off my sheepskin jacket and seaboots. One lone swimmer appeared alongside and I hauled him on to the float. We were eventually among the last to get on board from this side, and instinct had replaced cohesive thought.'

One by one the bunches of men were picked up. Among them was the group whose singing was being led by Stoker Colley. The Mate of the *Northern Gem* afterwards remarked that Colley 'Deserved a medal as big as a plate'. (He was later awarded the DSM.)

Finally, with eighty-one survivors on board, the *Northern Gem* circled the area in case she had missed anyone. None could be found, but among those who had been seen in the water yet were now missing were the gallant Bell, Cole and Bartripp.

Peyton-Jones describing the next few hours, wrote: 'Hustled below, I found myself in the warm and well-lit fo'c'sle surrounded by the majority of my fellow survivors. The *Northern Gem* was specially fitted for the rescue work and there were bunks, blankets and dry kits for everyone; and her crew, though heavily outnumbered, worked tirelessly on our behalf.

'After a couple of hours, by which time I felt well restored, I was sought out by the Mate and conducted aft to the ward-room, with many apologies for it not having been realized earlier that I was aboard. Here I found Davidson and Smith, the Gunner, both equally surprised to see me, and heard their accounts of their experiences.'

Then he went to the bridge to meet Aisthorpe, and to thank him. Aisthorpe and his crew were not strangers to this sort of work: the *Northern Gem* had acted as rescue ship in previous actions. Aisthorpe had, of course, lost touch with the convoy since coming to the rescue of the *Achates*' survivors, and he and Peyton-Jones discussed the best course to steer to catch up.

Later that evening there were many anxious minutes on board when another ship was detected closing from astern. She was in fact the *Obedient*. David Kinloch had decided to make a sweep astern of the convoy with the *Orwell*, in case any German ships were shadowing, and the two destroyers had been steaming along when radar reported a ship ahead. Both ships went to Action Stations, expecting to find an enemy, and were relieved when it turned out to be the *Northern Gem*.

Peyton-Jones shouted to Kinloch over a loud-hailer that the *Achates* had sunk. After passing the course to steer to overtake the convoy, Kinloch continued the sweep.

Now came the problem of dealing with the wounded aboard the tiny *Northern Gem*. The worst case was the young Sub-lieutenant, Barrett. He was in urgent need of a doctor but nothing could be done about that until they caught up with the convoy.

However, the *Northern Gem*'s radar operator, Ordinary Seaman E. G. Mayer, set to work. At the age of forty-two Mayer had volunteered to serve his country at sea and this was his first trip. His wife was a hospital sister and he had picked up some knowledge of first-aid which, helped by other willing but even less skilled hands, he put to good use.

Barrett and the other wounded had their wet clothing cut away; then they were carefully put in bunks in the Seamen's Mess and Mayer supervised the cleaning and bandaging of their wounds. Hot water bottles were tucked under the blankets to ease shock and those that could eat were given hot food.

But during the night the wind increased, making the little *Northern Gem* roll and pitch heavily as she struggled to overtake the convoy and get skilled medical help. The barometer was dropping once again and it began to look as if even when they did find the convoy the sea would be too rough for a doctor to get across to do anything for Barrett.

'The last evening of 1942 was for us memorable if only for the shock we felt at the loss of so many of our shipmates,' wrote Peyton-Jones, 'and our anxiety for the lives of those who seemed unlikely to survive.'

Finally the *Northern Gem* caught up with the convoy and by the time half-light came it was blowing a moderate gale, and the little trawler was being flung about by heavy seas. Aisthorpe signalled to Kinloch in the *Obedient* giving him the number and condition of the casualties and was told the *Obdurate* would put her doctor aboard.

He was Surgeon-Lieutenant Maurice Hood, who went to the *Obdurate*'s quarter-deck, had a life-line tied round his waist, and waited for the *Northern Gem* to come alongside—a manœuvre suggested by Aisthorpe as being the easiest and safest way of getting him aboard.

The *Obdurate*, now steaming before the wind, could not avoid yawing, and the *Northern Gem* was yawing and pitching as she came up on the port side. Aisthorpe then went down to the steering bridge and took the helm himself. He had to give her plenty of wheel to stop her from yawing too much. With watchful care and great patience borne of long experience—he had been at sea since he was fifteen, and received his Skipper's 'ticket' when he was twenty-two—Aisthorpe edged the *Northern Gem* closer and closer until only twenty feet of raging, swirling water separated the two ships.

255

Thick fenders hung over the sides of each vessel, but the manœuvre still looked like being extremely hazardous. Out of the corner of his eye Aisthorpe could see Hood waiting to leap, and he watched the gap, alternately widening and narrowing as great seas swirled under the two ships.

Then, grasping the right moment, he put the helm down, edged the trawler over and put her bow alongside the *Obdurate*'s quarter-deck. Hood, without a moment's hesitation, dropped more than six feet down on to the trawler's heaving foredeck, to be grabbed by three or four men, including Skippers Pooley and Buchan. His bag of instruments followed, and Aisthorpe immediately rang down 'Full Speed' and gave the trawler port helm to open up the gap and get clear. The *Obdurate* had some paint scratched, the *Northern Gem* a stanchion bent—a tribute to Aisthorpe's nerves and skill.

As soon as he was on board Hood washed his hands and began treating the wounded. He congratulated Mayer on the work he had done and then, despite the violent rolling of the ship, went from man to man, cleaning, cutting, stitching and bandaging. Helped by Mayer and Peyton-Jones, he often had to wedge himself to avoid being flung about while dealing with a particularly difficult wound.

It was vital to operate on some of the men, and Hood asked Peyton-Jones if he would administer the anaesthetic. He agreed, and within a few minutes was holding the mask over the face of the first patient, dripping on the anaesthetic according to Hood's instruction, while Mayer handed the doctor the instruments as he needed them.

The men worked all through the day; it was evening before they finished, worn out but pleased, with one exception, at the condition of their patients. The exception was Barrett, for whom Hood had been unable to do very much. He died uncomplainingly that night.[1]

---

[1] A year later on another Russian convoy the *Obdurate* was ordered to transfer Hood to a merchant ship which had a case of suspected appendicitis. As one of Sclater's own officers had pneumonia he was reluctant to let him go and was going to signal to that effect. However, the gallant Hood insisted on going and was transferred. The next night this merchantman was torpedoed. Hood managed to get his patient to a life-boat, but himself went down with the ship.

The Prayer Book which Skipper Aisthorpe handed to Peyton-Jones next morning had the pages containing the Burial Service well-thumbed from previous occasions. Permission was obtained from *Obedient* to stop the ship for a few minutes and a brief but moving service was held, attended by all the unwounded survivors of the *Achates* and the crew of the *Northern Gem*.

It was not the first time that Peyton-Jones had had to read the Burial Service, but on this occasion there was the added depth of feeling as they also said a symbolic farewell to more than a hundred of their shipmates who had perished the day before.

21

A Wife Waits

THE bare picture of the battle had begun to build up in the Admiralty in London in the form of a small pile of signals from Captain Sherbrooke. The messages had been necessarily terse even when transmitted but often words—even several groups of code—had been lost on the way, the Morse transmissions from *Onslow* far beyond the Arctic Circle being at times overlaid by the crackle and splutter of atmospherics. Gaps in the sentences were indicated by significant dashes on the signal forms or the words 'corrupt group'.

Few people walking through Admiralty Arch and into The Mall during the war realized the importance of the abominably ugly, stale-gingerbread-coloured building without windows which was on their left, past the statue of Captain Cook. Looking like some schoolboy's idea of a modern fort it was, in fact, called the Citadel.

Beneath it, many feet below the ground and protected from bombing by several feet of concrete, was the War Room. There, amid the noise of telephones and the constant hum of the air conditioning plant, the unreal glare of fluorescent lighting and the rattle-and-plop of message carriers falling out of pneumatic tubes, the staff worked twenty-four hours a day.

On vast charts the position of every British warship at sea all over the world was plotted; convoys were also shown, and many of them had symbols round or near them indicating U-boats attacking, lying in ambush or pursuing. The telephones in the room linked the staff—via naval wireless stations both at home and abroad—with any one of the ships, so that it could be diverted almost instantly to avoid danger, reinforce another ship or hunt a U-boat.

The Operations Division Staff were a mixed bunch of people. There were naval officers of all ranks, and civilian men and women, too. Some of the women were wives of serving officers, anxious to do their bit and also to have something to occupy their minds while their husbands were at sea. It was, perhaps, an advantage to work in the Operations Division if you were one of these wives: at least you could find out where your husband's ship was merely by looking at the Plot.

One of the strange things about working in the Operations Division was its air of unreality: you were remote from any actual action—whether a full-scale battle between capital ships, or just a scrap between a corvette and a German long-range bomber in the Atlantic; yet, because of the brief signals plopping monotonously out of the pneumatic tubes you felt you were in the midst of the action and, since you could see all the other ships indicated on the Plot, probably knew a great deal more about the over-all situation than the men doing the fighting. One's taste of battle was vicarious but exciting.

However, as your spell of duty ended you left the vast room to go out into the open air, mingling with people going to lunch, returning to their offices, and hurrying for trains. Yet you knew, hundreds of miles away . . .

When Mrs. Sherbrooke—for she was one of the people working in the Operations Division Signal Room—had gone off duty at noon two days before, on 29th December, the Plot showed that her husband's convoy was seemingly undetected: the German warships at Altenfiord had apparently not sailed, nor were any U-boats indicated near.

The first warning that JW 51B was menaced and likely to be attacked was Captain Sherbrooke's sighting report, which arrived about 0945 at the Admiralty. The desperate battle round PQ 17 was still fresh in everyone's mind—for it was here that the First Sea Lord Admiral Sir Dudley Pound had made his fateful decision.

The *Onslow*'s brief *One unknown bearing 325° distance 8 miles steering 140°* had been picked up by a warship at sea many hundreds of miles nearer the British Isles, passed to the naval wireless station at Scapa Flow and then relayed to the Admiralty. There it was decoded and, because it was vitally urgent, a roughly-scribbled copy (it would be followed later by a type-written one) was sent by pneumatic tube to the Director of the Operations Division.

In the Operations Room the staff were thankful for one thing: Mrs. Sherbrooke was off duty. She was due back at noon—in two-and-a-quarter hours' time—and perhaps by then everything would have sorted itself out. Admiral Pound had been warned, and up in the north of Scotland the Commander-in-Chief of the Home Fleet, Admiral Tovey,[1] was receiving duplicate signals. Since the convoy was under his operational command he was making what plans he could to help if it became necessary.

The convoy was so far away that there was little either of the Admirals could do, and anyway the signal simply said that a ship was near the convoy. It could be merely a straggler, some unfortunate merchantman wandering around the ocean after losing the convoy in the gale. . . .

A second signal arrived: *Three unknown.*

Then came Sherbrooke's signal, both stirring and bleak, which ruled out straggling merchantman: *Enemy in sight bearing 325. Three destroyers.*

That in itself was not too bad: he could deal with them, although few people in the Operations Division were optimistic enough to think it was likely to end there. It *was* possible that there were only three German destroyers patrolling, but it was more than likely that they were the scouts for a bigger force.

A fourth signal arrived, stamped 'EMERGENCY' like its predecessors. It had been transmitted from the *Onslow* four minutes after the previous one and, as they half-feared, it said: *One cruiser bearing 325.*

One cruiser and three destroyers. Not hopeless odds, but more than enough.

Sherbrooke's fifth signal said, *Am engaging one cruiser bearing 358°*, but after that there was silence for more than half an hour. Then came *Have been hit forward* followed by a garbled signal saying *Immediate . . . and in engine room. Am retiring on convoy making smoke.*

The *Onslow* herself was obviously badly damaged, but what

---

[1] As a young lieutenant-commander, Admiral Tovey had commanded another HMS *Onslow*, also a destroyer, in the Battle of Jutland in the First World War. For his bravery he was promoted to Commander and awarded the D.S.O.

of the rest of the escort? Were all the destroyers retiring on the convoy? And were they retiring because the enemy had been driven off or were they being forced back?

Ten minutes later a signal from the destroyers to Force R which had been transmitted as '*Convoy course 180°. Cruiser close to convoy*' was intercepted and received in the Admiralty as *Capital ships . . . cruisers closing the convoy.*

What were the two missing words? Could they be '*and two*'? Or even three? There must also be more than one capital ship. Against these odds—such a force would also have a heavy destroyer screen—Sherbrooke's destroyers and the convoy would be wiped out.

Recent air reconnaissance and intelligence reports showed that the Germans had the *Hipper, Lützow, Köln, Nürnberg*—and possibly the battleship *Tirpitz*—available; maybe all had put to sea to tackle JW 51B. They would have an escort of at least six destroyers. . . .

There were no more signals from the escort until, only a few minutes before Mrs. Sherbrooke was due in the Operations Room, one arrived which said: *Enemy in sight. Five unknown vessels bearing 060°.*

If this had been true it might well have indicated a very large German force making the final attack on the convoy—administering the *coup de grâce* in fact; but (although it was not realized in the Operations Division) there was an error in the signal. It was from *Obedient*, made when the *Hipper* came down after the convoy just before being attacked by Force R, saying an enemy was five miles away.

Yet it was a miracle that any of these signals were getting through to the Admiralty at all. Conditions were very bad, and the destroyers were more than one thousand miles from the wireless station at Scapa, with aerials affected by ice and their operators often tapping their Morse against the heavy overtones of enemy shells bursting nearby.

Had it not been for an operator in the battleship *Anson*, then at sea close to the east coast of Iceland with Admiral Fraser on board, they might not have got through at all.

This operator was aged about twenty-four, of medium height,

with dancing brown eyes. His sense of humour was infectious
and his spirit that of a crusader. Before he joined the Navy at
the beginning of the war he had been a monk. He was one of
the operators on Admiral Fraser's staff and an outstanding man.
The Staff Communications Officer, Lt J. E. Poulden, wrote later:
'He had acquired, within a matter of months of the completion
of his training, the sixth sense—the 'feel of the ether'—found
only in a very few telegraphists of great experience. It isn't an
easy thing to explain, but can best be summed up by saying that
a man with this sense seems to know exactly what is happening
"on the air" in the wave-band he is guarding, even when conditions are really bad and the air is thick with transmissions.'

This operator had heard a ship transmitting very weakly,
trying to raise Scapa Flow W/T Station, and noted that the
shore station had not answered. He then heard the ship transmitting what was clearly an enemy report. Realizing the importance of this signal he noted it down, and the petty officer in charge
of the watch immediately telephoned to Lt Poulden, who was
on the Admiral's bridge of the battleship, and reported the facts.

'As soon as I was told this,' wrote Poulden, 'I authorized the
Wireless Office to transmit to Scapa W/T the contents of the
enemy report they heard and to continue to relay any such
signals until they were confident that Scapa was hearing the
originator direct. As soon as I had given this authorization,
which was based on the fact the *Anson* was in a comparatively
safe area at the time, I reported to Captain Kinahan [command-
ing the *Anson*] that I had authorized an emergency breaking of
radio silence. He instantly concurred.'

Thus the operator in the *Anson* provided the tenuous but
vital human link between Captain Sherbrooke, fighting his lone
battle inside the Arctic Circle, and the Admiralty in London.

When Mrs. Sherbrooke arrived in the Operations Division
Signal Room for her spell of duty an hour before noon she
sensed at once that something had happened to JW 51B, and
almost immediately was taken to one side by a senior officer
who explained that, although things looked bad, there was still
a good chance. No doubt she would like to go off duty? Mrs.
Sherbrooke shook her head: she would prefer to carry on. It

was better to stay, knowing what was happening and having a job to occupy her mind, than to go home and wait in dread for the telephone bell to ring.

She had barely started her work when a signal from Admiral Burnett, reporting he had sighted a large vessel six miles away, showed that Force R were coming to the rescue of the destroyers.

Various other signals arrived telling of the ebb and flow of the battle. Then an hour and a half later a signal from *Orwell* to Admiral Burnett was intercepted. It half hinted that something had happened to Captain Sherbrooke, saying *Captain (D) out of action, Obedient taking charge*; but it was sufficiently ambiguous for it to be thought that it might refer to *Onslow* rather than Captain Sherbrooke personally.

Then a signal was received from Admiral Tovey preparing the Home Fleet in Scapa Flow. It said:

I anticipate that action between enemy forces and Force R will develop in easterly direction. Force R may subsequently be able to provide some cover for RA 51 [*the homeward-bound convoy*] *but may have to retire to Kola to refuel. Intend to proceed at 1530/31st December in HMS* King George V *with HM ships* Howe [*battle-ship*], Kent, Berwick, Bermuda [*cruisers*], Relentless, Raider, Musketeer, Queenborough *and O.R.P.* Poirun [*destroyers—the latter Polish*] *to take up covering positions for RA 51. . . .*

The hours passed. The two British cruisers had tackled the enemy force; a German destroyer had been left sinking. Beyond that, they knew nothing. Afternoon merged into evening, and then this last December evening of 1942 into night. Once it looked as if the fighting was going to rage round the convoy once more as *Obedient* signalled that she had sighted three unknown ships four miles away, but a further signal a couple of minutes later cancelled the report.

Midnight came, bringing the New Year. What could they look forward to in 1943? Precious little, it seemed, except the already proffered 'Blood, toil, tears and sweat'. Then, before half an hour of the New Year had passed, came the signal from the battered *Onslow* struggling towards Kola, trying to beat the bad weather. Onslow *damaged and proceeding independently* . . . still no news of whether or not Captain Sherbrooke was wounded or even alive.

263

22

Silent Night

DURING that eventful New Year's Eve, while four British
destroyers had held off a pocket battleship, a heavy
cruiser and six destroyers which had all the advantages
of surprise and concentration, the German Navy Staff in
Berlin had been almost completely without news of the battle.

At Fort Wolf Admiral Krancke, knowing Hitler would have
been fretting about the ships ever since he had been told the
night before that the *Hipper* and *Lützow* had sailed, had asked
the Operations Division to telephone any news immediately it
was received.

Thus at 1030 Admiral Krancke had been able to report to
Hitler that the cruisers had been in contact with the enemy since
0936. He read to him Admiral Kummetz's signal, *In action with
convoy in position 73° 27′ north, 28° 50′ east, course 090° speed
ten knots.*

When the time came for the noon situation conference, at
which all three services, the Army, *Luftwaffe* and Navy, in that
order, reported on the latest developments at the various fronts,
Krancke had some more news. The recital of the events on the
Eastern Front was not very cheerful; Field-Marshal Keitel
gestured over the unrolled maps and then listened to Hitler's
comments and answered his questions. Finally it was Krancke's
turn. What was the news of Operation Rainbow?

The Admiral had put two pink signal forms in front of him
on the table. Pasted on each of them was a message torn from a
teleprinter, and stamped in red ink were the words SECRET!
OFFICER ONLY.

Two signals had been picked up, Krancke told Hitler. The
first was from Admiral Kummetz, and said: *Break off engagement and retire to the westward.* That was timed 1149.

The second, timed 1145, was from *U-354*, the submarine which had first sighted the British convoy, and it said: *According to our observation the battle has reached its climax. I see nothing but red.*

From these signals, Hitler agreed, it seemed the main attack on the convoy had gone off to plan.

However, no more reports came in during the afternoon and evening except for a brief signal from Kummetz that the ships were returning to the rendezvous at 2200. From this, Admiral Krancke wrote later, 'I concluded that the naval forces had not suffered any damage, as their cruising speed was at least twenty knots. I also reported [to Hitler] that there was no wireless contact with the destroyer *Friedrich Eckholdt*.'

At the usual evening situation conference he had been reporting this to Hitler when an aide tiptoed into the bunker and handed Krancke a pink signal form. It was headed *By telephone from Wireless Monitoring Department* and it said:

Reuter reports 2005/31st December: Early today British ships came in contact with enemy forces in Northern waters. During the ensuing battle one enemy cruiser was damaged and withdrew. One enemy destroyer was hit several times and when she was last sighted was in a sinking condition. Operations continue.

It was only just over twenty-four hours earlier that Hitler, now watching him reading, had declared his ships were 'lying idle in the fiords, utterly useless like so much old iron'. Now Krancke had to tell him what was likely to turn out to be bad news—and it was from a British source.

'We thought it possible that this report was correct,' Krancke wrote. 'The Führer was uneasy and wanted to know why our own force had not yet reported. I explained that wireless silence was maintained at sea and that no message could be expected until our own ships returned to port.'

After the conference Krancke did what he could to get some news. 'In view of the Führer's impatience and because of the uncertainty of the situation I then suggested to the Operations Division, Naval Staff, that they should request the result of the action by a short radio signal. For example the cruiser force should reply "J" [presumably for "Ja"—yes] if the task had turned out successfully.'

The Operations Division put the idea up to Admiral Raeder, but even though he knew the reason, he refused to request ships at sea to make wireless signals. The danger of them having their positions plotted by British direction-finding wireless receivers and then being attacked was too great.

Krancke described the next move. 'After supper at 2200 I was ordered to attend a conference dealing with the organization of naval supply transport ships. This discussion lasted until 2350. At the beginning I was able to report that the return of the cruiser force would be delayed for three hours. The reason was not known; it could have been caused by damage to a cruiser, as reported by the British, but also by a breakdown in a destroyer, by heavy seas, or by weather.

'In any case, the Führer demanded that any report be passed on to him the moment it came in. He still hoped it might be possible to issue an announcement of the destruction of an enemy convoy this evening [31st December] or on the morning of 1st January. Since so far there had been no reports that enemy cruisers or similar vessels had taken part in the action, the Führer and I remained very optimistic.'

Although the conference lasted until 2350, it was not time for bed. Even had it been an ordinary night, Hitler would have started off on a light meal of tea and buns and, to an audience which would probably include one or two of his women secretaries, Martin Bormann, and Eva Braun, gossiped until nearly dawn, expounding prejudiced views and warped judgments on many subjects about which he knew very little, apart from the unrelated statistics stored in his retentive memory and frequently brought out for a pre-dawn airing.

The night of New Year's Eve was no exception. Just before midnight came a stream of telephone calls and personal visits to the Führer to wish him a Happy New Year: Field-Marshal Keitel, General Jodl, Marshal Göring, Ribbentrop—by now counting for little—Goebbels and several others involved in the familiar and disgusting gestures which were essential if one was to retain favour in this sycophants' paradise.

Hitler received their greetings and assurances of devotion and droned on. Every half an hour he telephoned Krancke to see if there was any news. Time passed—two o'clock, three o'clock, four o'clock—and Krancke in turn kept on telephoning the Operations Division. But they could tell him nothing.

'At 0415, shortly before the Führer went to bed, I visited him and informed him that I would submit incoming messages, so that he would have them the moment he awoke,' wrote Krancke. 'The Führer was very uneasy.'

After having made arrangements with the Duty Officer in Operations Division to telephone him as soon as there was any news, Krancke went to bed.

Admiral Kummetz steamed back to Altenfiord with his force as quickly as possible, and the *Hipper* had a singular escape from being torpedoed by a former German U-boat just before she entered the fiords leading towards her anchorage. As mentioned earlier, one of the British submarines patrolling this stretch of the coast with orders to keep an eye on the German surface ships was HMS *Graph*.

She had started off life as *U-570*, commissioned in June 1941 and sent to sea by Admiral Dönitz in August with a crew of forty-three, only four of whom had been on operations before. The U-boat had run into bad weather and was surfacing, after having dived to give the crew a rest, when a Coastal Command Hudson aircraft attacked and damaged her with depth-charges. This forced *U-570* to stay on the surface, and her captain surrendered by the novel method of waving one of his white shirts, frilled down the front and lightly starched, as a white flag. Other Coastal Command planes circled her for many hours, uttering dreadful threats in Morse should her captain try to escape. Eventually she was towed in by warships and her secrets probed. When repairs were completed she was put into commission with the Royal Navy. Now, after an anti-U-boat patrol in the Bay of Biscay, she was back off the Norwegian fiords, not far from where, under a German crew just over a year before, she had made her last departure for an intended operation against the British.

The *Graph* had been on patrol at the entrance of Soro Sound, the long and narrow fiord which led into the anchorage at Altenfiord when at 0106 on New Year's Day her captain sighted a cruiser about seven-and-a-half miles to the westwards, steaming for the Sound at high speed. It was impossible to manœuvre the submarine into an attacking position, so he contented himself with watching.

However he guessed she would be followed by other ships and steamed five miles to the westward on to the approximate track that the *Hipper* had used to enter the Sound. And three hours later his patience was partially rewarded—two destroyers were seen to the westward, steering south four miles away. Eight minutes later two destroyers were sighted steaming in the opposite direction. They stopped and the *Graph* attacked with torpedoes, but did not secure any hits.

The *Hipper* received a signal from Admiral Klüber, timed 0245, asking for a short survey of successes and the situation. Admiral Kummetz had in fact already prepared a brief report and it was coded up ready to be transmitted once the *Hipper* was inside the fiords, apparently safe from the Royal Navy and the RAF.

However, once she had got inside those sheltered waters the wireless transmitters had to be used for ordering tugs and generally passing various berthing instructions. It was not until 0410 that the first report went off, and it was brief. The 5th Destroyer Flotilla, Kummetz said, had patrolled the area with the *Hipper* and *Lützow* astern. *Hipper* had sighted the convoy, *Eckholdt* had shadowed, and then the *Hipper* had been in action with destroyers and later British cruisers. These at first had not been recognized as such. . . . *Lützow* and destroyers had also been in action. *Hipper* had damaged three destroyers and probably sunk another. *Eckholdt* had been hit by a cruiser while sinking a damaged destroyer. It had been impossible to give help. The force had retired to the west and the *Hipper* had been hit by a cruiser. . . . There was no mention of the British merchant ships.

268

The *Hipper* finally berthed in Kaa fiord at 0600 and, Kummetz noted in the log, in order to give a more comprehensive statement reports had to be got in from the other ships.

Everyone in the *Lützow* and *Hipper* was tired, and they appeared to be quite unaware that Admiral Klüber in Narvik, Admiral Carls in Kiel, Admiral Raeder in Berlin, and Admiral Krancke and Hitler at Fort Wolf, were waiting impatiently for news. They settled down to breakfast, swapping stories of the action.

Finally Klüber signalled at 1015 to Kummetz:

Request urgently additional information to that given in Hipper's *short report as this is required by Naval Staff.*

Meanwhile at Fort Wolf Krancke awoke just after 0900 expecting to find messages from the Operations Division awaiting him, giving news of the success of Operation Rainbow. There was none. Once again, by now completely exasperated, he telephoned the Operations Division.

All they could tell him was that the Duty Staff Officer at Group North, in Kiel, had reported at 0800 and said: 'At 0240 B. de K. Force passed the outer point [of Altenfiord]. Admiral Klüber [at Narvik] has received only an incomplete wireless message which was not picked up by Group North. According to the message B. de K. apparently scarcely penetrated the escort. During the battle he encountered two cruisers which had previously not been identified as such. *Eckholdt* was probably hit by a cruiser. Closer details are not known. *Hipper* had been hit in a boiler-room and had a fire in the aircraft hangar. This had been extinguished. Nothing was known about successes. Admiral Klüber expects to have a teleprinter or telephone conversation [with Admiral Kummetz].'

This, Krancke realized, was hardly cheering news to put before the Führer on New Year's Day.

On the basis of *U-354*'s signal 'nothing but red' the Führer was expecting to hear of a German victory—that the British destroyer escort had been driven back and the merchantmen carrying British and American arms for the Russians to use on his precious Eastern Front had been sunk. The success of the attack on PQ 17 had set a precedent for operations against these convoys. If the *Luftwaffe* could almost destroy a convoy, the Navy . . .

However, shortly after he put the telephone down a message was brought to him from Admiral Raeder in Berlin. It bore the instruction 'To be placed before the Führer' and said that the report of the force was on its way. Transmitting a message while under way at sea was a danger, Raeder said. A further report would be received when the *Hipper* moored up. In the meantime, in addition to a breakdown of all telephone lines 'it had been confirmed' that there was strong interference of wireless transmission which was probably due to the result of atmospheric disturbances.[1] 'I expect by tonight to have the answer to various individual questions,' Raeder concluded.

Warned at 1030 that the Führer was awake, Krancke reported that details of the operation should be coming over soon by teleprinter. Knowing that Hitler would definitely want news at the situation conference at noon, he did his best to get it. But despite repeated telephone calls to the Operations Division in Berlin and Group North in Kiel there was still no further message. 'I again pointed out the urgency of obtaining a report for the Führer,' he wrote. 'I was told that the telephone connection was damaged.'

Fearing the worst, Krancke went from his office to the noon conference, and later he wrote: 'I informed the Führer accordingly at the discussion. He said it was a disgrace that he as Supreme Commander had not received any news twenty-four hours after the action, and that the British had already given a report on the previous evening.'

Those remarks, however, were merely the first zephyrs heralding the storm of fury brewing up in the Führer's mind. It is obvious now that he regarded himself as being thwarted. He had dealt with the Army and secured complete operational control of it, despite the early resistance of the General Staff. The Navy was still something of a stronghold, which had held out mainly because he had never assaulted it. Now, having first

---

[1] This was subsequently denied by the Chief of Naval Communications. 'It was particularly good' at this time, he later told Hitler.

of all told him that a U-boat had 'seen red' they were unable to back it up with facts and figures.

'In a very excited state he ordered me to send a wireless message demanding a report from the naval forces,' Krancke continued. 'I conveyed this order to Wangenheim [Cdr. Hubert von Wangenheim, Liaison Officer at the Führer's headquarters].

'Then followed further remarks from the Führer, who was very excited. He spoke of the uselessness of the big ships, of lack of ability and lack of daring on the part of the older naval officers. I had to give up any attempt to explain or protest. He even stated that we dare to attack merchant vessels only if they do not answer our fire.'

Meanwhile on board the *Hipper* up in the far north Admiral Kummetz had received Captain Stange's report on the *Lützow*'s part in the battle and at 1216, while at Fort Wolf Krancke was being harangued by Hitler, sent off his second short report. He had written it without apparently realizing the atmosphere which had grown up in the past few hours at every stage of command from Narvik to the Führer's headquarters. It said:

'*Lützow* Group [experienced] poor observation conditions. Two hits by secondary armament observed. Hit on one ship followed by fire effect. No damage to *Lützow* group.

'According to observation from *Beitzen*, sinking of enemy destroyer by *Eckholdt* certain.

'The crews' conduct exemplary. The engine-room personnel of *Hipper* deserve special mention for repairing damage during the action. The task difficult in bad light during short hours of twilight. Have the impression that the commanding officers have done the best possible within the framework of their directives.[1] B. de K.'

Even after the noon conference Admiral Krancke was still without news and had no illusions about the dangerous

---

[1] Presumably a reference to the cautionary orders, culminating in the signal from Klüber after the *Hipper* sailed urging caution 'even against enemy of equal strength'.

situation that was building up. He kept telephoning the Naval Staff in Berlin, impressing on them the need for urgency, but there was nothing they could do. The news just had not arrived from Altenfiord.

To speed it up the Operations Division sent another signal to Admiral Carls at Group North. It said: 'Commander-in-Chief requests speedy report that he be informed about *Lützow* group, and that detailed survey of all reports with times of dispatch, receipt, etc., after beginning of battle. Admiral Northern Area [Klüber] and Group North [Admiral Carls] to give a report on the reasons for delay.'

Now, sitting in his office at Fort Wolf, Krancke could only wait patiently and trust the Führer would cool off. At 1700 the telephone bell rang: the Führer wanted to see him immediately.

The crisis had now arrived. The cruisers had been sailed to attack a British convoy; the battle had been fought; and now —although Hitler had no news to go on, apart from that given by Krancke and related earlier—the price was to be exacted for failure.

Krancke, of course, was unaware of this. In fact no one outside Altenfiord knew whether or not the attack had been a success. He walked into Hitler's office. This is his own account of what followed.

'At 1700 I was sent for by the Führer who asked me for news. He then walked up and down the room in great excitement. He said that it was an unheard of impudence not to inform him; that such behaviour and the entire action showed that the ships were utterly useless; that they were nothing but a breeding ground for revolution, idly lying about and lacking any desire to get into action.

'This meant the passing of the High Seas Fleet, he said, adding that it was now his irrevocable decision to do away with these useless ships. He would put the good personnel, the good weapons and the armour-plating to better use. "Inform the Grand Admiral [Raeder] of this immediately."

'I tried to point out quietly that after all we must wait for the report, but he would not let me get a word in and dismissed me. I then informed the Grand Admiral.'

Thus Hitler had disposed of his surface fleet: three battle-ships, two pocket battleships, two battle-cruisers, two heavy cruisers and four light cruisers were to be paid off. From now on the German Navy ceased to command anything larger than a destroyer.[1]

During the late afternoon Admiral Kummetz, after going through the reports of the *Lützow* and the destroyers, had drawn up a third signal giving in greater detail a description of the action. As it was rather long, it was decided to send the first two sections by wireless and the third by teleprinter from the cruiser *Köln*, which had a telephone line to the shore.

Then at 1700, while Hitler was working himself up into a fury and telling Krancke that he had decided 'to do away with these useless ships', Admiral Kummetz was called to the radio-telephone on board the *Hipper* to have a talk with Admiral Klüber at Narvik.

This conversation gives a good insight into Admiral Kummetz's mind and, taken from German records, is given here in full:

Kummetz: 'This is Flag Officer, Cruiser Force—Heil Hitler.'

Klüber: 'This is Flag Officer, Northern Area—Heil Hitler. I am ordered by C-in-C to transmit to you a series of questions and to summon you to this R/T conversation, and also to give you the following teleprinted message from C-in-C North [Carls] to you: "To Flag Officer, Cruiser Force, and *Lützow*: Request by return a detailed report and coherent summary about Operation Rainbow, as a report is urgently required by the higher commands. In this [Admiral Kummetz] should give a detailed account of the *Lützow* Group's action and results obtained. Approve breaking off action by the group on identifying enemy's strength.—C-in-C."'

Kummetz: 'Have you received the abridged reports, numbers one to three, the first two by wireless, the third by teleprinter?'

Klüber: 'I received your short message of 2100 last night

[1] The full significance of Hitler's decision is not given at this point because Admiral Raeder summarizes it later in the narrative.

273

[giving estimated time of arrival] by W/T and passed it on by R/T as well as "Most Immediate" teleprinter as requested. Then in the early afternoon we received the second message regarding the *Lützow* group, but have not received a third message.'

Kummetz: 'I am just informed that the third message has not yet been coded up because there are no suitable cipher facilities. It was therefore sent to Bossekop [the Naval H.Q. ashore] to be dealt with from there. You should receive it any moment now. I have mentioned everything in those three messages relevant to a short report. I will now endeavour to be more explicit and to answer the questions of Group North. As to ammunition expenditure, I have not got these details to hand— a "Most Immediate" teleprint will follow concerning them.

'To begin with, I should like to confirm that I do not understand how the impression arose at home of a great success. If I have no results, then I do not announce any. I have not yet decided to announce that I have none. It is not my fault if the impression has been created by the announcement of the U-boat commander that he "saw red". I could not verify that impression then, as I was on the way back.

'I believe that they do not recognize the difficulties of the task that was put before me. I did not doubt the existence of such difficulties for one moment, all the experiences of exercises and the war have shown that it takes a long time to overcome a well-disciplined close-range escorting force, even when they are only destroyers. And that it is seldom possible to reach the ships in convoy before having destroyed the close-escort force.

'The time at my disposal was extremely short. Practically speaking, at that latitude there are only two hours of twilight and the clouds did not improve that. My last attack on the convoy at about 1100 with the *Hipper* and *Lützow* groups in loose tactical formation, was quite a risk in the oncoming darkness, which I reluctantly took in compliance with my instructions. During this last attack the *Lützow* opened fire on some merchant ships with her heavy and medium-size guns but only observed two hits. [She then] had to turn her guns on to a destroyer. *Lützow* was being fired on by two destroyers. There was, as already mentioned, very bad visibility.

"By this time it was practically dark. Besides that, the scene of action was heavily smoke-screened. *Hipper* was again (as during the whole period of action) in an engagement with enemy destroyers. In addition another opponent came out of the mist at about 1130 to join the fight on the lee side, which was first of all thought to be a destroyer. As she probably fired base-fuse shells, the burst could not be recognized as 6-inch.

'That the C.O. of *Lützow*, who later at 1220 was in contact with this ship, was engaged only became apparent after the engagement was broken off. It was extremely difficult in that twilight to recognize the types of ships and to distinguish between friend and foe. For a long time there was doubt both in *Hipper* and amongst my staff as to whether cruisers or destroyers were involved. Because of that I reported before the action that no cruisers were in the escort.

'This group must have operated from the outer screen of *Hipper* with radar. I could not make a report on the sighting of the cruiser because I only learned later, as I have already said, that we were dealing with cruisers.

'The sharpest look-out had to be kept for torpedoes in such bad light conditions. With the risk of torpedoes I thought it impracticable to go in closer. On one occasion I restrained the Captain of *Hipper* and approved the tactics of *Lützow* during her engagement.

'It was necessary to keep the units together, i.e. the destroyers with the cruiser, as otherwise every perspective might have been completely lost. I was able on only one occasion to send in the *Eckholdt* group against a crippled destroyer. This task was taken over by *Eckholdt* alone. It held her up for some time. With the intention of running in still farther she encountered an enemy cruiser force which, as was confirmed later, consisted not of a cruiser and a destroyer, but two 6-inch cruisers.

'At 1140 *Eckholdt* signalled to *Hipper* by R/T: "Cruiser and destroyer in sight bearing 300°." At 1143 he made to *Hipper*: "They are firing on me." *Beitzen* then broke through and made

"No! British cruisers!" This R/T signal was acknowledged by *Eckholdt*. Subsequently she could no longer be contacted either by R/T or on any other wavelength.

'In all probability she thought she was closing *Hipper* which was in reality a British cruiser. This is how he was surprised. This strikingly illuminates the difficulties that existed in recognizing friend and foe and the types of ships. In this case one was dealing with a well-known, experienced Captain (D) of rare qualities. It would therefore have been wrong to send the destroyers away, otherwise the perspective would have been lost and indeed could scarcely have been regained.

'It was no day engagement but a twilight one. Only one part of the scene of action could be surveyed at a time. The destroyers took as a matter of course a big share in the engagement as far as gunnery and torpedo-range allowed. No torpedoes were fired as it was hopeless to fire at destroyers twisting and turning at such a great range, and there was no opportunity for their use. *Hipper* had an opportunity to fire torpedoes at a cruiser but could not fire because she had to alter course violently to withdraw from effective fire before having time to use her own heavy guns. The use of heavy guns was delayed due to blurred vision.

'I will now see which questions [a reference to a previous signal from Klüber] I have not yet answered. I have already answered most of them in the incoming report.

'To (1) Yes; I was in sight of the convoy. Saw at least six ships and a number of escort-vessels, the number and types of which I could not make out. I was under the impression that in the first action, in which *Hipper* was engaged without a destroyer escort, she attracted the enemy's escort to the extent of four or more destroyers, which left only corvettes with the convoy.

'To (2) I hoped that *Lützow*, coming from the south, would approach the ships. I knew that the visibility would be worse in the south. It was however bad luck that *Lützow* only saw the convoy in the dusk and snowsqualls. She was fired on, saw columns of smoke and could not go further in this uncertain situation without taking risks. I agree with his decision. He then turned and ran eastward, coming into action in the more favourable north-east sector with *Hipper*, as was previously stated. His destroyers had closed him quite early. He had not sent them in for the same reasons as *Hipper*.

'To (6) Special reports of results were not available. At that time I did not even consider as probable the sinking of the destroyer by *Eckholdt*. Consequently I considered that I had nothing special to report. Then of course I had to make the wireless message as short as possible.

'About our own losses I could only report the interruption of communications with *Eckholdt*. The damage in battle to *Hipper* could not at this time be assessed. I had as yet received no report from that ship. I did see black smoke rising from the funnel; it must have been a hit in the engine-room. I did not immediately observe any decrease in her speed. I also made no report about that. I could not do that later, because I had to keep wireless silence; all the more so because the situation was becoming gradually difficult. First it seemed as if No. 3 engine was going to "pack up". Then it stopped altogether. Then No. 2 engine began to miss, and finally stopped. Then water ran short, so that I had to run at fifteen knots even when clearing the burners. Otherwise I could maintain eighteen knots. When I made my first signal, I was still counting on twenty-five knots. I believe that I have now said everything there is to be said on the matter.'

Klüber: 'Good. Thank you very much for your account and comprehensive report. I will assess and distribute as quickly as possible, so that everything will be in order. For us ashore, the fact remains that we, at first, took a too favourable view of your W/T message and consequently took further action by directing our U-boats and aircraft to the scene of action instead of farther along the convoy's course. A short pointer in that direction would have been very useful to me. The judgment thereof should simply be left to higher commands.

'I am certain that no one can make or will make any objections to your technical achievements, since these can only be left to the decision of the man on the spot. We have attained much that is positive in so far as it concerns your forces, as well as [mine], and if this year you are assigned to a similar difficult

277

task, I wish you better tactical conditions and all success.—
Klüber.'

Kummetz: 'Many thanks. Two more points. First, I may
state again that I would have reported any successes, no matter
of what importance. Also any casualties on my side worthy of
mention. I have always been under the impression that no report
means that one has nothing to report. Secondly, with reference
to Aurora, I am of the opinion that in these long nights the task
is impossible for the ships' captains. A single ship is not suited
for a night-encounter. Every night-action is more or less a
question of luck. Here up north there is not enough light for
daylight operations. The operational area is limited because of
the ice-boundary. The area is constricted and avoiding action
is difficult to take. The risk bears no relation to the successes.
Heil Hitler.—Kummetz.'[1]

Klüber: 'I will transmit your views to C-in-C North and
thanks very much. Heil Hitler.'

The detailed report mentioned earlier and referred to by
Admiral Kummetz in his conversation with Admiral Klüber as
not yet coded up 'because there are no suitable cipher facilities,'
was subjected to a series of fantastic delays.

Once it had been written by Kummetz aboard *Hipper*—
which was still at anchor in Kaa Fiord—it had to be coded up
in the cipher used for transmitting top secret signals either by
wireless or teleprinter. These ciphers were changed on the first
day of each month.

Since the *Hipper* and *Lützow* had been at sea for the last two
days of December they did not have a copy of the new cipher
key and because both were still at anchor instead of on their
usual buoys they were not linked to the shore by telephone
lines and thus could not use their teleprinters. It was decided,
therefore, to send the report over to the cruiser *Köln*, which
was moored up nearby, since she would have copies of the new
cipher key and was linked to Group North by teleprinter. The

[1] Aurora was the operation in which *Lützow* was to sail on and then act
alone after Rainbow.

Köln could transmit the first two parts of the signal and the third by teleprinter.

The *Hipper*'s one and only boat capable of making the trip was therefore sent off to the *Köln* with an officer carrying the report with him. It was past 1600 and darkness had fallen some time earlier. The boat puttered away from the *Hipper* but did not get far before the engine broke down.

The mechanic and coxswain worked at it feverishly but the boat was drifting about for more than an hour before they managed to coax the engine to life again and continue their trip to the *Köln*. They finally arrived alongside and the officer from the *Hipper* went to the Signals Officer to have the report coded up.

The Signals Officer, however, was most apologetic: although today was indeed the 1st January, the key for the new cipher had not yet arrived . . . there might be a copy at Bossekop. . . .

Bossekop was a village fifteen miles north of Kaa Fiord where the *Hipper* was lying, and it nestled below the mountains at the mouth of the River Alten-Eve, famous for its salmon. A German naval base had been established there since telephone lines already linked Bossekop with the outside world.

Once again the *Hipper*'s boat went off into the Arctic night. It had nearly fifteen miles to go in the darkness before it came to Bossekop, and very soon the darkness became swirling and impenetrable—they had run into thick fog. Within a short while they were lost.

The boat eventually arrived at Bossekop and the report was taken ashore, coded up and sent over the teleprinter. It arrived at the Operations Division in Berlin at 1900, three hours late. Admiral Raeder was immediately called and he read it. Then the grim little man put a telephone call through to Fort Wolf and at 1925 spoke to Krancke. Briefly he dictated a report on the battle for the Führer, and Krancke took it down by hand. When the Grand Admiral had finished and they had exchanged their 'Heil Hitlers', Krancke had the report typed out. The Führer was having his usual early evening sleep, so Krancke left word that he was to be called as soon as he awoke.

The call came shortly after 2015, and the Admiral took the

report through. Although it was headed Operation Rainbow, it painted the action in sombre colours; and it was a far from cheerful text that Hitler read. '. . . Our forces had been unable to penetrate the defensive screen of the enemy. . . . *Hipper* was surprised and received three hits . . . her speed was thereby cut down to eighteen and at times fifteen knots. . . . *Eckholdt* mistook a British cruiser for the *Hipper*; thereupon she closed the enemy force, was surprised and sunk. . . . After *Hipper* was damaged . . . gave orders to break off action and retire. . . .'

Shortly after this was given to Hitler, the usual evening situation conference was held. The Führer had not cooled off, nor had the contents of Admiral Raeder's message caused him to have second thoughts. He had made his decision in a fit of rage, without any logical, reasoned thought, without any discussion, without even hearing the result of the battle even though his decision was allegedly based on it.

The conference took the course that Admiral Krancke feared 'There was another outburst of anger with special reference to the fact that the action had not been fought out to a finish. This, said the Führer, was typical of German ships, just the opposite of the British, who, true to their tradition, fought to the bitter end.

'He would like to see an Army unit behave like that. Such Army commanders would be snuffed out. The whole thing spelled the end of the German High Seas Fleet, he declared. I was to inform the Grand Admiral immediately that he was to come to the Führer at once, so that he could be informed personally of this irrevocable decision.

'I informed the Commander-in-Chief, Navy, of this order by telephone, in a somewhat toned-down form. After the discussion the Führer kept Field-Marshal Keitel and Colonel Scherff with him. According to private information from Scherff, he then recorded in writing his decision and the underlying reason.'

Krancke realized that it would be most dangerous for Admiral Raeder to come to Fort Wolf from Berlin at the moment and meet Hitler, who would be in a rage for many hours. He therefore had a talk with Hitler's Naval Adjutant, Captain von Puttkamer, to see how best to delay the meeting for as long as possible. He finally arranged that Raeder should arrive at Fort Wolf on 4th January.

One thing now remained to be done: inform the world about the battle. The British had stepped in quickly with their statement on the evening of 31st December. Then, on 2nd January, the German communique was issued. It was not a distortion of the truth, a mere manipulation of words so that the action was presented in the most favourable light. It was simply a collection of lies which were not even based on wild possibilities:

It said, in full:

'German naval forces near Bear Island, in the Arctic, attacked a British naval formation consisting of cruisers and destroyers escorting a convoy. In the course of the battle, lasting several hours, our cruisers damaged several enemy cruisers and destroyers as well as merchant ships by artillery.

'Observation of this success was made difficult by weather conditions. An enemy destroyer damaged in the engagement was sunk by a German destroyer. A German U-boat torpedoed four ships of the convoy but could not observe the sinkings owing to the conditions of the engagement. One of our destroyers has failed to return from this engagement.'

In fact, far from damaging 'several cruisers', they had inflicted slight splinter damage on the *Sheffield* and *Jamaica* but caused no casualties; one merchant ship had been hit with a few splinters; the 'destroyer' claimed to have been sunk was in fact the minesweeper *Bramble*. Not one ship of the convoy or escort had even seen a torpedo let alone been sunk by one. And ironically enough the Germans did not claim their one other success—the *Achates*.

From the Admiralty point of view the communique revealed one interesting fact: the German force had not realized that the two cruisers were not operating as part of the close escort of the convoy. For once Britain had scored in the propaganda war.

23

Sherbrooke, V.C.

L T CDR Tom Marchant brought the battered *Onslow* along-side Vaenga Pier near the entrance to Kola Inlet at noon on New Year's Day. The fourteen men killed in the battle and the three who died of their wounds had been buried at sea the night before; now all efforts were concentrated on the wounded. There were twenty-three cases, and even before the ship had berthed Holland, the surgeon, and Hanley had labelled all the men, detailing their names, diagnosis and treatment already given.

Waiting at the quayside was a doctor from the Royal Navy hospital at Vaenga and three ambulances. It was decided to take Captain Sherbrooke and two other badly-wounded men in the first ambulance and Holland travelled with them. The journey fortunately took only five minutes, as the thermometer was registering zero Fahrenheit.

The hospital was merely a technical description of the build-ing in which two naval surgeons, Lts MacEwan and Robinson, did their best in spite of appalling difficulties. It was impossible to heat the wards and operating theatre to more than fifty-five degrees, and the frequent failure or inadequacy of the electricity supply made X-rays often impossible (the secondary lighting, bearing in mind it was almost continually dark outside, was two battery-fed Aldis lamps and a torch).

There was no bathroom, no place where crockery could be washed up, and the sanitary arrangements were most primitive. Fortunately the *Onslow* was able to supply some paraffin for the sterilizers. Yet despite all this the doctors worked cheerfully, getting little or no rest for the first few days.

Having got the wounded ashore the rest of the *Onslow*'s crew spent the afternoon clearing up the ship as much as possible, and in the evening the Russian Technical Mission arrived on board to inspect the damage with a view to repairs. The Mission comprised two engineers of the Russian Navy and Nina Alexandrina, a blonde female naval constructor who doubled up as interpreter.

The party took very little time to walk round and inspect the damage, and notes were conspicuous only by their absence. However, after spending twenty minutes with the *Onslow*'s officers in the wardroom they cheered up immensely.

The *Onslow* could not move from Vaenga Pier because the steam-pipes to the forward capstan had been shot away. Accommodation had been arranged ashore by the Russians for the *Onslow*'s crew in a building furnished with huge pictures of Marshal Stalin and Timoshenko but very little else. There were no washing facilities or toilets—a wooden one was in the process of being built outside, where there was continuous frost throughout the twenty-four hours—only half the rooms had lights and all were filthy. In view of this it was decided that the sailors would prefer to 'rough it' on board.

On Sunday 3rd January the Russian Technical Mission arrived on board once again. They fielded the same team, with the exception that they were led by an Engineer Captain. Nina Alexandrina again acted as interpreter, and in the wardroom afterwards she told Tom Marchant that repairs to the *Onslow* would be made in Vaenga, and there would be no need for the ship to move to Rosta, which was nine miles nearer Murmansk and in the bombing area—the Luftwaffe arriving daily.

'My satisfaction on hearing this,' Marchant reported later, 'was shortlived as within twenty seconds I was called to one side by the Engineer Captain and informed that repairs would be carried out at Rosta and would be started as soon as the ship arrived.

'This seemed a bit odd and on passing it on to the interpreter she could only shrug her shoulders and, with hands outstretched, palms upwards, and head on one side, looked as though to say "Aw pliss", but she actually said "If he say so, may be", which was all very confusing.'

The Russians had, from the very beginning, refused to

believe that the *Onslow* had been in action with an 8-inch cruiser. Whether this disbelief was genuine or politically inspired (for Stalin was bitter over the decision to stop convoys during the autumn) is not known. Fortunately part of the base of one of the *Hipper*'s 8-inch shells was found on board, and the Russians were invited, with the aid of a pair of compasses, to measure it. They did this correctly and were finally convinced of its origin.

On 8th January the time came for the *Onslow* to move up to Rosta for the repairs to be made. The *Northern Gem* had arrived earlier with the convoy and secured alongside her at Vaenga Pier. Skipper Aisthorpe had just manœuvred the trawler out of the way to let the *Onslow* leave when suddenly he heard someone blowing a trumpet on the wing of his bridge. All the shouting stopped and there was silence throughout the anchorage as Skipper Buchan, a soloist in the Salvation Army in the days of peace, played 'Auld Lang Syne' as a simple tribute to the gallant destroyer.

Once the *Onslow* arrived in Rosta the Russians lost no time in 'boxing in' the damaged fo'c'sle. Several of the shipyard workers were women; others were young boys. However, they all knew their job.

Two days later, on Sunday after church, word reached the destroyer that the King had awarded the Victoria Cross to Captain Sherbrooke. Marchant immediately cleared the lower deck and read the message to the crew. With a third of their shipmates dead or wounded, everyone's feelings on hearing of this honour were deep. Then Marchant read them a message from Sherbrooke himself. Written while he was propped up in bed and almost blind, it told them that the award was a tribute to them all, not to one man. (See picture 23.)

By this time it had become clear that because it was impossible to remove the splinter, it might be fatal for Sherbrooke to stay in Russia. It was finally decided to take him home to the United Kingdom as quickly as possible, accepting the risk to his life should the ship run into heavy weather.

Next day, 11th January, he was carried aboard the *Obedient*, with the rest of the more seriously wounded, for the passage back. Mercifully it was completed without incident.

Onslow herself sailed from Vaenga Bay on the 29th in company with convoy RA 52, being detached three days later to carry on alone back to the United Kingdom 'at best speed'. The voyage, however, was not without incident. At 1425 on 2nd February the officer of the watch, Sub-lt Baber, reported two ships to the east-north-east. Marchant could make out the mastheads of two ships and they were about fifteen miles away. It was quite clear that they were cruisers.

With the *Onslow* carrying just over half the normal complement, the fo'c'sle only patched up, the funnel held together by a wire strop, A gun useless because of the dent in the barrel and B gun wrecked, Marchant had no intention of getting mixed up with two German cruisers; but they had to be reported since the convoy was not far behind. On the other hand, they might be British. . . .

After studying the chart for a few moments he decided to make an enemy report of the two cruisers but transmit it on low power, so that the signal would just about reach the two cruisers and not much more. Thus if they were British they would reply on low power; if they were German they would ignore the bait and Marchant, thus warned, could transmit it again on full power so that it would be received by the Admiralty.

So the enemy report went out. For many moments they waited anxiously. The team on the bridge was different from the one which had waited a month earlier for the *Hipper* to open fire—Peter Wyatt, Bird and Henderson had been transferred at Vaenga to the new Senior Officer's ship—and fortunately the result this time was more peaceful. A signal from the two cruisers soon revealed that he had sighted Force R, and he cancelled his enemy report.

On 4th February the *Onslow* arrived back in Scapa Flow to receive more surprises. The battleship *Anson*, which had provided the wireless link with the Admiralty during the battle, was leaving with Admiral Fraser on board, and Marchant altered course to give her a wide berth. He was startled to get a signal from the battleship saying *Pass close to me*.

As the *Onslow* approached they could see that the decks of

the great battleship were black with men, and over the loud-speakers they heard: 'Three cheers for the *Onslow*—Hip, Hip Hurray! Hip, Hip . . .'

They were still recovering from their gratified embarrassment when they approached Switha and met the battleship *Malaya* coming out. Once again the little destroyer was cheered as she passed. A few moments later came the order that the *Onslow* was to steam past all the ships of the fleet now at anchor to receive their congratulations. She had been away for forty-three days; she had fought bravely in defence of a convoy. Though only a few men knew it, and they were in Berlin or at Fort Wolf, she had played a great part in defeating the German surface fleet.

The German Naval Staff managed to delay the meeting between Hitler and Raeder, planned to take place on 4th January, for two days, in the hope that by then the Führer would have cooled down; but they were disappointed.

Admiral Raeder flew in the afternoon from Berlin to the small airfield at Rastenberg, and drove through the pine forests to Fort Wolf for the fateful conference. It is doubtful if he was worried by the recent turn in events; there had been other crises before this one, and they had always sorted themselves out in the end. Several times before the war he had been on the verge of resigning as Commander-in-Chief. On one occasion, in October 1938, he had reported to the Führer about new types of ships and the Navy's plans for their further development. At once 'the Führer, in a manner defying explanation, began to attack everything that we had built and were building, including the plans for the *Bismarck*, and then declared them wrong', Raeder said later.[1]

'Later I found out that things like that happened whenever some people of his entourage, who knew very little about such things, gave him their opinion; that he always followed it up, probably wanting—as I told myself later—to check whether the things he had been told were actually correct.'

[1] To the International Military Tribunal, Nuremberg, 18th May, 1946.

After the war began, he said: 'The Führer became more nervous when I made reports and flared up in a rage when there were divergences of opinion or if there had been any incidents as, for instance, a technical defect or a poor performance by a ship. It happened again and again that his entourage influenced him before I could actually explain matters to him, and I was called in subsequently to set him straight on these matters. In that way unpleasant scenes ensued which wore me out.

'One point about which the Führer was especially sensitive was the large ships. He was always uneasy when our large ships were out on the high seas and were carrying on raids against shipping. The loss of a ship . . . he considered a tremendous loss of prestige; and matters like that, therefore, excited him tremendously. That went on until the end of 1942.

'Then there came—and this particularly impressed me—my defeat in consultation with the Führer on questions dealing with Norway, France and, above all, Russia. In the final analysis he always listened more to the Party people as, for example, Terboven, than to an old officer.[1] That led to a situation which could not be tolerated for any length of time.

'One of the basic characteristics of the Führer was a tremendous suspicion towards anyone and everyone, but especially directed against old officers who had come from the old Wehrmacht and of whom he always assumed—despite all well-intentioned treatment—that in their hearts they did not share these feelings which he had to demand of them. . . .'

Eric Raeder was, of course, one of the 'old officers', and was first and foremost a sailor and a strategist. Born near Hamburg in 1876, the son of a minor official, he had joined the Navy when he was eighteen. By a lucky chance he was appointed navigating officer of the Kaiser's yacht *Hohenzollern* in 1910. Although very short—it is said that his small size prevented him from ever getting command of a ship—he was very efficient. The

---

[1] Hitler attended Terboven's wedding on 28th June 1934, and went on to organize Ernst Rohm's murder in the 'Night of the Long Knives' two days later. Terboven became Reich Commissioner for Norway.

Kaiser knew and liked him, and it was in the *Hohenzollern* that he came to know Admiral Franz Hipper. When the First World War came Hipper took Raeder as his Chief of Staff. In that post he fought at the Battle of Jutland.

After the war, although highly regarded as a staff officer, he could not, like so many of his colleagues in the Services at the time of the Weimar Republic, keep his fingers out of home politics. And, because he was politically naïve, he got them burned at the time of the Kapp Putsch. He openly proposed that the Officer Corps should support Kapp; but Kapp failed and Raeder was one of the people who paid the price—a small one, in his case, and one which was to pay good dividends. He was appointed, in semi-disgrace, to the Department of Naval Archives for a couple of years.

However, he was a shrewd observer of foreign affairs and made good use of those two years' enforced leisure. Realizing how a powerful fleet could back a vigorous foreign policy, he was quick to relate that to Germany's position—a Germany which had been involved in six wars in just over one hundred years, two of them ending in disastrous defeats.

He formed his own idea of the future strategic needs of a German Navy. He saw, for instance, Germany's need for cruisers. Since she had no overseas bases, long-range cruisers were highly effective weapons for commerce raiding. The result was that he wrote a treatise on cruiser warfare which later was to become a textbook on the subject.

By 1922 Raeder was reinstated, made a Rear-admiral, and given the job of Inspector of Training and Education. His great chance came, however, when he succeeded Admiral Zenker as the Commander-in-Chief. He took over his new appointment on 1st October 1928,[1] and started the long task of rebuilding the Navy. He was one of the few men in Germany—if not the only one—able to do it successfully.

And when Hitler came to power as Chancellor in January 1933 Raeder gave his allegiance to the Nazis, and in return was given a comparatively free hand to construct a fleet. The Treaty

---

[1] Eighteen years later, to the day, Raeder was sentenced to twenty years' imprisonment by the International Military Tribunal at Nuremberg.

of Versailles, limiting the size and composition of the fleet, was repudiated when convenient. The Anglo-German Naval Treaty was signed in its place; but its terms were ignored.

Thus in 1936, while Britain and America were hamstrung with various treaties which limited the size of their fleets, Germany considered herself free to 'go it alone'.

Although a brilliant Commander-in-Chief of the Navy, Raeder had little or no influence over Hitler; yet he was professionally an extremely able man compared with those who formed Hitler's 'Court'. The reason, perhaps, lies in the fact that, apart from Hitler being a land animal, the Navy had never shared in the early days of the Nazi Movement before it came into power. No naval officer had been among the group of thugs and opportunists who rode on Hitler's bandwagon—like Göring, Himmler, the cruel, sadistic pseudo-mystic who ran the SS, or Goebbels, the shrill, warped 'intellectual' of the Party, or even Sepp Dietrich, a crude thug who headed Hitler's beerhouse bodyguard and, on that recommendation, later became an SS General.

No, Raeder was not one who shared those nostalgic, to Hitler, romantic days of the *Kampfzeit*, sapping at Germany's power, racing from meeting to meeting, beating up hecklers, plotting, planning, waiting and striking. Yet these were the days that, during the war, Hitler liked to remember.

One remark of his perhaps gives a clue to his feelings about the Navy—essentially still those of a corporal, even when he was Supreme Commander. At one of his interminable night sessions he was describing[1] how, during the Great War, 'I had the chance of going for a short trip in a submarine, and the sailors, smart, efficient, turned out as always as if for a review, were magnificent. It made one ashamed to be seen in their company. I suppose this accounts for the slight inferiority complex which the land forces feel in the presence of the Navy.'

Perhaps it was not entirely Hitler's fault. Raeder had 'certain human characteristics' which put him at a disadvantage when presenting to the Supreme Command the unpopular viewpoint

[1] *Hitler's Table Talk.*

of the Naval Staff. He was not gifted with a persuasive manner nor with the necessary tenacity of will to force his opinions on his listeners:

This must have had a deleterious effect on the co-operation between the Navy and the *Luftwaffe* and, in addition, it limited Raeder's influence over Hitler. It appears from the War Diary that Raeder, in his anxiety to dispose of a difficult point, would interpret a nod from Hitler as an indication of consent, which frequently led to misunderstandings.

It is here remarked that Hitler was not always frank in his dealing with Raeder. Occasionally, usually when he was alone with Hitler, Raeder would succeed in overcoming his reticence enough to convince Hitler of the wisdom of his arguments. Unfortunately, as soon as he left the Führer's headquarters, other influential people would take advantage of his absence to bring Hitler round to the opposite view. . . .[1]

Perhaps, as the car now took him through the twisty lanes to Fort Wolf, Admiral Raeder planned what he was going to say to Hitler: the explanations of the way the action went, excuses for the delay in getting the reports, the exhortation to leave the fleet in being . . .

But when the time came, when the car stopped and he was sitting before the Führer, with Field-Marshal Keitel and shorthand writers present, he had no chance to speak; instead the Führer had plenty to say.

The following account of the meeting was signed and approved by Admiral Raeder:

The Führer talks for an hour and a half about the role played by the Prussian and German navies since they came into existence. The German Navy was originally patterned after the British Navy, and proved to be unimportant during the wars of 1864, 1866, 1870–71. The first distinct contribution of the German Navy was the development of the torpedo boats. Special care was taken to perfect

---

[1] From *Aspects of The German Naval War* written for the Admiralty by two German Naval Staff officers.

this weapon. Submarines constituted the most important branch of the German Navy in the last war [1914–18] and must be considered today.

The High Seas Fleet made no notable contribution during the [First] World War. It is customary to blame the Kaiser for this inactivity, but this opinion is unwarranted. The real reason was that the Navy lacked men of action who were determined to fight with or without the support of the Kaiser. As a result of this inactivity a large amount of fighting-power lay idle, while the Army was constantly heavily engaged.

The revolution and the scuttling of the Fleet at Scapa Flow do not redound to the credit of the German Navy.[1] The Navy has always been careful to consider the number of their own ships and men as compared with the enemy before entering an engagement. The Army does not follow this principle. As a soldier, the Führer demands that, once forces have been committed to action, the battle be fought to a decision.

Due to the present critical situation, where all fighting power, all personnel, and all material must be brought into action, we cannot permit our large ships to ride idly at anchor for months. They require constant protection by the Air Force as well as by numerous smaller surface craft. The same situation would hold in case of an invasion of Norway, where the Air Force would be of more value in attacking an invasion fleet than being obliged to protect our own Fleet. For this reason, the Fleet would not be of great value in preventing the enemy from establishing a beachhead.

Until now light naval forces have been doing most of the fighting. Whenever the larger ships put out to sea, light forces have to accompany them. It is not the large ships which protect the small, but rather the reverse is true. (This remark is indicative of Hitler's lack of understanding.)

Owing to the mining of the Baltic the large ships find it more and more difficult to engage in manœuvres. The Coast Defence could use the guns from these large ships very effectively. Heavy naval guns, if mounted where invasions on a large scale would be practical, could possibly prevent such landings. In this connection consideration

---

[1] A young midshipman in HMS *Canada* watching the German Fleet steaming in to surrender was R. StV. Sherbrooke, then aged seventeen.

should be given to the North Sea area. It should not be considered a degradation if the Führer decides to scrap the large ships. This would be true only if he were removing a fighting unit which had retained its full usefulness. A parallel to this in the Army would be the removal of all cavalry divisions. The Führer also points out that the Italian Fleet uses the complements of her large ships for duty in the destroyers.

The Navy shall consider the following:

1. Should the three aircraft carriers which were planned be retained? Should other ships be converted into aircraft carriers (especially in case the *De Grasse* cannot be used)? Are the *Hipper* and the *Prinz Eugen*, because of their great speed, more suited than the *Lützow* and the *Scheer*, which have a more extensive operating radius? If the latter were lengthened, could they develop greater speed and could they be given a larger landing deck?

2. Where would the heavy guns of these ships best be mounted on land?

3. In which order should the ships be paid off? Probably the *Gneisenau* would be the first, since she will not be ready for active duty until the end of 1944. Next would probably be the ships which are now due for overhauling and repairs. Personnel of these ships will remain with the Navy.

4. Can the submarine programme be extended and speeded up if the large ships are eliminated? The C-in-C, Navy, shall prepare a memorandum giving his views on the above. These comments will be of historical value. The Führer will carefully examine the document.

The C-in-C, Navy, rarely had an opportunity to comment, but his final impression was that the Führer, even though he described his decision as final, would reconsider some of his views if sound arguments were presented. Concerning the question of the C-in-C, Navy, whether the *Scharnhorst* and *Prinz Eugen* are to be sent to Norway, the Führer replied in the affirmative and said that for the present Norway is to be defended as strongly as possible.

During a private conversation between the C-in-C, Navy, and the Führer, the C-in-C, Navy, tried to explain the reason for the delay in communications on 31st December–1st January. . . . At that time the C-in-C, Navy, explained that Kummetz and the individual commanders had obeyed orders to the letter. The orders of the Naval Staff strictly limited the extent of the operation.

What Raeder did not include in this report of his talk with Hitler was that he had tried to resign. He made up for the omission after the war at Nuremberg, when he told the International Military Tribunal:[1]

After the Führer concluded his speech I asked to be permitted to speak with him alone. Field-Marshal Keitel and the shorthand writers left and I told him I was asking for my resignation as I could see from his words that he was extremely dissatisfied with me and therefore this was the proper moment for me to leave. As always, he tried at first to dissuade me, but I remained adamant and told him that a new Commander-in-Chief who would have complete responsibility would definitely have to be appointed.

He said it would be a great burden for him if I were to leave now since for one thing the situation was very critical—Stalingrad was impending—and secondly, since he had already been accused of dismissing so many generals. In the eyes of the outside world it would incriminate him if I were to leave at this point.

I told him I would do everything I could to prevent this happening. If he wanted to give the appearance as far as the outside world was concerned that I had not resigned because of a clash, then he could make me a general inspector with some sort of nominal title, which would create the impression that I was still with the Navy and that my name was still connected with the Navy. This appealed to him at once and I told him on 6th January that I wanted to be dismissed on 30th January. At this point I had concluded ten years' service under him. He agreed to this proposal and asked me to suggest two successors, so that he could make a choice.

The two men that Raeder nominated were Admiral Carls and Admiral Dönitz. Admiral Rolf Carls was one of the senior and most capable officers in the Navy and commanded Group North. Dönitz, commanding the U-boats, was a very junior admiral (he was at the top of the captains' list in 1938 when Carls was fourth on the list of thirty-two admirals).

[1] Evidence given on 18th May 1946.

24

A Bloodless Victory

A CHASTENED Raeder, realizing he was now fighting for the very existence of the Navy which he had built up, almost alone, and commanded since 1928, returned to Berlin to prepare the memorandum. He had been unable to reason with the Führer, and Krancke had also been shouted down. That meant there was no one left on the Navy's side who had the Führer's ear. Göring was seizing his opportunity to put the Navy's case in the worst possible light; Martin Bormann (the Führer's chief assistant and confidant) and Himmler were unsympathetic. Only Keitel could possibly have swayed Hitler, had he chose; but Keitel was a subservient lackey, a yes-man, the contemporary standard-bearer for the once-proud Officer Corps. Nothing was too degrading or too much trouble for Keitel, provided it boosted his reputation with the Führer. It was this pliability, this facility for not questioning where, metaphorically speaking, the housekeeping money came from but to concentrate on the cooking, which led him to the gallows at Nuremberg, condemned legally as a war criminal and morally a pandering self-seeker. Raeder could not look to him for help.

No, everything—the whole future of the Navy, the war and the prospects of victory, and certainly the future of the Grand Admiral himself—rested on the memorandum that a group of senior officers in the Operations Division were given a week to write. The final draft came out at more than 5,000 words, and was taken to the Grand Admiral. He read it through and made several careful corrections. These were, in general, aimed at deleting phrases which could, by misinterpretation, appear politically offensive. (By this time Hitler had, of course, like the majority of people who obtain power, become very sensitive to criticism and flared up at the slightest actual or imagined hint of it.) Also removed from the memorandum were some detailed calculations showing the possible use of guns and other equipment from dismantled ships. Where, however, it spoke of the role of the German Navy in the war, Raeder's final corrections brought out his point of view in the clearest and most outspoken form.

After the memorandum had been re-typed for presentation to Hitler, the Admiral wrote a brief letter addressed to 'The Führer and Supreme Commander of the Armed Forces'. It contained the last plea of the Navy: 'The paying off of the large surface vessels,' wrote the Grand Admiral, 'will be a victory gained by our enemies without any effort on their part. It will cause joy in the hostile camp, and disappointment in the camp of our allies, especially Japan. It will be viewed as a sign of weakness and of a lack of comprehension of the supreme importance of naval warfare in the approaching final stage of the war.'

The memorandum itself was a cleverly-written restatement, carefully phrased in layman's language, of Raeder's concept of what German naval strategy ought to have been and, up to a point, had been. It is as true today as when it was written.

Germany's naval forces have been designed and built for use against the weak points of hostile naval powers. These weak points lie in the vulnerability of Anglo-American sea communications. The very existence of the English people rests on these communications, which also form the prerequisite to the entire British war effort. The enemy is superior in manpower, raw materials and industrial potential. His chief problem is to maintain the vital shipping links within the British Empire, to the United States and to Russia, so that he can transport men, material and supplies to the points where he wishes to bring his offensive power to bear.[1]

[1] It should be noted that this lesson of the First and Second World Wars has yet to be learnt by the United Kingdom's politicians. Vote-catching defence cuts have whittled down the Royal Navy's escort force to negligible proportions at a time when Russia has five hundred U-boats. Germany had fifty-seven at the beginning of the Second World War.

After describing the shortcomings of the Kaiser's Navy, the memorandum outlined the efforts of the Navy under the Nazis to build, by 1944–45 'a navy capable of attacking the British communication lines in the Atlantic with an adequate number of ships'. It added tactfully: 'Construction of this naval force had just begun when war broke out in 1939, five years prior to the date planned upon.'

This meant, it said, that the British sea lanes could not be cut and the opportunity to put a speedy end to the war was lost: all emphasis had to be placed on U-boats. The occupation of Norway and France increased their opportunities.

'Our ships, few but aggressive, utilizing the element of surprise for their operations, constituted such a danger to the British sea communications that the British looked upon the possibility of a numerical increase of our forces from French sources [i.e. at the fall of France] as an unbearable threat. . . .'

The concentration of the German fleet in northern waters was also a serious threat to Britain. 'In order to protect his North Atlantic sea route he had to commit the Home Fleet, his most modern battleships, several aircraft carriers and a large number of cruisers.'[1]

The Naval Staff pointed out, quite tactfully, that the *Luftwaffe* had failed to support the Navy's Operations sufficiently; and Italy's entry into the war meant that 'Axis naval strategy was capable of exercising such pressure on the British naval command that by the spring of 1941 it was no longer able fully to carry out its naval task. Help from the United States was requested and received in the form of light naval forces transferred in exchange for British bases'. Japan's entry into the war brought a very strong navy to the side of the Axis and further stretched Britain's Navy, as well as occupying the Americans.

Having set the scene, as it were, the memorandum then declared:

[1] The Home Fleet in January 1943 comprised four battleships, four 8-inch and five 6-inch cruisers, and about twenty destroyers. It did not, at this particular time, have any aircraft carriers.

This strategic over-all situation would undergo a fundamental change with the dismantling [*Abwrackung*] of the German nucleus fleet [*Kernflotte*], that is *Tirpitz, Scharnhorst, Gneisenau, Scheer, Lützow, Prinz Eugen* and *Hipper*. Such an action would constitute a bloodless victory for the enemy.

For us, the result would be that the enemy could operate in our coastal waters at his discretion. It is not possible to maintain air forces in sufficient strength and in constant readiness for defence, especially in northern waters. Even if this were possible, weather conditions such as low cloud ceiling would prevent their successful operation at times.

We would be practically offering our coastline to the enemy. Light naval units alone cannot ward off such operations. . . . If ships' guns were to be mounted as coastal batteries, their fire power would be immobile, making it impossible to use them at points where they might be needed most. . . .

After warning that the Luftwaffe was increasingly unable to defend vital coastal shipping, and inward- and outward-bound U-boats would be threatened, the Naval Staff put up its final arguments.

If Germany's large ships are paid off, the repercussions will be disastrous not only for our situation but for the over-all naval strategy. There will be speedy and serious consequences in the other theatres for our allies. If we withdraw our threat from the Atlantic, the enemy will be able to concentrate his power somewhere else, and no effort on his part will have been required for the achievement of such a decisive success.

He will be able to use this situation to settle conclusively the Mediterranean problem; or he can mass all the power of his best ships for a decisive blow against the Japanese Fleet. In either event, he will regain the initiative which he has lost or which at least has been seriously limited.

It is impossible to foresee the consequences.

After that extremely accurate round-up of the situation which, had Hitler read it dispassionately, might have persuaded him to alter his 'irrevocable decision', the Naval Staff gave some figures. Paying off the fleet would have the following 'advantages' for the German war effort:

1. About three hundred officers and 8,500 ratings would become available. This represents not quite 1·4 per cent of the total naval personnel.

2. If the ships were scrapped, 125,800 tons of steel would be obtained. This is less than one-twentieth of the German monthly requirements.

3. There would be a saving in raw materials, fuel, yard facilities, shipyard workers, etc. A large part of these savings would be consumed by mounting ships' guns as shore batteries.

4. Fifteen batteries could be constructed from the guns thus made available. The first of these batteries would be ready for action a year after the order to scrap the ships, the fifteenth battery after twenty-seven months.

5. The scrapping would require the work of 7,000 men in five large shipyards for a period of about one and a half years.

6. Effects on the submarine construction programme would be slight. Of the three hundred officers available for reassignment, only about fifty would be gained for the submarine branch, the others being too old or otherwise unsuitable. If the entire amount of steel from the scrapping of the ships was used for submarine construction, seven more submarines per month could be built, providing that 13,000 to 14,000 specialized workers could be allocated for this job.

7. The paying off of the big ships would make it imperative to increase the number of destroyers and torpedo boats.

8. Paying off the big ships constitutes a final and irrevocable act; it would take years to rebuild them.

9. The disappearance of the nucleus fleet will affect not only the war but will continue to be felt in the years of peace. During the early years after the war the Navy will not be able to carry the flag of the Reich to foreign shores.

Then Raeder, after repeating that the Allies would be able to free many of their ships at present pinned down by the need to 'contain' the German ships, concluded:

I believe that the small gain in personnel and material which may be accomplished by paying off the Fleet cannot outweigh the grave political and naval consequences that will result.

I am firmly convinced that with the nucleus fleet the German Navy is no longer capable of carrying out the task assigned to it in the Greater German War for Freedom.

The memorandum, with Raeder's letter pinned to it, was delivered to Hitler on the 15th January, but nothing more was heard in Berlin until the 18th, when Krancke reported to the Naval Staff from Fort Wolf. His communication, dated Führer's Headquarters, 17th January, showed that the Supreme Commander either had not read the memorandum or was crazy.

After today's situation conference [it said] the Führer asked me to stay and again stated that he could not see any further use for the big ships in this war. The situation in the East is so critical that he must scrape together all forces to help out. More than ever before it has become obvious that tanks are decisive, but despite all our efforts we are still turning out too few. He must put everything into the effort to increase production figures.

Hence he must have all the labour that was working on projects that will not be ready for operations until after 1945–46, that is perhaps after the end of the war, for the production of tanks. It is not yet possible to say whether these workmen can be returned later. Therefore no more ships can be constructed or converted unless they are necessary for the submarine war or the expansion of our coastal defences (motor minesweepers to destroyers). All workers hitherto employed on this work must immediately be made available for tank production. I got him to confirm that he means in this connection all aircraft carriers as well as the large ships that were to be converted into transports.

I mentioned that the number of workers that would be released is not so very large, in any case not nearly so large as the 20,000 he mentioned. The reply was: 'Even if it is only 5,000 it will help.' I had several opportunities to say a few words about the value of the big ships. Yet the Führer interrupted me and said: 'This time it must be done, for there is no other way.'

The commitment and maintenance of big ships presupposes foreign bases, he said, which we unfortunately do not possess and furthermore could not obtain in this war. His idea of acquiring bases in Iceland or in Portuguese islands in the Atlantic had not been shared by the Naval Staff, which had declared this was impossible. It has become more and more obvious that it is not possible for a fleet of big ships to operate in coastal waters where enemy air forces can penetrate. Aircraft carriers, too, are useless in the vicinity of coastal airfields as land-based planes are superior, he stated. . . .

I again referred to the struggle against the Anglo-Americans with their gigantic sea power, for this battle is after all at least as decisive for the outcome of the war as the war in the East. The Führer said that this is absolutely correct, and therefore every effort must be concentrated on maintaining submarine warfare, and everything connected with it must be reinforced if at all possible. Yet we have to realize that all this will be of no use unless we can defeat the Russians in the East. So we must manage without big ships.

The conversation went off quietly in the main, so that I was able to get in a word more than once. To my mind the cancellation of work on all large vessels including aircraft carriers and the release of workers employed on them is to be regarded as an order.

The fact that Hitler's orders now also affected the aircraft carrier programme was 'entirely new' to the Naval Staff, according to a note in the margin of Krancke's communication.

Three days passed before news of Hitler's reaction to the Grand Admiral's letter as such filtered through to the Naval Staff. According to the War Diary, Admiral Fricke, who was Chief of Staff to the Naval Staff, reported 'in the smallest circle' that the following information had been received by telephone from Fort Wolf:

'The Führer has made several comments concerning the memorandum. These comments which were more or less sarcastic dealt with minor questions only. Therefore Admiral Krancke concluded that the main points of the memorandum have not failed to impress the Führer. To what extent this conclusion is correct only the future can tell.'

The Alice-in-Wonderland atmosphere at Fort Wolf must have been increased by the arrival there on 22nd January of a report by the Chief of Naval Communications concerning the delays there had been in forwarding Kummetz's report about Rainbow. When he read it, Hitler could not be blamed if he wondered what on earth was going on at Naval Headquarters in Berlin. The report said:

[Grand Admiral Raeder] in a report to the Führer on 1st January said that speedy reports were made difficult by the interruption of telephone lines to Norway and numerous disturbances in W/T traffic which were particularly unfavourable.

This report [i.e. by the Chief of Naval Communications] proves the reason for the delayed reporting did not lie in the aforementioned lines of communication. The radio link at the time of the operation in the Arctic coast area was particularly good and usable between there and home, and the times required for transmission were normal and unavoidable and did not result in essential delays in transmission.

Between relevant commands on land there were at all times official telephone connections. . . .

After outlining the difficulties caused by the fact that the *Köln* did not have the new cipher key and the *Hipper*'s motorboat broke down, he adds: 'Why the *Lützow* did not transmit his first action report by W/T on entering harbour as *Hipper* did (this W/T message from Admiral Kummetz was received by Operations Division and Group North) is beyond my comment. . . .'

For the fortnight following his disastrous talk with Hitler Raeder had kept secret the fact that he had put in his resignation. Then on 20th January he met all the heads of departments in the Navy and told them that he had repeated his request, first made in 1941, to be permitted to pass the office of

Commander-in-Chief on to a younger man in view of his 'advanced age and failing health'.

At this time there was no indication of which candidate Hitler had chosen to take over. Would it be Carls, whose policy would probably be the same as Raeder's? Or Dönitz, the thrusting chief of the U-boats, whose Party fanaticism and loyalty to the Führer was unquestioned?

It is not clear on what day Hitler made up his mind, but in fact he chose Dönitz—the obvious choice if he was going to place the emphasis on U-boat warfare—and ordered him to report at Fort Wolf for a conference on 25th January. No record of what was said at this conference was ever discovered among the German Naval archives captured at the end of the war, but the events are shown in the Naval Staff's War Diary.

'According to information received by telephone from Admiral Krancke, the Führer informed Admiral Dönitz of his decision concerning the memorandum. . . . The arguments put forth . . . have not moved the Führer to give up his decision to dispose of the Fleet in favour of direct submarine warfare. . . . After the decisive conference with the Führer, Admiral Dönitz transmitted by telephone the orders from the Führer. . . .' The War Diary then recorded an extract from Hitler's orders, which said that all German ships larger than destroyers were to be paid off.

Two days later the Naval Staff sent to all the commands concerned the following directive:

On 26th January the following order from the Führer was transmitted by Admiral Dönitz to the Chief of Staff, Naval Staff:

1. All work on big ships under construction or being converted is to cease immediately; this also means any further work on aircraft carriers, auxiliary carriers, and troop transports. Exceptions: (a) Repairs to continue on *Scheer* until it has been decided whether or not she is to be converted to a training ship. (b) ships to be kept in commission for training purposes are always to be maintained in the state of repair required for this function. Details will be settled later.

2. Unless required for training purposes battleships, pocket battle-

ships, heavy and light cruisers are to be paid off. The date for paying off will be announced by the Führer in accordance with suggestions submitted by the Commander-in-Chief, Navy.

3. Naval personnel, workers, yard facilities and weapons becoming available as a result of this directive should be used to speed up submarine repairs and construction.

4. The appropriate measures will be taken to arrange all details needed for the execution of this order before 2nd February, at which date all suggestions are to be submitted to me.

Then there followed a list of questions which required clarification. The order ended: 'In view of the political and psychological effect of this order it will be communicated to the smallest possible number of officers.'

On 30th January, ten years to the day after the Nazis seized power and Hitler had become Chancellor, the change in the leadership of the German Navy was announced to the German people in a proclamation.

That was the official end; but there was a private end next day when Raeder bade farewell to the Naval Staff. In his speech he was at pains to disguise the real reason for his resignation.

His successor, Dönitz, had his first conference with Hitler after taking over as Commander-in-Chief on 8th February and told him of 'proposed personnel changes at the highest level of the Naval High Command'. These were aimed at getting rid of several admirals senior to Dönitz and who might be regarded as hostile and exponents of Raeder's policies.

Dönitz also put forward a time-table for paying off the big ships, to which Hitler agreed.

The battle-cruiser *Gneisenau*, which had been badly damaged, was already paid off and the light cruiser *Leipzig* was following within a week or two; the heavy cruiser *Hipper* and the light cruiser *Köln*, which we have already met in this narrative, would go on 1st March; the old battleship *Schleswig-Holstein* on 1st April, the old *Schlesien* on 1st May; the battle-cruiser *Scharnhorst* on 1st July. The battleship *Tirpitz* would be paid off in the autumn. The remaining ships, the heavy cruiser *Prinz Eugen*, the two pocket battleships *Admiral Scheer* and *Lützow*, and the light cruisers *Nürnberg* and *Emden* were to be assigned as training ships and no longer ready for action.

Nearly three weeks later Dönitz again reported to the Führer, who had meanwhile moved his headquarters from Fort Wolf to Vinnitsa in the Ukraine. Continuing his liking for the name 'Wolf' in the naming of his headquarters, this new one became '*Werwolf*'.

During those three weeks Karl Dönitz had been having second thoughts. Perhaps the immensity of the task set him had finally sunk in. Hitler had virtually turned the Navy over exclusively to U-boat warfare, yet at this conference Dönitz was forced to report that during the first fourteen days of February U-boats had not sunk any Allied ships 'because nothing was sighted'. The month of February, he said, 'may be considered as typical for the present submarine warfare'.

Dönitz then reported that the *Hipper*, *Leipzig*, and *Köln* had been paid off and the *Schlesien* and *Schleswig-Holstein* were to follow shortly. Then he put forward a suggestion which, considering what had gone before, was extraordinary. 'The Archangel convoys would make excellent targets for the large ships,' he said, and he 'considered it essential that the *Scharnhorst* be sent to Norway to strengthen the forces there. The *Tirpitz*, the *Scharnhorst*, and for the present the *Lützow*, together with six destroyers, would be a fairly powerful force.'

Hitler reacted strongly and was opposed to the idea of any further operations by the surface ships 'since, beginning with the *Graf Spee*, one defeat has followed the other. Large ships are a thing of the past'. The minutes of the meeting say:

When the C-in-C, Navy, mentioned that ships were severely limited by the imposed restriction that they must not be sacrificed, and therefore commanding officers of ships at sea could not be censured, the Führer replied that he had never issued an order restricting commanding officers in this manner. If in contact with the enemy, ships must go into action. However, he no longer valued their effectiveness. . . .

Thereupon the C-in-C, Navy, declared that instead of paying off the two heavy ships [*Tirpitz* and *Scharnhorst*] he would consider it his duty to send them into action whenever possible and as long as suitable targets could be found. The Führer finally agreed to let the *Scharnhorst* join the force, as recommended by the C-in-C, Navy. He asked how long it would be before a suitable target would be found. The C-in-C, Navy, thought in the next three months. The Führer replied: 'Even if it should require six months, you will then return and be forced to admit that I was right!'

There was something bitterly ironical about Dönitz's position now as Commander-in-Chief. For years he had been preaching the gospel that the war at sea would be won entirely by his U-boats, but Raeder, with his greater strategic grasp of the situation, had subordinated them to what he considered their proper role. Now Dönitz, from February 1943 onwards, was the boss, able to throw all the weight of the Navy into the U-boat attack.

But at the same time the Allies were beginning to get the measure of the U-boat threat: more aircraft carrying highly-developed radar, highly-efficient escort groups including carriers, and a general increase in the strength of convoy escorts meant mounting U-boat losses in the first four months of the year. In May thirty-seven U-boats were sunk—30 per cent of those at sea. As a result Dönitz, facing his biggest crisis yet, withdrew them from the Atlantic while he worked out counter-measures. And in July the number and tonnage of Allied merchantmen launched from the shipyards exceeded those sunk for the first time in the war. Although at this time neither the Germans nor the Allies realized it, the Battle of the Atlantic was, for all intents and purposes, over.

Just over ten months passed before Dönitz reported to the Führer over the *Scharnhorst*. On 25th December 1943 the battle-cruiser had sailed from Altenfiord to attack convoy JW 55B. Unfortunately for her, Admiral Sir Bruce Fraser (who had taken over from Admiral Tovey as Commander-in-Chief of the Home Fleet) anticipated this and was at sea with the battleship *Duke of York* and the cruiser *Jamaica,* who had distinguished herself almost exactly a year earlier against the *Hipper* and four destroyers.

Vice-admiral Burnett—appointed to command the 10th Cruiser Squadron during that same battle—was covering this convoy with the *Norfolk, Belfast* and *Sheffield.* In addition the *Onslow,* now repaired, and the *Orwell,* were among the escorts of JW 55B.

Admiral Burnett had found and attacked the *Scharnhorst* in a gale on Boxing Day when the battle-cruiser was just over thirty miles from the convoy. The German ship had been hit, but escaped because of her superior speed in heavy weather. Admiral Fraser had picked up Admiral Burnett's enemy report and steered to intercept. After heavy attacks—including torpedo attacks by destroyers—the *Scharnhorst* was sunk off North Cape.

It was the last foray of the war by a German capital ship. The *Tirpitz* stayed in Altenfiord, under constant attack by the Royal Navy, Fleet Air Arm and RAF. The pocket battleship *Admiral Scheer* was bombed and capsized, the *Hipper* was set on fire, and the *Emden* damaged in air raids in April 1944. When the war ended only the *Prinz Eugen, Lützow* and the *Nürnberg* remained of Germany's fleet. (The first was later sunk in the atomic-bomb tests at Bikini Atoll in the Pacific, the third was handed over to the Russians and renamed *Admiral Makarov.* The *Lützow* was badly damaged when she was captured by the Russians.)

Thus the Navy which was to help build the Thousand Year Reich perished. Under the wilful leadership of Hitler it had lasted, in name at least, for thirteen years.

25

Hitler's Harvest

THE Battle of the Barents Sea[1] was fought and won; the German fleet was reduced to the status of a training squadron; there remains only the final analysis of why Hitler made his 'irrevocable decision'.

Overriding every other consideration was the fact that the whole of the Nazi war machine was run in much the same way as that of the most sadistic and brutish court of a king of the Dark Ages.

As long as the Foreign Minister was personally in favour with the Führer then his foreign policy was in favour; as long as the Air Minister was personally one of the Führer's favourites then the *Luftwaffe* could do no wrong. There was no Chiefs of Staff Committee to integrate the war effort of the Navy, Army and Air Force, only the Führer.

Under this Nazi law of the survival of the craftiest the final judge in each case would be the Führer.

At the time that the *Hipper* and *Lützow* sailed to attack convoy JW 51B, Hitler was beset on all sides by requests for men and materials: more steel to build tanks to fight on the Eastern Front; more soldiers to replace those falling in swathes before the unexpectedly tough Russians; more anti-tank guns and more mortars, more shells, and more fighters. The Army was, not unnaturally, his own favourite. With it he had done wonders. By overrunning Europe, he had founded the Thousand Year Reich, and he certainly was not going to see it go short so that the process of consolidation would be endangered. The Army then, had the lion's share of what was going. Göring was still at this time a favourite, the man who, should the Führer die,

---

[1] The official title. Those of the 17th Destroyer Flotilla originally called it the Battle of Cape Misery—the name of the nearest land, on Bear Island.

would take over the leadership in Germany's great struggle. The *Luftwaffe* therefore seldom went short.

But the Navy had no friend at court; apart from the need for U-boats and oil it had no pressing demand to make on the Führer and perhaps for this reason the great man assumed it had too much, mistaking the silence of sufficiency for the silence of surfeit.

The Army had made spectacular advances and fought spectacular battles; its victories yielded land—tangible lines firmly drawn on large maps—and propaganda. The *Luftwaffe* was closely linked with these victories. And the Navy . . .?

(Had the war begun in 1945—the date by which Raeder planned to have his powerful fleet completed—it might have been a different story.)

All this, then, was in the back of Hitler's mind, stored as a disorderly hodge-podge of prejudices, dislikes and suspicions. To the forefront of his mind was the realization that Raeder had said in August 1942 that it was possible that the Allies would invade North Africa while he, the Führer, had said that Norway was the 'zone of destiny'. Raeder had been right and he, the Führer, wrong. . . . Yet being the kind of man he was, he could not accept that.

He, the Führer who ten years ago had taken a crushed, dissident, broken and dissatisfied Germany and moulded it into a great nation destined by its traditions, superiority and strength to lead the world, could not be wrong. Other people could be wrong; but not he.

It is the all-too-common reaction found among so many men who have any authority at all: they have an inner aching uncertainty, an inner insecurity which they subconsciously feel will germinate and grow fat if they admit openly they have been mistaken. It is the inadequate husband raging at a patient wife; it is the boss faced with falling sales who blames his staff, never his own mistakes, the very man who will brook no criticism of his methods and decisions.

Any man who surrounds himself with sycophants, who refuses to listen to ideas, comments, criticisms and suggestions freely made by men with ability, eventually has to face the fact that a mistake has been made by the only man capable of making it—himself. And almost every time he reacts in the same way. He metaphorically kicks the dog.

In the case of Hitler, facing the harvest of his mistakes in 1942—on the great battlefields of Russia, the sands of Libya, the mountains of North Africa, and the icy wastes of the Arctic —he had created his own scapegoat. Hedged round with his own restrictions and injunctions to take no risks, the Navy failed him. It was quite inevitable. It was not up to the job in any case; and Hitler had given it impossible tasks.

So the Führer wreaked his vengeance on the Navy. As a corporal in the trenches in the Kaiser's war he had envied the Navy's self-assured smartness; he sneered at it because the sailors never had mud on their boots. The Navy had not been a breeding-ground for that *élite* group that was the early Nazi party. So it paid the price for its shortcomings; it also paid the price for all the defeats that Germany had suffered. And in making it pay that price Hitler knew he was not putting himself in any great jeopardy; having opened the Second Front in North Africa he knew Italy would be the Allies' next target. There would be no invasion of Norway and therefore no need of a Navy to defend it. The U-boats, he thought, could cut the Allied sea lanes.

In Britain early in 1943, while Captain Sherbrooke, V.C., D.S.O., was in hospital undergoing a series of operations, the reports on his gallant destroyer action were studied, along with the reports of Admiral Burnett's Force R. The convoy had been saved, it had been a classic destroyer action, and at least one lesson learnt was that the Germans were excessively scared of torpedoes.

However it was not until the end of the war, when the German naval archives were captured and translated, that the Allies discovered, to their great surprise, that Sherbrooke's action had had such fantastic results. It is perhaps unnecessary to add that even if he and his men had known at the time what was at stake they could not have fought more bravely or skilfully.

Appendix 1

THE following awards for gallantry were made after the Battle of the Barents Sea on 31st December 1942:

HMS *Onslow*

The Victoria Cross: Captain R. StV. Sherbrooke, D.S.O.

Distinguished Service Cross: Lt Cdr T. J. G. Marchant; Lt P. J. Wyatt; Lt L. King, R.N.Z.N.V.R.; Surgeon-Lt C. B. Holland, R.N.V.R.; Cdr (E) H. B. Samways; Lt (E) E. W. K. Walton.

Distinguished Service Medal: Leading Seaman R. T. Uren; PO Telegraphist F. V. Lovett; ERA R. Howarth; Stoker PO A. W. Heaman; SBA T. Hanley; Yeoman of Signals W. E. Moorman; Leading Seaman E. Wilcox; Able Seaman T. Cunningham.

Mentioned in Despatches: Lt F. H. Foster; Lt J. M. A. Wilson; Lt M. P. Vaux, D.S.C.; Gunner (T) F. C. Tibbs, M.B.E.; CPO Telegraphist W. Bearpark; Leading Telegraphist D. Grant.

HMS *Obedient*

Companion of the Distinguished Service Order: Cdr. D. C. Kinloch.

D.S.C.: Lt P. F. Cole.

Mentioned in Despatches: Lt J. P. Donovan; Lt (E) H. Good, D.S.C.

HMS *Obdurate*

Bar to the D.S.O.: Lt Cdr C. E. L. Sclater, D.S.O.

D.S.C.: Lt C. A. H. Owen.

Mentioned in Despatches: Lt (E) G. L. Densham; Sub-Lt C. R. A. Senior, R.C.N.V.R.

HMS *Orwell*

Bar to the D.S.O.: Lt Cdr N. H. G. Austen, D.S.O.

Bar to the D.S.C.: Lt H. J. Lee, D.S.C.

Mentioned in Despatches: Lt P. G. Satow; Lt (E) R. H. Tribe.

HMS *Achates*

D.S.O.: Lt L. E. Peyton-Jones, D.S.C.

Conspicuous Gallantry Medal: ERA H. Hawksworth.

D.S.C.: Gunner (T) G. W. Davies.

D.S.M.: Stoker J. Colley; Able Seaman C. Brightmore; Able Seaman H. Platt; CPO D. Hall; Stoker E. Drummond; Stoker L. Meacock; Yeoman of Signals A. W. Taylor.

Mentioned in Despatches: Chief Stoker W. Brown, D.S.M.; Leading Seaman R. C. Wells; PO F. Batchelor; Telegraphist E. J. Dickenson; Stoker W. Wilkinson.

Posthumously Mentioned in Despatches: Lt Cdr A. H. T. Johns; Lt (E) P. A. Wright, R.N.R.; Surgeon-Lt J. L. B. MacFarlane; Stoker PO R. Bell; Supply PO J. R. Cole; Able Seamen K. MacIver; Able Seaman C. W. Coe; PO Telegraphist W. Bartripp; Officers Steward A. Jones; Canteen Manager G. Drummond; PO C. Carpenter.

HMS *Northern Gem*

D.S.C.: Skipper Lt H. C. Aisthorpe, R.N.R.

Mentioned in Despatches: Skipper J. W. Pooley, R.N.R.; Ordinary Seaman E. G. Mayer; Acting Coxswain S. A. Kerslake; Engineman J. J. Edmonds; Leading Seaman D. E. S. Parnell; Steward J. J. Fleming.

HMS *Bramble*

Posthumously Mentioned in Despatches: Cdr H. T. Rust, D.S.O.

HMS *Rhododendron*

Mentioned in Despatches: Lt Cdr L. A. Sayers, R.N.R.

HMS *Hyderabad*

Mentioned in Despatches: Lt S. C. B. Hickman, D.S.C., R.N.R.; Lt R. Adams, R.N.V.R.

HMS *Vizalma*

Mentioned in Despatches: Lt J. R. Angleback, R.N.V.R.

HMS *Sheffield*

D.S.O.: Rear-admiral R. L. Burnett, C.B., O.B.E.; Captain A. W. Clarke.

D.S.C.: Lt Cdr E. F. S. Back; Lt Cdr O. G. Cameron; Lt G. L. Hogben.

D.S.M.: Leading Seaman W. T. Robertson; Able Seaman G. Parkinson; Ordinary Seaman J. Moore; PO A. C. Connal; PO A. Murray; PO N. M. Johnson; Sergeant S. G. Hills, R.M.

Mentioned in Despatches: Temp. Gunner C. H. Reynolds; Ordinary Seaman F. H. Jennings; Chief ERA L. C. Frost; Chief Mechanician D. G. Whitman; Chief Stoker J. W. Burdett; PO C. W. Knight, D.S.M.; Able Seaman K. Atkinson.

HMS *Jamaica*

D.S.O.: Captain J. L. Storey.

D.S.C.: Lt Cdr J. E. Scotland; Lt Cdr H. H. R. Moore; Sub-lt R. T. Walker.

D.S.M.: Able Seaman R. Morrison; Chief Yeoman of Signals W. C. Cosh; CPO T. R. Alderson; Colour Sergeant T. I. Gauntlett, R.M.: PO R. E. L'Amy.

Mentioned in Despatches: Lt E. W. Brien, R.C.N.V.R.: Acting Gunner G. Simpson; Marine J. J. Cooke; CPO Cook F. B. Bowen; Acting Yeoman of Signals F. S. Street; Chief ERA H. D. Davidson; Chief ERA F. F. C. Nelmes.

Commodore of Convoy

Mentioned in Despatches: Captain R. A. Melhuish, R.I.N.

Appendix 2

The following table shows the merchant ships and their cargoes sailing in convoy JW 51B

	Vehicles	Tanks	Fighters	Bombers	Fuel	Aviation Spirit	Misc. (in tons)
Empire Archer (Br.)	141	18	21	—	—	—	4,376
Daldorch (Br.)	264	—	—	—	—	—	1,744
Empire Emerald (Br)	—	—	—	—	2,580	7,400	—
Pontfield (Br)	—	—	—	—	5,500	5,250	—
Chester Valley (USA)	2	25	10	4	250	—	4,371
Puerto Rican (USA)	14	23	15	8	100	—	5,345
Executive (USA)	130	—	13	4	450	—	4,210
R. W. Emerson (USA)	160	45	—	5	780	—	5,090
Ballot (USA)	115	25	18	—	—	—	5,534
Jefferson Myers (USA)	376	—	—	4	500	—	5,336
Vermont (USA)	299	—	—	4	300	—	4,058
Yorkmar (USA)	188	—	—	—	150	—	5,326
J. H. La Trobe (USA)	191	58	10	4	640	—	4,397
Calobre (Panamanian)	166	8	—	—	250	—	4,534
TOTAL	2,046	202	87	33	11,500	12,650	54,321

Appendix 3

Allied convoys to Russia between 1st August 1942 and 11th January 1943

Convoy	No. of Ships	Sunk	Arrived	Escort Losses	Enemy Losses
PQ 18	40	13	27	nil	3 U-boats 41 aircraft
QP 14	15	3	12	1 destroyer 1 minesweeper 1 oiler	2 U-boats
QP 14	28	2	26	nil	nil
JW 51A	16	nil	16	nil	nil
JW 51B	14	nil	14	1 destroyer 1 minesweeper	1 destroyer
RA 51	14	nil	14	nil	nil

Index

315